"*Katie Chin's Global Family Cookbook* is an invitation to a much needed global culinary adventure from a seasoned chef who treats you like her best friend. She brings 'everyday ease' to exotic recipes from every corner of the globe, and the cultural celebrations with her friends and family make it all the more fun."
—**Ben Ford**, chef and founder of Ford's Filling Station

"This cookbook is packed with flavorful and colorful dishes that definitely reflect Katie Chin's personality. Her recipes are easy to follow and will allow any home cook or chef to have success in the kitchen."
—**Dorian Hunter**, *MasterChef* season 10 winner

"Katie invites us to explore a flourishing array of flavors, colors, textures and stunning presentations, both classic and delightfully original. The holiday celebrations are prepared with notable chef friends who make you feel like you've been invited to their tables."
—**Barbara Lazaroff**, co-founder of Spago, Chinois and the Wolfgang Puck brand

"Chef Katie Chin brings the taste of the world into our kitchens and onto our plates. This cookbook is a delicious celebration of cultures and cuisines."
— From the foreword by **Margaret McSweeney**, author and founder/ host of the award-winning program *Kitchen Chat*

"The recipe titles in this cookbook read like a list of all of the dishes you've ever been torn between ordering in restaurants—but the good news is that they're all here for the cooking! Katie shows us that bringing new flavors into our kitchens is a wonderful way to break out of any cooking rut and expand our horizons."
—**Katie Workman**, creator of *themom100.com* and author of *The Mom 100 Cookbook* and *Dinner Solved*

Welcome to My Global Family Table!

Thank you for joining me on my latest culinary journey—please pull up a seat.

My late mother Leeann Chin taught me the importance of sharing my table and opening my kitchen and heart to all walks of life. Cooking is an expression of love, an act of friendship and a bridge to new cultures. Food can transcend our differences, and when we break bread, we form new relationships and at times, heal fractured ones.

While I was growing up, I was fortunate to have a gourmet Chinese chef for a mom, but the only exposure I had to other types of ethnic cuisine was the occasional dinner at the home of a friend whose parents were also immigrants. Our family's diet consisted mainly of my mother's famous Cantonese dishes and the Scandinavian cuisine popular in neighbors' homes at that time in Minnesota. A visit to our local Mexican restaurant was about as exotic as it got for our family.

That was then, this is now. We're living in such an exciting time for food and cooking. Hallelujah! Over the years, our palettes have become more receptive to cosmopolitan flavors through travel and the internet. World cuisines provide a sense of adventure that we all seek, whether dining out or experimenting in our home kitchens.

Global flavors have hit center stage, with popular mainstream restaurant chains offering everything from Thai-style Pizza

Above Chef Katie Chin in her kitchen with Weeknight Steak Frites (page 124), Thai Cauliflower Pineapple "Fried Rice" (page 163) and Chopped Greek Salad (page 93).
Left Cheesy and nutritious Oven Baked Eggplant Parmesan (page 45).

to Sriracha Burgers. A trip to the mini-mall used to be limited to burgers, sandwiches and pizzas, but now you can easily find a Poke Bar or an Empanada Cafe on your street corner.

Popular cooking shows have exposed our families to exciting flavor profiles that can be cleverly combined for a fusion of taste. It's not uncommon to hear someone sitting next to you at a restaurant mentioning a dish's piquant note or its hint of umami. We've been educated, we're adventurous and we're hungry!

Being a working mom to stepdaughter Kyla and 12-year-old twins Dylan and Becca, I know how hard it is to get dinner on the table and how much we all want our families to enjoy the experience of sitting down together. Adding fun, fresh and interesting new flavors to your routine is just the ticket. And while we all enjoy the delicious, diverse and exciting world flavors available to us today while dining out, I know many people are still intimidated by the thought of trying their hand at making Moroccan Chicken or a Banh Mi Street Tacos in their home kitchen.

I thought, "Wouldn't it be great to create a resource featuring a wide array of delicious, globally-infused recipes that are easy to make with ingredients found primarily at our local grocery stores and using everyday pots, pans and utensils?" Of course it is!

This book celebrates food from multiple cultural backgrounds, including fusions of new and traditional as well as local and global: from Bacon, Date & Goat Cheese Potstickers and Chicken Tikka Masala Pizza to Thai-inspired Poutine French Fries and Greek-style Nachos. I also wanted

to take traditional comfort foods for a global spin, such as my Umami Burger and Whole Roasted Peruvian-style Chicken. You'll also find international classics like Quick and Easy Penne Bolognese and Bouillabaisse along with American creations like Vegan Mac and Cheese and Kid-friendly Brussels Sprouts.

I infused the recipes in this book with the flavor and memories I've gleaned from my many international travels, visits to ethnic enclaves all over the U.S., along with the countless delicious meals I've enjoyed from my vast network of ethnic friends (cooked mostly by their moms).

All my friends, and my darling hubby Matthew, know I'm a party girl. Yup, I'm addicted to throwing parties (can you relate?). I've included a section on multi-cultural entertaining in this book,

and you're invited! Come join my party posse and explore the colorful ethnic celebrations—Greek Easter, Lunar New Year, Hanukkah and Cinco de Mayo—with my dear friends.

Thank you for spending time at my table. I hope these recipes bring you and your family joy, inspiration and put you on the path to a lifelong exploration of global flavors.

Happy Cooking!

Facing page Succulent Grilled Tequila Lime Shrimp (page 142).
Above left Katie and her son Dylan prepare a weeknight stir-fry together.
Above right Katie and friend Kimlai prep for a dinner party.

The kitchen is the heart of the world, and food is its universal language.

Foreword by *Margaret McSweeney*

Chef Katie Chin brings the taste of the world into our kitchens and onto our plates with this new cookbook. It's a delicious celebration of cultures and cuisines.

Chef Katie and I met several years ago through the International Association of Culinary Professionals (IACP). Immediately, we connected as friends and fellow foodies on a culinary journey honoring our late parents. Chef Katie is honoring her mother, and I am honoring my father. Chef Katie and I share a parallel path, having grown up with a parent who was passionate about food. Chef Katie's mother imbued her with the confidence to start cooking after a career change, and I am discovering my late father's joy of connecting and cooking in the kitchen.

Gathering at the table creates community, and when we share a meal, conversations take place that can create bridges of better cultural understanding. In the kitchen, we discover that we all share many similar ingredients in our pantry. It's just the preparation and the recipe that might be different. And food is always the centerpiece of any celebration, whether it's a special holiday or even a personal milestone. And of course, beverages and desserts are also an important enhancement to any meal. In this special cookbook, Chef Katie Chin brings us into her "global kitchen" to sample and celebrate the tastes of the world. Her gracious hospitality welcomes each of us as we also journey into the kitchens of some of her international foodie friends to learn recipes and to expand our palates and our minds. And through this culinary adventure, we will discover how truly delicious and small the world is.

As I say on my *Kitchen Chat* podcast, always remember to take a moment and savor the day!

Margaret McSweeney
Author and Founder/Host of the award-winning program *Kitchen Chat*

My World Pantry Primer

Stocking your pantry with the right ingredients is key to infusing global flavors into your kitchen for everyday meals and entertaining.

Achiote/Annatto Seed

Ground achiote (or annatto) is mainly used to color tamales, rice, meats, soups, stews and beans. It's used heavily in Latin and Caribbean dishes.

Ancho Chili Powder

Ancho chili powder is a staple in Mexican cooking, especially for tamales. It's smoky, rich and deep, and has a subtle raisinlike flavor. The powder is made from dried and ground ancho (poblano) chilies, which are known for their mild to medium heat.

Balsamic Vinegar

Balsamic vinegar is made from grape must (the skin, juice and pips left over from grape pressing). It's flavorful, dark and intense. The three types of balsamic vinegar are *Aceto Balsamico Tradizionale di Modena* (traditional balsamic vinegar of Modena), *Aceto Balsamico Tradizionale di Reggio Emilia* (traditional balsamic vinegar of Reggio Emilia) and *Aceto Balsamico di Modena* (balsamic vinegar of Modena).

Bamboo Shoots

Popular in Asian cooking, bamboo shoots come from a bamboo plant that is harvested before it matures. The tender, cream-colored "meat" inside the shoot is what is eaten. Sold fresh, canned or bottled, smaller shoots are often used in soups and stir-fries, while the larger shoots can be sliced for curries.

Banana Leaves

Used in Asian, Caribbean and Latin cuisines, banana leaves are beautiful and fun to use as an aromatic wrap for meat, rice, fish and veggies. I like to run banana leaves under hot water to make them more pliable. You can find them in Asian and Latin markets. They store well in your freezer. I love the subtle grassy flavor that is transferred to any food that is wrapped up in a banana leaf. They're great for dressing up platters too. You can use lotus leaves or cabbage leaves as a substitute.

Basil (Italian)

Italian Sweet Basil is an herb in the mint family that is used throughout Italian and Mediterranean cuisines. Its distinctive flavor features licorice and clove notes, and it serves as the basis for pesto. It's also used in sauces, salads, soups, sandwiches and the list goes on! It's best used fresh and is often added to recipes at the last minute to preserve its flavor. My hubby's favorite salad—Insalata Caprese—

is made with buffalo mozzarella, extra virgin olive oil and lots of fresh Italian basil. I love buying my basil at our local farmers market, and we store it in our fridge in plastic bags as soon as we get home.

Basil (Thai and Holy)

Basil is an essential ingredient in Thai cooking and it is called for throughout this book. Thai basil and Holy basil are the two most commonly used varieties of basil in Thai cooking. Thai, or Asian basil is a tropical variety with a strong peppery, anise flavor that stands up really well to cooking. It has purple flowers, red-tinged stems and pointy green leaves. Holy basil is so named because it is held as sacred in the Hindu culture. It is revered in Thai cooking for its subtle minty flavor that comes alive when heated. When buying either variety, choose bunches that are fresh, fragrant and show no signs of wilting. Separate the leaves from the stems and wash and dry them well before use. A substitute for either variety is fresh Italian basil (the kind found in most supermarkets). Italian basil isn't quite as fragrant or flavorful as Thai or holy basil, so you may want to add a bit more than is called for in the recipe.

Black Beans, Fermented

Fermented black beans are salted black soybeans. They have a distinctive flavor and a pungent aroma. They're often combined with garlic and ginger, resulting in a richly flavored dish often used when steaming whole fish. Black beans should always be rinsed in warm water to remove excess salt. Fermented black beans are also sold jarred or as a pre-made sauce.

Black Mushrooms

Black mushrooms are also known as dried shiitakes or fragrant mushrooms. They are used in everything from soups and stews to stir-fries and eggrolls. Dried black mushrooms need to be hydrated in warm water before cooking. Once hydrated, they plump up and have a juicy, meaty texture with a savory, umami flavor. They are incredibly versatile and a great pantry item to have on hand whenever you want to drop an umami bomb into your next dish.

Cardamom

Cardamom is used throughout Indian, Middle Eastern and Scandinavian cuisines. It has a distinctive herbaceous piney-citrusy flavor with a pungent aroma with notes of lemon, smoke and mint. It can be purchased as seeds in pods or ground. In Indian recipes, you can find cardamom used in spice blends and masala chai and whole cardamom pods used in preparing basmati rice and various curries. In Middle Eastern recipes, ground cardamom is used in preparing certain desserts. In Scandinavia, cardamom is found in everything from meatloaf to baked goods.

Chicken Stock or Broth

Chicken stock or broth is used widely in the recipes in this book. If you have time, make your favorite chicken stock recipe and freeze batches for ease and convenience. Otherwise, store-bought chicken stock or broth is totally fine and always great to have on hand in your pantry.

Chinese Rice Wine

Also known as Shaoxing wine, Chinese rice wine is made from fermented rice and yeast. It is used in dumplings, stir-fries, clay pot dishes and marinades. It is fragrant and slightly nutty with a rich amber hue. This is an essential ingredient to keep on hand for Chinese recipes. If you can't find Chinese rice wine, dry cooking sherry is a fine substitute.

Chipotle Peppers (Chipotles) in Adobo Sauce

Chipotle peppers in tangy red abobo sauce are intense, smoky and sour-sweet. They are sold canned and are used in stews, sauces and marinades, to name just a few applications. Use less if you like it mild and more if you like it hot! You can also remove the seeds for less heat. This is a staple ingredient I keep in my pantry for Mexican and other Latin recipes. Chop up a pepper with some of its sauce and add it to anything you'd like to add smoky, spicy, sour-sweet flavor to. Chipotle peppers in adobo sauce can be found at Latin markets and many well-stocked grocery stores.

Cinnamon

Cinnamon has been around for hundreds of years and is considered an essential spice in India and many other countries. It comes in stick form or powdered and is known for is delicate flavor which compliments both savory and sweet dishes. In Middle Eastern and Asian recipes, the spice is used to flavor eggplant, lamb, rice and curries. It's also used throughout the world for baking in sweet recipes, and is a core ingredient in the Indian spice mix *garam masala*. Not only is cinnamon a versatile and delicious spice. it has numerous health benefits including being a powerful antioxidant.

Coconut Milk

Coconut milk is used throughout Thai cooking, adding sweet, creamy-rich flavor to any dish. It's used in soups, sauces, drinks, curries and desserts. When a coconut is first pressed, it produces a thick cream. Later pressings result in the thinner coconut milk found in cans at the market. You can find canned coconut milk at Asian markets and well stocked grocery stores. Make sure to shake well before opening. You can find lite coconut milk with fewer calories

if you're watching your waistline. It's also great for those who are lactose intolerant (like me!) and it's loaded with antioxidants!

Coriander Leaves (Fresh)

Also known as Chinese parsley or cilantro, fresh coriander leaves are one of the most popular fresh herbs in the world. Coriander leaves are used widely throughout this book because the herb is so popular in many global cuisines, including Middle Eastern, Mediterranean, Indian, South Asian, Mexican, Latin American, Chinese, African and Asian cuisines! It's citrusy with a mild spicy bite that's perfect for salads, salsas, soups, chilies, stir-fries and so much more.

Cotija Cheese

Cotija cheese is one of Mexico's most popular cheeses. It has a salty and strong flavor and is used mainly as a topping or mixed into sauces. It's a seasonal cheese named after the town Cotija, Michoacan where it originated and is made by artisan cheese makers. Sold at Latin markets and well-stocked markets in both block or grated form.

Cumin

Cumin has a pungent, nutty and peppery flavor, and it's one of the most popular spices in the world. It is a common ingredient in Mexican, Indian and North African cuisines, and serves as an essential spice in many curry blends. It's also known for aiding in digestion. It's sold in seed form or ground.

Curry Paste

Curry pastes are usually made with a blend of chilies, garlic, galangal and lemongrass, which are ground into a paste in a mortar and pestle. The results are intense and aromatic. Adding yellow curry powder results in yellow curry paste. Green curry paste contains green chilies, which yield a bright, sharp flavor. Red chilies are found in red curry paste for a bold, spicy flavor. Curry pastes can be found at Asian markets and well-stocked grocery stores. I prefer the Mae Ploy brand. Keep your curry paste well-sealed in the refrigerator for up to one month.

Curry Powder

Made from ground turmeric, coriander, cumin and dried red pepper, curry powder is a spice blend used widely throughout the world. It becomes yellow curry when added to curry paste giving it its distinct yellow hue. It's often heated and combined with coconut milk to make a delicious curry sauce where its flavors open up and come alive. It is widely available at well-stocked grocery stores and Indian and Asian markets, where it tends to run on the spicier side.

Edamame

Edamame is the Japanese word for immature soybeans, probably because they were originally sold with the stems attached. The pods can be boiled or steamed or even microwaved and are best served with salt. In the US, frozen edamame is widely available, sold in the pod or shelled. They are a great plant-based protein source in meals or as a snack. Swap out garbanzo beans with shelled edamame for edamame hummus.

Fennel Seeds

Fennel seed is a spice with warm aromatic flavor used in Mediterranean cuisine and other cuisines around the world. It has a sweet and licorice-like flavor that is sometimes confused with anise. Fennel is known to aid in digestion. It is roasted and eaten after dinner to freshen breath in countries like Pakistan and India. It is also a key ingredient in Chinese five spice powder.

Dark Soy Sauce

Dark soy sauce is aged longer and is slightly sweeter and thicker than regular soy sauce. It is made from fermented soybeans. Caramel and molasses are added to deepen its color and thicken its consistency. It has a rich, deep flavor and is used in stir-fries, sauces and gravies. Dark soy sauce can keep for several months when stored in a dark, cool place. You can find dark soy sauce at Asian markets and some specialty stores. The Indonesian version of dark soy sauce is called *kecap manis*.

Extra Virgin Olive Oil

Olive oil is a major component of the Mediterranean diet. Extra-virgin olive oil is an unrefined oil and the highest-quality olive oil you can buy. It has a rich golden-green color and distinct flavor. The process used to make extra-virgin olive oil results in more pronounced olive taste and lower oleic acid levels than other olive oils, while also retaining many more of the vitamins and nutrients from the olives. If you can't find extra-virgin olive oil then substitute with non-extra-virgin olive oil or canola oil—or blend the oils together if you're running low. Extra-virgin olive oil is more expensive than regular olive oil, but worth every penny.

Fish Sauce

Fish sauce is a popular ingredient and condiment used widely in Southeast Asian cooking. It's typically made by layering anchovies with salt allowing it to ferment for several months in a sealed container. When buying fish sauce, look for a clear, light amber color. Fish sauce puts the "salty" in the sweet-sour-salty-hot flavors of Southeast Asian cuisine. Like salt, it enhances and brings out the flavors in any dish. A good substitute for fish sauce is soy sauce mixed with a splash of oyster sauce or anchovy paste. One teaspoon of fish sauce roughly equals a teaspoon of salt.

Feta Cheese

Feta cheese is a rich and creamy soft cheese from Greece. It is traditionally made from whole sheep's milk, although many varieties are now made with goat's milk or a mixture of the two. It has been around for centuries, and is commonly featured in Greek meals. The better varieties are aged four to six weeks, cured in a salty whey and brine. The flavor of feta becomes sharper and saltier with age. It is creamy white in color with small holes, a crumbly texture and is normally found crumbled or in square cakes with no rind.

Five Spice Powder

Also called Chinese five spice powder, this blend is comprised of five ground spices: star anise, Sichuan pepper, fennel, cloves and cinnamon. It is spicy, pungent and mildly sweet with a hint of licorice. Five spice powder can be found in Asian markets and well-stocked grocery stores.

Flat-leaf Parsley

Sometimes confused with cilantro because of its flat leaves, flat-leafed parsley (or Italian parsley) has a more robust flavor than its curly cousin. It's one of the main ingredients found in Chimichurri and is used all over the world, and it's especially popular in Mediterranean and Middle Eastern cuisines. Because it's so flat it is easy to chop, and minced flat-leaf parsley makes an excellent garnish. It's available year round and it's also easy to grow at home.

Garam Masala

Known as a staple in Indian cooking, the word *garam* simply means "hot," and *masala* means "spices." However, garam masala isn't particularly hot. Garam masala is a blend of whole spices which have been roasted and ground, such as cumin, coriander, cardamom, cinnamon, cloves and nutmeg. It's a key ingredient in the popular Indian dish, tikka masala.

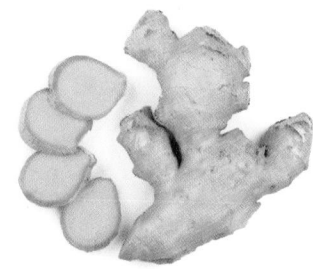

Ginger

Fresh ginger is widely used in Asian cuisines. With its sweet, spicy and peppery notes, ginger adds a tangy zest to any dish. It can be used in stir-fries, soups, salads, marinades, sauces, desserts and drinks. It's also known for its ability to aid with digestion and morning sickness. A great trick my mom taught me is to peel and mince a large amount of ginger in a food processor. Freeze the results in strorage bags and voila! You just snap off whatever you need.

Gochujang

Gochujang is a Korean red chili paste made with glutinous rice, fermented soybeans, salt and sometimes sugar. Smoky, earthy, sweet and spicy, gochujang is the new Asian "it" condiment used in marinades, sauces, stews, soups, stir-fries and much more! It's a great paste to mix with ketchup or barbecue sauce that will add a hit of flavor to anything you're making. In case you were wondering how to pronounce it, the "jang" rhymes with "chong" as in Cheech & Chong.

Haricots Verts

Haricots verts is French for green beans. They have a more delicate flavor than garden variety American green beans and tend to be younger, longer and thinner. Their petite and slender shape make for a pretty presentation, especially in salade niçoise and the Niçoise Deviled Eggs found this book. Oh la la!

Harissa

Harissa is Tunisian hot chili pepper paste typically made from roasted red peppers, caraway, cumin and garlic paste. Harissa is sweet, smoky, tangy and bit spicy. So versatile, you can add a teaspoon to a sauce, soup or marinade, and add a punch of amazing flavor. I like to add some olive oil and drizzle it over grilled meats or veggies. It's easy to make harissa from scratch, but it's widely available in jars, tubes or cans at Middle Eastern markets and some grocery stores.

Hoisin Sauce

Hoisin sauce is used in Chinese cuisine. It has a dark color and thick consistency with salty, sweet and tangy flavors. It's made from a combination of fermented soybean paste, garlic, vinegar, sesame oil, chilis and sugar. It can be used as a marinade, glaze or a dipping sauce. Its strong flavor can be overpowering, so use it sparingly if you're new to hoisin sauce. It can be found at most well-stocked grocery stores and Asian markets.

Kaffir Lime Leaves

Kaffir lime leaves, also known as makrut lime leaves, are used in Thai cooking and have notes of orange, clove, lime and citrus. Their leaves have an hourglass shape and a glossy shine. They have a complex fragrance and a strong citrus flavor, and are used in curries, stir-fries, soups like tom yum and more. It's important to remove the Kaffir lime leaves before serving, much like you would with a bay leaf. They can be purchased fresh, frozen or dried at Asian markets. One of easiest substitutes is lemon or lime zest.

Kalamata Olives

Kalamata olives are a staple of Greek cuisine and are named after the city of Kalamata in the southern region of Greece where they were first grown. Contrary to their "black olive" nickname, they are actually dark purple. They are sold marinated in olive oil or vinegar and are often eaten plain or sliced and added to recipes. Kalamata olives are rich in anti-oxidants and healthy fats.

Kimchi

Kimch is a staple in Korean cuisine and is made from salted and fermented cabbage seasoned with chili powder, green onions, garlic and ginger. It's made by lacto-fermentation, the same process used to make sauerkraut. Sour and tangy, it's most frequently served as a side dish, but can also be served as an entrée. Kimchi is loaded with vitamins and contains excellent probiotics which helps with gut health. Traditionally, kimchi was stored underground in jars to keep cool in warm months and so it wouldn't freeze during winters. Nowadays, kimchi is best stored in your fridge.

Lemongrass

I like to call lemongrass "ginger's frisky cousin" because of its lemony-woodsy flavor without the acidic sharpness of lemon. The best way to prepare lemongrass is to cut off the stalk leaving the lower 3–4 inches. The outer fibrous layers need to be removed to reveal the most tender and edible part. Chopped, sliced or ground, fresh lemongrass is used in curry pastes, soups, stir-fries, salad dressing and more. You can find fresh lemongrass at Asian markets, some farmers markets and well-stocked grocery stores. When shopping for lemongrass, look for stalks that feel firm, smell fragrant and look fresh. Avoid any that appear dried out, brown or yellow. A substitute for lemongrass is sliced lime leaves, or sliced lime or lemon rind. If fresh lemongrass isn't available you can also use frozen lemongrass or minced lemongrass in a tube.

Mexican Oregano

Mexican Oregano is similar to regular oregano but has a more robust and pungent flavor with subtle hints of citrus. It's used in Mexican, Southwestern US and Central American dishes. Used in salsas, chile sauces, pozole, black beans and meat dishes, it's a versatile spice you can use whenever you're craving authentic Southwestern flavor.

Miso Paste

Miso is a Japanese paste with rich umami flavor. It's made from fermented soybeans mixed with salt and koji (a mold that's used to make sake) along with barley, rice, or other grain. It's a staple of Japanese cuisine, including miso soup. There are three different types of miso: white (light and mild), red (intense flavor due to longer aging) and mixed (bolder flavor from the blending of white and red). Miso is used in salad dressing, sauces, marinades, baked tofu and vegetable dishes, imparting a unique flavor to everything it touches.

WORLD NOODLE VARIETIES

Dried Glass Noodles
Also known as cellophane noodles, bean thread noodles and Chinese vermicelli, are transparent noodles that, when cooked, look like glass. They are delicate thread-like noodles which are made from green mung bean flour. Dried glass noodles need to be presoaked in hot water for a few minutes before cooking, unless they are added to a soup or deep-fried. They're a great option for those on a gluten-free diet. Like tofu, they absorb the flavors of the other ingredients in a dish.

Rice Sticks
Rice stick noodles are made from rice flour and water and come in a variety of widths. Thin sticks work well for soups and steamed noodle dishes. Wider rice sticks are ideal for stir-fries, pad thai and pad see ew. You can find fresh rice noodles at Thai markets, but they are most commonly sold dry at Asian markets and well-stocked grocery stores. Dried rice sticks need to be hydrated in very hot water before using them, where they become soft, chewy and translucent.

Rice Vermicelli Noodles
Also known as rice threads, vermicelli rice noodles are similar to bean threads except they're made with rice flour. They are usually sold dried in little blocks. The noodles need to be presoaked in hot water when being used in spring rolls, stir-fries and salads. They can also be dropped straight from the package into soups or into hot oil to make crispy noodles for recipes like Chinese Chicken Salad (page 95).

Flat Wide Rice Noodles
Wider than rice sticks, flat wide rice noodles are most famously used for the popular Asian noodle dishes beef chow fun and Thai rad na. In Thailand, they're also known as river noodles. They hold up better in heavy gravy than thinner noodles. They're sold fresh or dried. If using fresh, I recommend placing them in boiling water for a few minutes to loosen them up.

Udon Noodles
Udon is a type of thick wheat flour noodle used frequently in Japanese cuisine. It is often served hot as a noodle soup in its simplest form, as kake udon, in a mildly flavored broth called *kakejiru*, which is made with dashi, soy sauce and mirin.

Yakisoba Noodles
Yakisoba literally means "fried noodle" in Japanese. Fresh yakisoba noodles are similar to ramen noodles and are used to make yakisoba, the Japanese-style stir-fried noodles that are one of Japan's best known street foods. Yakisoba noodles are great in many stir-fried dishes. They are sold fresh in bags at Asian markets and in the refrigerated section (usually near the tofu) at well-stocked grocery stores.

Oyster Sauce

Oyster sauce is used widely in Chinese cuisine. Brewed from dried oysters, salt and water, oyster sauce has a deep, rich brown color. It is salty and sweet and surprisingly not fishy tasting. A staple in stir-fries, oyster sauce is a versatile condiment and flavoring that can also be used as a marinade and barbecue sauce. A good substitute for oyster sauce is combining fish sauce with a bit of soy sauce. Vegetarian/vegan versions of oyster sauce are made from mushrooms and can be found at Asian markets.

Roasted Red Chili Paste

Roasted chili paste is an intense and complex paste that is used throughout Thai cooking. It's made from a blend of crushed red chilies and other ingredients like garlic, onion, dried shrimp and tamarind. It's used in soups, sauces, stir-fries and stews. A little bit packs a punch and goes a long way toward adding authentic Thai flavor to all of your dishes.

Saffron

Saffron is harvested from the *Crocus sativus*, a flower better known as the "saffron crocus." It is one the most rare and expensive spices in the world. It has a strong, exotic aroma and a bitter taste. It's used to color and flavor many Middle Eastern, European and Mediterranean dishes, and is famously known for its starring role in the Spanish dish paella and bouillabaisse soup.

Sage

Sage is native to the northern Mediterranean coast and is known for its strong herbal aroma and earthy flavor with notes of eucalyptus, cedar, lemon and mint. It's used in savory recipes and is a common ingredient in holiday stuffing. It makes an excellent paring with roasted butternut squash, Italian veal and French meat dishes. Sage has long narrow leaves and a distinctive fuzzy texture. Use it sparingly, as sage's strong flavor can overpower a dish.

Sambal Oelek

Sambal Oelek is a fiery red Indonesian chili-garlic paste. It's used as an ingredient and condiment throughout Malaysia and Thailand. It's typically made from a combination of crushed red chilies, vinegar and salt. It provides heat but not in an overpowering way, much like cooking with fresh chilies. One tablespoon is roughly the equivalent of a small chopped jalapeno pepper.

Sesame oil, toasted or dark

Sesame oil is made from toasted sesame seeds and has a distinctive, nutty aroma and flavor. Deep amber in color, it can enhance the flavors of all sorts of dishes, from meats and vegetables to stir-fries and salads. It's generally used as a flavoring and not as a cooking oil.

Smoked Paprika

Otherwise known as pimentón, smoked paprika brings a deep, smoky flavor and aroma to everything it touches. It's made from pimiento peppers that have been smoked and dried over oak fires. It can range in flavor from mild and sweet to hot but it's usually known for being mild and slightly sweet. It's used in meat and vegetable dishes and sauces and stews. You can substitute with sweet paprika but you'll sacrifice the smoky flavor.

Sriracha Sauce

Traditional sriracha sauce is made chili peppers, vinegar, garlic, sugar and salt. It's named after the seaside town in Thialand where it originated. It's nicknamed "rooster sauce" because of the distinctive rooster featured on the bottle of the popular Huy Fong Foods brand. It's spicy with rich and complex flavors and has become the go-to hot sauce for many people all over the world. Combining sriracha with mayo makes for a creamy-hot dipping sauce.

Spring Roll Wrappers

Spring roll wrappers can be found at Asian markets and well-stocked grocery stores, and come in 4-inch or 8-inch squares. They fry up light and crispy and are used for the Banana Walnut Wontons recipe in this book (page 216).

Star Anise

This star-shaped spice is the seedpod of a small tree found throughout Asia. It's pungent with a licorice-like flavor and aroma. It's a constituant spice in Chinese five spice powder as well. It is used in Vietnamese pho and is a popular ingredient in curries, soups, sweets and teas. It can be used whole or ground for a more intense flavor. You can substitute star anise with a blend of cloves and cinnamon.

Straw Mushrooms

Straw mushrooms have a mild and sweet taste and a smooth texture. Their shape resembles little helmets. They get their name from the way they're grown on beds of straw. They are used in Chinese and Thai dishes such as soups, curries, salads and stir-fries. Straw mushrooms are generally sold in cans and can be found at Asian markets and most well-stocked markets.

Tamari

Tamari is a type Japanese soy sauce made with very little or no wheat. It's less salty than Chinese soy sauce and a bit thicker, which makes it ideal as a dipping sauce. Tamari is great option if you're

on a gluten-free diet, but always check the label for wheat.

Tomatillos

Also known as or husk tomatoes, tomatillos are a staple in Mexican cuisine. Tomatillos look like unripe green tomatoes and come wrapped in a crinkly husk. Once the husk is peeled away, its green and glossy fruit is revealed. They have a citrusy flavor and are used both raw and cooked in salsas, sauces, soups and more.

Turmeric

Tumeric is a bright yellow spice powder made from the root of a plant in the ginger family. Earthy, sweet, slightly bitter and peppery, turmeric is used in curries, marinades and rice dishes. Be careful when handling turmeric as it can stain your clothes and hands. Tumeric has many health benefits, including being a natural anti-inflammatory.

Wrappers

From wontons and egg rolls to potstickers and dumplings, everything tastes better wrapped up and steamed or fried. Most wrappers or skins are made from flour and water and are differentiated mainly by their shape, thickness and size.

Wonton Wrappers are square and thin. Many people use wonton wrappers to make ravioli. (I know, who knew?) **Potsticker Wrappers** (also called dumpling wrappers or gyoza wrappers) are similar to wonton wrappers but are round. When making potstickers or other dumplings, like shu mei, you can substitute with wonton wrappers by using a cookie cutter to create a round shape. **Eggroll Wrappers** are the same as wonton wrappers but come in large squares, 9 x 9 inches (23 x 23 cm). **Spring Roll Wrappers** are naturally used to make spring rolls, which have a crispier, more delicate texture than egg rolls. Spring rolls are white in color and contain no eggs. They are usually sold in the freezer section at Asian markets and must be pulled apart to separate the sheets before using. I like to keep all types of wrappers on hand in my freezer because they're so versatile and great for last minute entertaining. **Rice Paper Wrappers** are made from rice flour and water which are spread out into thin sheets and sun dried. They're used for roll ups, like chilled spring rolls, and must be moistened in warm water before using.

Yard-Long Beans or Long Beans

Also known as snake beans or asparagus beans, summertime brings an abundance of fresh yard-long beans or long beans farmers markets and Asian markets. They are similar to the common backyard green bean except that they can grow to about yard, hence their name. They have a pronounced flavor that isn't quite as sweet as regular beans, and they also cook much more quickly. They really come alive when stir-fried, deep-fried or sautéed, and they make for a crunchy, juicy and flavorful side dish when combined with soy sauce, ginger and oyster sauce.

WORLD CHILI PEPPER VARIETIES

serrano peppers if you can't find Thai chilies. Deseed chilies if you prefer less heat or omit altogether or choose a milder type if cooking for young children.

Anaheim
Known in Mexico as "chile verde del norte," Green Anaheim chili peppers are defined by their long, curved bright-green pod and their mild, sweet flavor. The chili's skin is waxy, glossy and semi thick. Raw Anaheim chilies are very mild and slightly peppery in flavor. When sold fresh they should be bright and green and when sold dried they should be red.

Jalapeño
This popular moderately spicy Mexican pepper is one of the most popular chili peppers in the world because of its bright, grassy flavor. A common misconception is that jalapeños are crazy hot, but they are only moderately spicy (2,500–8,000 on the Scoville scale). They're used throughout Latin cuisines and other cuisines around the world. Jalapeños are widely available and make a great substitute as a go-to pepper if you can't find the more exotic chili that you're looking for.

Serrano
Serrano peppers are similar to jalapeños peppers but are smaller and notably hotter. Fleshy in texture, they are typically eaten raw and have a bright flavor and are used often in pico de gallo and other sauces. They are a good substitute for Thai chilies.

Habanero
Habanero chili peppers are hot hot hot! They're named after the Cuban city of La Habana and are rated at 100,000–350,000 on the Scoville scale! Unripe habaneros are green, and they most commonly turn orange and red as they mature. Because of their intense heat and flowery aroma, they are a popular ingredient in salsas and hot sauces, as well as cocktails, like Spicy Habanero Margarita (page 209). Be sure to wear rubber gloves or wash your hands thoroughly after touching habaneros to avoid getting the oil on your face or in your eyes. Also, wash cutting surfaces after chopping chilies or you may transfer the heat to other foods.

Thai Chili (Bird's Eye)
Thai chilies happen to be some of the hottest in the world (rated 50,000–100,000 on the Scoville scale). They get their "bird's eye" nickname because of their unique appeal to birds. Thai chilies are used in everything from curries and soups to sauces and flavored vinegar. Wear rubber gloves when cutting fresh Thai chilies, or be sure to wash your hands thoroughly afterwards to avoid getting the oil on your face or in your eyes. Also, wash cutting surfaces after chopping chilies or you may transfer the heat to other foods. I recommend using fresh

Shishito
Holy shishito! I love these peppers. Shishito peppers are slender with a thin skin and a bright green color. In Japan, it's known as the lion-head pepper as the word *shishi* means "lion." They are relatively mild and can be eaten raw, broiled, grilled or pan-fried. The popular restaurant method of pan-frying until charred and crisp is featured in this book (page 70). Before cooking, it's important to poke a hole in the shishitos to prevent hot air from expanding and bursting the peppers.

Arborio Rice
Arborio rice is an Italian variety of short-grain rice. It is named after the town of Aborio in the Po Valley of Italy. It is high in amylopectin starch, so when the firm, rounded grains are cooked, they become creamier and chewier than other rices. They are the signature ingredient in risotto and paella recipes.

Japanese Rice/Sushi Rice
Everyday Japanese rice (often labeled "sushi rice" in the US) is the staple of the Japanese diet and consists of short, translucent grains. It is sticky, making it easy to be picked up and eaten with chopsticks after it's been steamed. It's important to soak the raw grains for 20 minutes before cooking. You can substitute with Calrose rice if you can't find sushi rice.

Jasmine Rice
Jasmine rice gets its name from the fragrant jasmine flower. Native to Thailand, it's the most popular rice in Thailand and all over Southeast Asia. Jasmine rice has a subtle floral aroma and is sweet, buttery and mild. It cooks up soft, moist and sticky. Like all white rices, it's important to wash the raw grains several times until the water runs clear to eliminate excess starch during the cooking process.

Basmati Rice
Basmati is a variety of long grain rice grown in the Himalayas and in Pakistan. It is one of the best known varieties in the world. It is fragrant and nutty, and is served with many Indian curries. It is also popular in rice pilaf dishes.

Long-Grain White & Brown Rice
Long and slender, long-grain white rice is the most widely grown rice in the United States. It is nearly four to five times longer than it is wide. American long-grain brown rice is unhulled, meaning it's a whole grain with its bran and outer layer of fiber intact. Long-grain white rice cooks up firm, dry, fluffy and loose. It has a somewhat bland, sweet-grain flavor. Brown long-grain rice has a chewier, nuttier flavor. Being unhulled, brown rice is a whole grain so it contains all the vitamins and minerals lacking in white rice. Brown rice requires double the amount of water and takes at least twice as long to cook as white rice.

Quinoa
Quinoa (pronounced "keen-wah") is actually a seed, but can be used in all the same ways you'd use a grain. It's become hugely popular because of its health benefits and pleasant nutty taste that pairs well with spices. This little powerhouse has the highest protein content of any grain. And it is a complete protein, meaning it has all nine essential amino acids and gets its superfood status from its B vitamins along with folate, vitamin E, iron, magnesium, phosphorus, zinc and potassium. Quinoa comes in various colors including black, red, yellow and white, and it is quick-cooking—ready in 15 minutes. All this, and it's gluten free! It makes a great side dish for any meal or as a bed for stews or grilled fish or meat. It's so versatile that you can use it casseroles, salads and breakfast bowls (like the one in this book—page 60), and you can substitute it for rice in fried rice recipes.

Techniques for Cooking Globally

If you like to cook, chances are you already feel comfortable with the techniques for cooking the recipes in this book. I promise that nothing is too out there and that most of the recipes involve traditional techniques such as pan-frying, steaming, grilling, broiling, stir-frying, deep-frying and braising. If you're new to cooking, I think you'll find that the recipes will clearly explain what you're supposed to do (pinky swear). Here are few techniques and tips I wanted to share which are applicable to several styles of cuisine and are great tidbits to keep in your front apron pocket.

HOW TO BLANCH

Along with steaming, blanching vegetables is a basic technique every cook should know. Briefly boiled and then plunged into ice water, vegetables turn and stay a vibrant color and remain tender-crisp when cooked. Blanched vegetables may be used in crudité platters, salads, sushi rolls and stir fries, or refrigerated or frozen for later use. The recipes in this book will let you know if vegetables need to be blanched.

To blanch successfully: Bring a pot of water to a boil. Submerge veggies in the boiling water for about 1 minute (some vegetables like spinach leaves need less time). Transfer the veggies to an ice bath for at least 1 minute. Drain and use as directed in recipe.

HOW TO DEEP-FRY

A lot of my friends are scared to deep-fry. They think: 1) oil will splatter all over the place, and 2) the food usually turns out soggy.

Well, I'm here to debunk these deep-frying myths. First of all, you need to use a pan that's deep enough to eliminate the splatter factor. You don't need to use a wok when deep-frying but you must always use a deep pan to adequately cover the item you are frying. For example, if you are using 2 inches (5 cm) of oil, you must leave 6 inches (15 cm) of space above the oil. If your oil begins smoking, turn off the heat for a few minutes and let the oil return to 350°F (175°C). Heat oil uncovered to prevent overheating.

Secondly, deep-frying requires very high heat levels (350°F–375°F / 175°C–190°C). Make sure the oil isn't too hot, because food will over cook on the outside and will be undercooked on the inside. Also, if the temperature is too low the food will soak up too much oil. Don't try to fry too many pieces at one time or the oil temperature will dip. It's also important that anything you intend to deep-fry is first dried completely, especially before you dip items into batter or marinade.

If you have a deep fat frying thermometer, use it. If you don't have a thermometer, the oil is ready when a 1-inch (2.5-cm) cube of white bread dropped into the oil browns in 60 seconds.

I recommend using vegetable oil or corn oil for deep-frying because they have "high smoke points," meaning they don't break down at high deep-frying temperatures. In other words, don't use olive oil to deep-fry.

Lastly, always be prepared with a paper towel-lined sheet pan to rest and drain your items on after they've been fried.

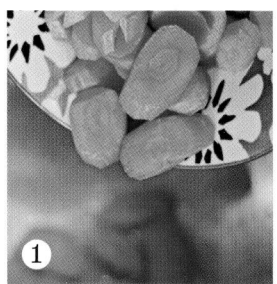 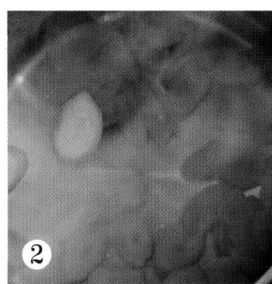  

 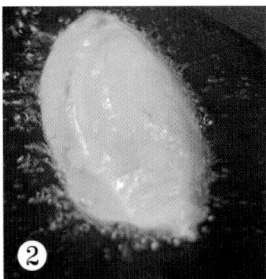 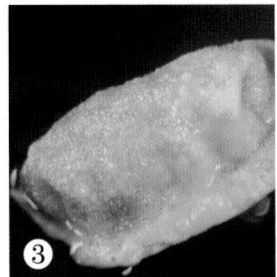 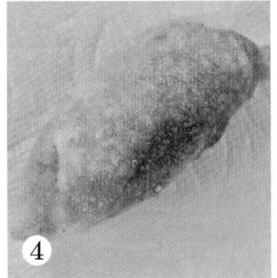

HOW TO STIR-FRY

Chinese stir-frying is all about the prep. Once you have all your stir-frying ingredients cleaned, cut and ready to go, the rest should be easy peasy and super-duper fast. I mean really, REALLY fast. The key to great stir-frying is heating your wok or skillet up very hot so you get a nice sear on your proteins and your veggies are tender but crisp at the same time. You also want to keep things moving in the pan. The term stir-frying is a bit of a misnomer because the action is more about tossing and flipping than it is about stirring.

It's also important to allow the wok or skillet to heat up first before adding the oil which you then swirl to coat. The wok or pan is ready for oil when a drop of water sizzles and evaporates right away. Ensure that your skillet has high enough walls so the ingredients don't fly out.

I also like to use a firm spatula—not a flimsy one. A firm spatula helps you take control of your stir-frying and allows you to get underneath the ingredients to toss while you cook. I'll say it again, folks. Stir-frying is not about stirring, it's more of a toss-and-flip action so all of your ingredients are evenly cooked.

HOW TO SEASON A WOK

I've been asked if seasoning a wok involves spices. In actuality, seasoning a wok is a process to make your wok rust resistant and it creates a natural non-stick finish at the same time. It also improves the flavor of stir-fried dishes. "Seasoning" only applies to iron, cast iron, steel and carbon steel woks because they are porous materials prone to rust. You don't need to season a non-stick wok.

By creating layers and layers of burnt oil coatings on the surface of the metals, you can cover the pores and protect them from rusting or corroding due to water or acid exposure.

Here's how to season your NON non-stick wok:

1. New woks have a thin factory coating that must be removed before the first use. To do this, wash the wok inside and out with a stainless-steel scrubber, dish soap and hot water. Rinse and dry it over low heat.

2. Heat the wok over high heat. Tilt and turn the wok until it becomes a yellowish-blueish color. Remove from the heat.

3. Using a paper towel, wipe the inside of the wok with a small amount of vegetable oil.

4. Turn the heat to medium-low. Place the wok on the burner for 10 minutes.

5. Wipe with a fresh paper towel. There will be black residue on the paper towel. Repeat steps 3 and 4 about three times, or until there is no longer black residue on the paper towel when wiped.

6. Ta-dah! You just seasoned your wok. Time to stir-fry!

HOW TO SEASON A CAST IRON PAN

Preheat the oven to 300°F (150°C). Place a layer of foil on the bottom rack of your oven. Place the pan on the top rack. Heat the pan for 10 minutes and remove. Using a cloth or paper towel, coat the pan with about 1 tablespoon of vegetable shortening. Place the pan back in the oven for another 10 minutes. Remove and pour out any excess fat or oil. Turn the pan upside down and return it to the top rack of the oven (directly over the foil to catch drips). Bake for 1 hour, turn off the oven, and let the pan cool in the oven.

HOW TO CLEAN YOUR SEASONED WOK OR CAST IRON PAN

Now that you've created a beautiful non-stick coating on your wok or cast iron pan, you'll want to protect it. Don't use anything too abrasive like steel wool to clean it. You should also never use soap on your wok or cast iron pan. Just run it under hot water and use a soft cleaning brush or sponge to remove food bits. You may need to soak it in hot water for few minutes to remove stubborn bits.

The best way to dry a wok after it's been cleaned is to place it on low heat until all the water evaporates. If you put your wok away before it's completely dry, it will develop rust spots, which is quite sad.

HOW TO COOK A PERFECT POT OF RICE

I'm going to let you in on a little secret. Shhhhh. Any white rice needs to be washed before you steam it. This has been a life-altering epiphany for some of my friends. When you wash your rice, you eliminate the excess starch that would otherwise get released into the cooking water and then reabsorbed while cooking, resulting in mushy rice. Once you get rid of that excess starch you will enjoy the lightest, fluffiest rice ever. You can thank me later. In many Chinese families, it is the job of the youngest child to wash the rice. Being the youngest in my family, I'm a bona fide rice washing expert!

How to wash your rice

Fill a pot with 1 cup (200 g) uncooked long-grain white rice and cool water. Swirl the water around with your hands and wash the rice by rubbing it gently between your fingers and drain. Repeat this process until the water runs clear, usually about 5 or 6 times. Drain the water carefully from the pot.

How to measure water the Mount Fuji way

As in many Asian households, I was taught to measure the water when preparing rice by using my finger, otherwise known as the Mount Fuji technique. With the tip of your index finger just touching the surface of the rice, add water until it reaches your first knuckle. You may feel most comfortable using a measuring cup or using the lines on the side of your rice cooker machine bowl as a guide, but know that millions of Asian families swear by this technique. Only use the Mount Fuji technique for preparing white rices, not brown, black or red.

How to cook your rice

Use the Mount Fuji technique and add water to the 1 cup of washed rice or add 1 cup (250 ml) water. Bring the pot of rice and water to a boil over high heat. As soon as the water is boiling, lower the heat to a simmer and cover the pot.

Cook at a gentle simmer until the water is completely absorbed and the rice is tender, about 12 minutes. Remove from the heat and let the pot sit for 10 minutes with a lid on before serving. One cup (200 g) of raw rice will yield 3 cups (450 g) of cooked rice.

If you're using a rice cooker, wash the rice in the rice cooker bowl. Follow your instruction manual to cook using the 1 cup (200 g) rice to 1 cup (250 ml) water ratio.

HOW TO STEAM

Steaming is one the healthiest cooking methods. When steaming, make sure to bring the water to a rolling boil and maintain the heat level while cooking. You can use your stockpot to steam; simply use two cans (such as empty tuna fish cans) to raise a platter 2 inches above the water. When steaming dumplings, you can use sliced carrots under the dumplings to prevent them from sticking. Parchment paper with holes cut in it works for this purpose too. It's important to use enough water so it doesn't completely evaporate and leave you with a scorched pot. Whether you use a wok, stockpot or traditional steamer, make sure items are raised above the water and that you use a secure lid.

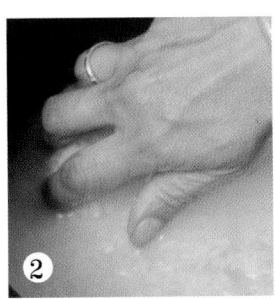

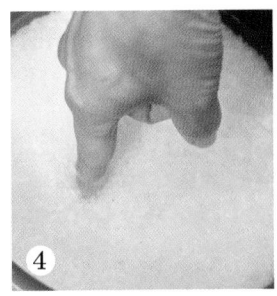

HOW TO MINCE LEMONGRASS

1. Remove the first 4–5 tough, fibrous outer layers of the lemongrass stalk with your fingers to reveal the softer, yellower part of the stalk that you'll be using. The remaining layers will still be slightly fibrous.
2. Using a sharp serrated knife, slice off the bulb (the bottom 2 inches / 5 cm) and discard.
3. Now, using the back of a knife, oblong pestle or rolling pin (or wine bottle if that's all you have), smash the bottom 6-inches of the lemongrass stalk to release the essential oils and separate the fibers. Next, use a sharp knife and finely chop the bottom 1/3 of the stalk.

HOW TO TOAST SPICES AND SESAME SEEDS

Toasting spices and sesame seeds intensifies their flavor. To toast spices, simply put your whole spices in a pan over medium heat and toast for about 2 minutes, or until you begin to smell their fragrance. Follow the same steps to toast sesame seeds.

HOW TO SLICE HOT CHILI PEPPERS

It's important that you use a latex rubber glove on one hand while handling hot chili peppers that you're slicing, such as Thai or bird's eye chili peppers. Remember to slice finely as you don't want your guests or family to inadvertently place a large piece of hot chili into their mouths. As noted in the recipes, feel free to deseed hot chili peppers or use another type of chili if you prefer less heat. If cooking for young children, feel free to select a milder chili or omit them altogether.

QUICK TIPS

Be organized: Before you start cooking, lay out all of your ingredients on the counter and organize them in the order you'll be needing them. Mince, chop, blanch, etc. all of your ingredients before you start adding anything to the pan. Don't get caught with burned garlic because you forgot to open the can of artichokes in time! The same goes for pots, pans, bowls and utensils. Read and re-read recipes before starting.

Bake your bacon instead of frying it: Place bacon strips on a wire rack on a rimmed baking sheet and cook for 20 minutes at 400°F (200°C), and then drain on paper towels. The bacon turns out crisp and perfect every time and saves you from an oil-splattered stove top.

Mince ginger and freeze it: Peel and cut about 1 lb (500 g) of fresh ginger into medium pieces and finely mince them in a food processor. Put the minced ginger in a resealable plastic food storage bag and flatten. Place the bagged ginger in the freezer. Once frozen, just break off the amount you need for your recipe!

Freeze beef before slicing: It's easier to slice raw beef when slightly frozen, as it's firmer in this state. Place the meat in the freezer for about 20 minutes before slicing for stir-fries.

Getting your kids to try new flavors: I always involve my 12-year-olds when I'm cooking because they're always excited to try whatever they help me make. Enlist their ideas and help and it will pique their curiosity. I always have my kids label ingredients with numbered post-it notes in the order I need them. Before I know it, they want to help cook the meal (and of course, try it right away, too).

Place leftover chicken stock in ice cube trays and freeze: Freeze the stock or broth in ice cube trays and then transfer them to a large resealable plastic food storage bag. Simply take out however much you need for future recipes.

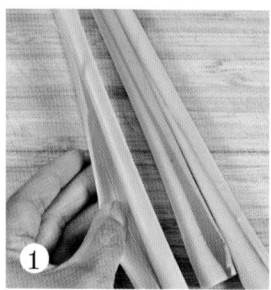 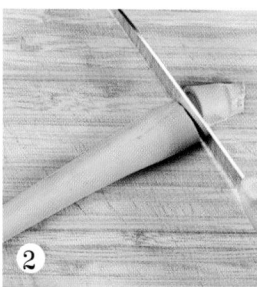  

Tips on Tools and Utensils

The beauty of the recipes in this cookbook is that you can conjure delectable international flavors using many of the tools and utensils you likely already have in your kitchen cabinets.

NON-STICK SKILLET
No one likes sticky situations. The majority of the recipes in this book can be made in a large non-stick skillet. Why non-stick? Because they require less oil (healthier) and proteins don't stick to the pan (much easier clean-up). Look for non-stick pans that are PFOA, lead and cadmium free. I prefer ceramic non-stick pans. Just make sure to use a plastic spatula to avoid scratching the non-stick surface of the pan. If you'd prefer to use a NON-non-stick skillet, that is totally fine—you just may need to use a bit more oil. When deep-frying, make sure to use a NON-non-stick skillet, as non-stick pans can't withstand the high heat levels required for deep-frying.

CAST IRON PAN
My hubby is in love with his cast iron pan. A love like this is versatile, durable and functional (not exactly the most romantic sounding relationship—but great qualities in a pan). Cast iron skillets can be used for sautéing, pan-frying, searing, baking, braising, broiling, roasting and even more cooking techniques. They're unmatched at retaining high heat levels and are easy to clean, as a natural non-stick surface is created over time when you season your cast iron pan. Never use detergent on a cast iron pan; simply wipe it clean with a damp towel. If you need to scrub your cast iron pan, use a bit of salt!

DUTCH OVEN
A dutch oven is a heavy cooking pot (usually made from cast iron) with a tightly fitting lid that is good for braising. Dutch ovens are also excellent for making soups and stews and can be used on the stove top or in the oven. Its significant weight is a reason why you probably won't use a dutch oven every day, but it's a great tool for slow cooking and doubles as an attractive serving vessel for stews and braised dishes.

WOK
The wok was invented in China over 1,000 years ago. It is central to Chinese cooking and other Asian cuisines because of its unique concave shape and ability to heat up quickly. It's incredibly versatile and used for everything from stir-frying and deep-frying to steaming and braising.

The most common types of woks are cast iron and carbon steel. I recommend carbon steel because they heat up quickly and retain heat. The most user-friendly size is 14 inches (29 cm). Larger woks can become unwieldy. Look for a wok with sturdy handles and a lid. I use both a cast iron wok and a carbon steel wok in my kitchen. Some wok purists turn up their noses at non-stick woks but I say go with whatever works for you. If you're going to use non-stick then I recommend a premium brand like Calphalon, Circulon or All Clad.

A flat-bottomed wok is the best shape for an American stovetop. If you have a powerful range, like Viking or Wolf, then you can get away with a round bottom wok with a wok stand as they produce enough heat to thoroughly heat a round bottom.

If you purchase a carbon steel or cast iron wok, you must season it first to create a natural non-stick finish. As with cast iron pans, never use detergent on a seasoned wok. Always wash with hot water and a scrub brush.

CHEF'S KNIFE
A quality chef's knife is one of the most important tools to have in your arsenal. Invest in quality knives and keep them sharp. A standard 8-inch (20-cm) chef's knife should do the trick along with some paring knives. If you're feeling insecure about using a sharp chef's knife, take a knife skills class at a local cooking school.

MANDOLINE
A mandoline is a cooking utensil used for slicing and for cutting with suitable attachments. It can make crinkle-cuts and can julienne vegetables.

by the rice or grains in the pot. It then miraculously switches to a warm setting so you don't have to do a thing and you don't have to worry about your rice burning. This is especially great when you're entertaining and trying to juggle a few recipes at once.

SPIRALIZER

A spiralizer is an inexpensive tool that turns fresh veggies into faux-noodles (such as zucchini noodles, called "zoodles") essential for making low-carb dishes which replace pasta with veggie "noodles." They function like a large pencil sharpener and the result is a pile of extra-long, gently curled ribbons.

CHEESE CLOTH

Cheesecloth is a cotton cloth that is loosely woven and resembles gauze. It comes in seven grades, from open to extra-fine weave. The grade is determined by the amount of threads per inch or centimeter constructed in each direction. It is a great tool for straining water and capturing solids in various recipes, and always handy to have on hand.

TONGS

An obvious but important item to have in your toolkit, especially when dealing with very hot foods—particularly when deep-frying. Tong tips that are coated in non-stick material are easier to clean up.

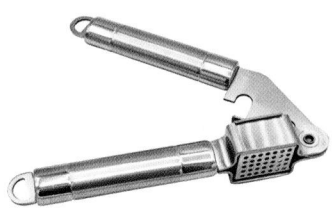

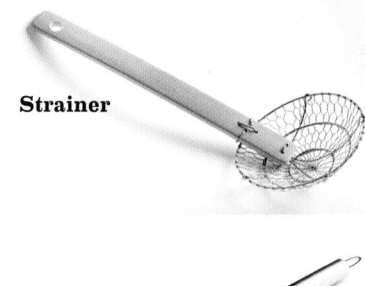

Strainer

Slotted Spoon

MICROPLANE OR ZESTER

A microplane or zester is a kitchen utensil for obtaining zest from lemons and other citrus fruit. A kitchen zester is approximately four inches long, with a handle and a curved metal end, the top of which is perforated with a row of round holes with sharpened rims.

GARLIC PRESS

A garlic press (also known as a garlic crusher in Australia, New Zealand and the United Kingdom), is a kitchen utensil to crush garlic cloves efficiently by forcing them through a grid of small holes.

RICE COOKER

Rice cookers are handy for making rice along with many other types of grains such as quinoa. Who doesn't need a device that can do the thinking for you? Rice cookers can determine through an internal temperature sensor when boiling water has been absorbed

STRAINER OR SLOTTED SPOON

I recommend a traditional Chinese style strainer with a long bamboo handle. A lot of people call this utensil a "spider." I'm not sure why but it sometimes makes me feel like a superhero, especially when I'm trying to fry eggrolls for 100 guests. It's made out of wire mesh and is great for removing deep-fried foods from oil as well as removing blanched foods from boiling water. You can find this type of strainer at an Asian market or specialty gourmet stores. I find it to be an indispensable tool in my kitchen. You can also use a wide, Western-style slotted spoon in place of a Chinese style strainer but not for deep-frying if it's made of plastic.

BAMBOO STEAMERS
I stock up on all different sizes of bamboo steamers because I steam so many different things in them—from dumplings to whole fish—and because they're so pretty and fun to use when I entertain. I guess you could call me a basket case! For everyday cooking, one large bamboo steamer with lid should be adequate. If you like to entertain, then I'd buy a stackable set, which usually comes with three baskets. Make sure your basket fits snugly in your wok or pan and that the pan is about 3 inches (7.5 cm) wider than the basket. Always make sure you have enough boiling water in the pan and that the basket sits about 2 inches (5 cm) above the water. Cover tightly with the lid before steaming.

SPATULAS
Every kitchen needs spatulas to cook. If using non-stick pans or woks, it's essential that you use non-stick spatulas so as to not scratch the Teflon surface. It's a key tool for stir-frying, as ingredients cook quickly and you need a sturdy spatula to keep things moving. I also recommend having rubber spatulas at the ready in different sizes. My friend Amy bought me some tiny rubber spatulas for Christmas and they've made all the difference in my scraping abilities!

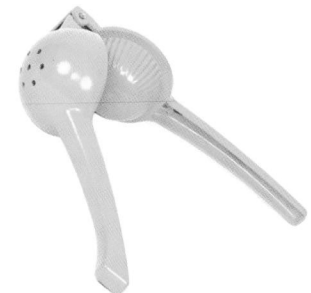

LEMON/LIME SQUEEZER
Many recipes in this book call for freshly squeezed lime or lemon juice, so it's a good idea to have a manual or electric lemon/lime squeezer. If you're in a pinch, you can buy store-bought juices, but nothing beats the real thing. My mother taught me to press and roll limes on a counter with your hand a few times before juicing to get the most juice.

FOOD PROCESSOR
I get by with a little help from my friends. My food processor has become my BFF and my cleaver is getting jealous. If you're like me, always trying to squeeze as much as possible into the day, I look for things to make life easier. Food processors can blend salad dressings, mince ginger, finely chop and grate vegetables, blend dumpling filling, and it goes on and on. Go for a standard model and get the attachment blades so you can grate, shred and do other nifty stuff.

COOKING SPRAY
I always have cooking spray on hand because it's important to have it available for grilling. As you'll see in many of the recipes that call for grilling in this book, I recommend coating the grill rack with cooking spray in advance to avoid sticking.

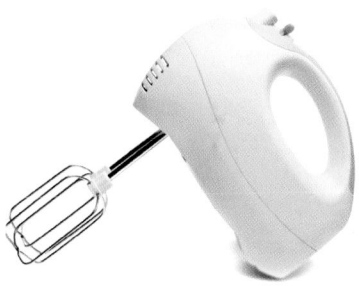

ELECTRIC HAND MIXER
If you've ever had to beat heavy cream into fluffy peaks without a hand mixer, you've felt my pain. Everyone should have a hand mixer in their kitchen to save time and make blending an ease.

PASTRY BRUSH
A pastry brush, also known as a basting brush, is a cooking utensil used to spread butter, oil or glaze on food. Traditional pastry brushes are made with natural bristles or a plastic or nylon fiber similar to a paintbrush, while modern kitchen brushes may have silicone bristles.

Global Go-to Sauces You Need to Know

My friends tell me I'm a connector and I'm pleased to introduce you to my favorite globally-inspired sauces. This chapter will make you "Sauce like a #BOSS!" Who doesn't want a stable of go-to sauces with global flavors to make your everyday meals come alive with flavor and spice? I've spent hours perfecting these versatile sauce recipes which I use all the time for my family and friends. These saucy gems can be used to dip, grill, stir-fry, marinate, baste, simmer and drizzle. I've integrated them into many of the recipes in this book but I recommend keeping batches on hand to add a little magic to whatever you're making: turn that plain, grilled chicken breast into a **Korean BBQ Sauce** beauty or simmer some shrimp in **Lemongrass Curry** for an aromatic feast for the senses. Spicy **Thai Peanut Sauce** transforms a stir-fry into a symphony of sweet, salty, sour, hot flavors. **Gochujang Sauce** will surprise and delight you with its smoky, sweet heat when tossed with some grilled veggies. **Chimichurri Sauce** will awaken all your senses with its bright piquant flavors and is amazing drizzled on any kind of meat, **Lemony Basil Pesto** turns your everyday sandwich into a supernova of flavor, and **Miso Butter Sauce** adds a luxurious umami touch to pan-fried scallops or anything else it touches.

Chimichurri Sauce

In a hurry? Whip up some Chimichurri! A few simple ingredients plus a quick whirl in your food processor equals a delicious and versatile Latin pesto that will add a fresh burst of spicy garlicky flavor to anything you cook. You can also use it as a marinade or salad dressing, a dipping sauce for grilled meats or even as a condiment on burgers or hot dogs.

Makes ³/₄ cup (185 ml)
Prep Time: 15 minutes + 10 minutes resting time

1 cup (25 g) packed fresh Italian parsley
¹/₃ cup (80 ml) red wine vinegar
4 tablespoons roughly chopped fresh coriander leaves (cilantro)
2 cloves garlic, peeled
¹/₂ teaspoon dried crushed red pepper
¹/₂ teaspoon dried oregano
¹/₂ teaspoon ground cumin
¹/₂ teaspoon salt
¹/₂ cup (125 ml) extra virgin olive oil

Place all the ingredients except the extra virgin olive oil in a food processor and purée. Slowly drizzle in the extra virgin olive oil. Transfer the sauce to a bowl. Cover and let it rest to integrate the flavors.

Gochujang Sauce

This sweet, smoky and spicy sauce makes anything from chicken wings to noodle bowls come alive with authentic Korean flavors. So versatile, you can add it to your scrambled eggs or even use it in place of pizza sauce.

Makes 3/4 cup (185 ml)
Prep Time: 10 minutes

1/4 cup (55 g) gochujang paste (Korean chili paste)
1/4 cup (35 g) finely chopped green onions
2 tablespoons soy sauce
2 tablespoons toasted sesame oil
2 tablespoons rice vinegar
1 tablespoon toasted sesame seeds
4 teaspoons white sugar
1 tablespoon peeled and minced fresh ginger

Whisk all the ingredients together in a medium bowl. Store in a airtight container in the refrigerator for up to 1 one week.

Korean BBQ Sauce

(Marinade, glaze, stir-fry sauce)

This Korean BBQ sauce is spicy sweet, garlicky and oh-so divine! This recipe calls for gochujang paste, which can be found at most grocery stores. Throw a spoonful into your next stir-fry or use it to marinate chicken breasts next time you're grilling. It's a signature flavor in Korean recipes and will make your dishes sing like K Pop!

Makes 3 cups (750 ml)
Prep Time: 15 minutes
Cook Time: 15 minutes

3 tablespoons cornstarch
3 tablespoons water
1 1/2 cups (350 ml) reduced-sodium soy sauce (do not use regular soy sauce)
1 1/2 cups (300 g) light brown sugar, packed
1/2 cup (125 ml), plus 2 tablespoons water
1/2 cup (125 ml) sake
4 tablespoons store-bought gochujang paste (Korean chili paste)
4 tablespoons honey
2 1/2 tablespoons rice vinegar
3 tablespoons minced garlic
2 tablespoons minced fresh ginger

Whisk the cornstarch together with the water. Set aside. Combine the remaining ingredients in a saucepan and bring to a boil. Add the cornstarch mixture in a steady stream. Return the sauce to a boil for one minute until thickened.

Thai Peanut Sauce

(Salad & noodle dressing, dipping sauce, stir-fry sauce)

My friend Jen Preuss goes a little nutty for peanut sauce and this recipe makes her give out a tiger sized ROAR! She helped me serve hundreds of servings of this yummy sauce tossed with rice noodles at a recent fundraiser. I use this recipe all the time as a salad dressing, dipping sauce and it's also great drizzled into a wok of stir-fried tofu and bok choy.

Makes 1 cup (250 ml)
Prep Time: 10 minutes
Cook Time: 15 minutes

6 tablespoons smooth peanut butter
6 tablespoons coconut milk
2 tablespoons water
2 teaspoons red curry paste
1 tablespoon freshly squeezed lime juice
2 tablespoons chicken broth
1$^1/_2$ tablespoons soy sauce
1$^1/_2$ tablespoons brown sugar
$^1/_2$ teaspoon sriracha sauce

Heat the peanut butter, coconut milk, water, red curry paste, lime juice, chicken broth, soy sauce, brown sugar and sriracha sauce over medium heat in a saucepan until the mixture begins to simmer, stirring constantly. Reduce to low heat and simmer for 10 minutes.

Lemongrass Curry

(Noodle sauce, simmering sauce)

This is a quick and easy way to bring the taste of Thailand to your family table any night of the week. Within minutes, your kitchen will be filled with the exotic aroma of coconut milk, lemongrass and fish sauce. Toss with your favorite noodle or brown some chicken or shrimp, add the sauce and simmer until cooked through for a soul satisfying easy weeknight dinner.

Makes 3$^1/_4$ cups (815 ml)
Prep Time: 15 minutes
Cook Time: 15 minutes

1 tablespoon oil
2 teaspoons green curry paste
3 cloves garlic, minced
2 shallots, finely chopped
6 tablespoons minced lemongrass
1 fresh hot red or green chili pepper, preferably Thai (deseeded if you prefer less heat), finely sliced
3 tablespoons fish sauce (*nam pla*)
2 teaspoons freshly ground black pepper
1 teaspoon brown sugar
1 cup (250 ml) chicken stock or broth
2 cups (500 ml) coconut milk

Heat the oil in a wok or large non-stick skillet over medium heat. Add the curry paste, stirring to break up paste, about 1 minute. Increase heat to medium-high. Add the garlic, shallot, lemongrass and chili peppers and stir-fry until fragrant, about 30 seconds. Add the fish sauce, pepper and brown sugar, and stir to combine. 1 minute. Add chicken stock or broth and coconut milk. Bring to a boil. Reduce heat and simmer for 4–5 minutes.

Miso Butter Sauce

Miso happy to share this recipe with you! I'm not sure if a sauce can be considered luxurious but I feel like my taste buds are being wrapped in a silky, buttery umami blanket every time I slurp this sauce up with noodles or stir-fry some shrimp with it. Add a luxury to your menu-planning life with this easy and divine sauce.

Makes 1 cup (250 ml)
Prep Time: 15 minutes
Cook Time: 12 minutes

One 4 oz (113 g) stick butter
3 cloves garlic, minced
4 tablespoons minced shallot
4 green onions (scallions), finely chopped (white and green parts)
1/2 cup (275 g) white miso paste
4 tablespoons soy sauce
4 tablespoons sake
4 tablespoons basic chicken stock or broth, or vegetable stock
1 tablespoon oyster sauce

Heat a wok or large non-stick skillet over medium-high heat. Add the butter, garlic, shallot and green onion. Sauté for 30 seconds until fragrant. Add the miso, soy sauce, sake, stock or broth and oyster sauce and sauté for 1 minute, breaking up the miso paste and stirring constantly. Reduce heat to low and simmer for 10 minutes.

Lemony Basil Pesto

Easy, peasy, lemon squeezy sums up this light, bright and fresh pesto recipe that you can whip up in minutes. Toss it with pasta, drizzle on grilled meats or seafood, or spread onto a sandwich. My sister Jeanie even throws a spoonful into her chicken noodle soup—it's that tasty.

Makes about 2/3 cup (160 ml)
Prep Time: 20 minutes
Cook Time: 8–10 minutes

3 tablespoons pine nuts
3 cloves garlic
2 cups (50) fresh basil leaves
1/2 cup (12 g) fresh flat-leaf parsley leaves or spinach leaves
4 tablespoons grated cheese (Parmigiano-Reggiano)
1 1/2–2 teaspoons lemon zest
1 tablespoon freshly squeezed lemon juice
1/4 teaspoon salt
1/8 teaspoon freshly ground black pepper
1/2 cup (125 ml) extra virgin olive oil
Salt and freshly ground pepper, to taste

Preheat oven to 350°F (175°C).

Toast the pine nuts: Place the pine nuts on a baking sheet and bake until golden, 8–10 minutes. Remove from the oven and set aside.

In a food processor, combine the garlic, toasted pine nuts, basil, parsley or spinach, cheese, lemon zest, lemon juice, salt and pepper, and purée until a smooth paste is formed.

With the machine running, slowly drizzle in the extra virgin olive oil until the desired consistency is reached. Season with salt and pepper.

COOK'S NOTE
You can substitute walnuts for the pine nuts. Basil leaves darken when exposed to air so cover with plastic wrap until ready to serve.

FAMILY DINNERS
Four Ways

We all know Meatless Mondays, Taco Tuesdays, Pizza Night and Sliders are popular meal options for family dinners. Here are four ways and 16 different recipes to add excitement, a fusion of flavors and downright deliciousness into your meal planning—or to amp up your game night or Super Bowl party! Some highlights include: a Latin twist on Taco Tuesday with **Cuban Fish Tacos with Citrus Mango Slaw**, **Crispy Tofu with Orange Glaze** for Meatless Mondays that will satisfy your kids' orange chicken craving, a **Chicken Tikka Masala Pizza** for pizza night that will have you performing a Bollywood number in your kitchen and finally, home run-worthy **Korean Fried Chicken Sliders** for Slammin' Slider night.

Cuban Fish Tacos with Citrus Mango Slaw

I used to travel to Miami for business all the time, and one of the great perks was getting to treat myself to a delicious meal at one of the many colorful Cuban seafood restaurants in and around Miami Beach. This Cuban fish taco recipe is inspired by a cafe in the Coconut Grove district that my Miami-based friend Michael Dagnery took me to. These tacos are bursting with clean and bright flavors from the lime and orange juices, and fresh herbs and spices, which pair beautifully with tender grilled fish and a crunchy and tangy slaw.

Serves 4
Prep Time: 25 minutes
Cook Time: 10 minutes

Fish

4 tablespoons extra virgin olive oil
Juice of 1 lime
4 tablespoons freshly squeezed orange juice
3 cloves garlic, minced
2 green onions (scallions), finely chopped (white and green parts)
4 tablespoons finely chopped fresh coriander leaves (cilantro)
1 tablespoon finely chopped fresh oregano
1/4 teaspoon paprika
1/2 teaspoon cumin
1 teaspoon salt
1/2 teaspoon freshly ground black pepper
1 lb (500 g) skin-on mahi mahi or salmon
Corn or flour tortillas, warmed
Cotija cheese, for serving
Finely chopped fresh coriander leaves (cilantro), for serving
Lime wedges, for serving

Citrus Mango Slaw

2 cups (200 g) shredded purple cabbage
1 ripe mango, diced
1/3 cup (15 g) finely chopped fresh coriander leaves (cilantro)
4 tablespoons finely chopped red onion
1 jalapeño pepper, finely chopped (deseeded if you prefer less heat)
2 teaspoons extra virgin olive oil
1/2 tablespoon freshly squeezed lime juice
1/2 teaspoon salt
Zest of one blood orange
1 tablespoon freshly squeezed blood orange juice

Whisk together the extra virgin olive oil, lime juice, orange juice, garlic, green onions, cilantro, oregano, paprika, cumin, salt and pepper in a medium bowl. Place the fish in a 9 x 13-inch (23 x 33-cm) baking dish, pour the marinade over the fish. Cover and refrigerate for at least 15 minutes and up to 4 hours.

Make the **Citrus Mango Slaw**: Place all the slaw ingredients in a medium bowl. Toss to combine.

Spray a grill pan or cast iron skillet with cooking spray and heat over medium-high heat (you may also use an outdoor grill). Add the fish, skin side down, and sear for 3–4 minutes, brushing the fish with the marinade as it cooks. Flip and cook until desired doneness. Remove the skin.

To serve, break the fish into pieces. Warm the tortillas. Place some fish pieces on top of tortillas. Top with slaw and sprinkle with cotija cheese and cilantro and serve with lime wedges.

Banh Mi Street Tacos

Word on the street is that this taco recipe is all about Mi, Banh Mi that is! This recipe was inspired by a trip to New Orleans when I was a guest chef at the Food & Wine Festival. I took my sous chef Stacy Mears to one of the many local Vietnamese restaurants in town for a Banh Mi sandwich. One day I was reminiscing about our trip and craving a traditional Vietnamese Banh Mi—but not the doughy bread and carbs from the French roll. I decided to throw all of the amazing sweet, sour, salty and hot ingredients into a corn tortilla and ta-dah: the Banh Mi Street Taco was born!

Serves 4
Prep Time: 25 minutes
Cook Time: 10 minutes

Marinade
- 2 tablespoons freshly squeezed lime juice
- 1 tablespoon oil
- 1 clove garlic, minced
- 1/2 shallot, minced
- 1 tablespoon fish sauce (*nam pla*)
- 1 tablespoon brown sugar

- 2 boneless, skinless chicken thighs or breasts
- 4 tablespoons pâté or liverwurst
- Corn tortillas, warmed
- 2 fresh jalapeño peppers, thinly sliced (deseeded if you prefer less heat)
- 3/4 cup (45 g) fresh coriander leaves (cilantro)
- 1 English cucumber, sliced thin
- 2 bunches radishes, sliced thin
- Soy sauce, to drizzle
- Fish sauce (*nam pla*), to drizzle
- 2 limes, cut into wedges, for serving
- Sriracha sauce, for serving

Slaw
- 8 oz (226 g) daikon radish, peeled
- 1 carrot, peeled
- 1/2 cup (125 ml) unseasoned rice vinegar
- 1 tablespoon sugar
- 1/2 teaspoon salt

Make the **Marinade**: In small bowl, whisk together the lime juice, oil, garlic, shallot, fish sauce and brown sugar. Place the chicken thighs or breasts in a large resealable plastic bag and pour the mixture over the chicken thighs or breasts. Place in the refrigerator and let marinate for 20 minutes.

Make the **Slaw**: Shred daikon and carrot in a food processor fitted with a medium shredding disk or with a mandoline. Place the vinegar, sugar and salt in a medium bowl. Add the shredded vegetables and toss to combine. Let the slaw stand, stirring occasionally, for 15 minutes. Drain slaw and set aside.

Heat a grill over medium-high heat. Spray with cooking spray. Grill chicken thighs or breasts for 4–5 minutes per side or until cooked through or until an internal thermometer registers 165°F (75°C).

Remove from the grill and let stand for 10 minutes. Slice thinly.

Spread pâté or liverwurst in the center of each tortilla. Place chicken slices on top of the spread, top with some slaw, jalapeño, cilantro, cucumber slices and radish slices. Drizzle with soy sauce and fish sauce. Serve with lime wedges and sriracha sauce.

Verde Chicken Tacos

Lean, clean and green, these Verde Chicken Tacos are loaded with tons of flavor and not a lot of fat. We're always looking for ways to bring some unexpected and exciting flavors to our Taco Tuesday Table and this recipe is a winner. My friend Steven Durbahn made these at a recent test kitchen session and proclaimed that Tuesday was the new favorite day of the week and he couldn't wait to make them again! You can find store-bought salsa verde at any grocery store.

Serves 4
Prep Time: 25 minutes
Cook Time: 10 minutes

2 tablespoons oil, divided
4 bone-in chicken thighs with skin on
1 tablespoon ancho chili powder
Salt and freshly ground black pepper
2 cups (500 ml) chicken stock or broth
1 tablespoon freshly squeezed lime juice
1/2 tablespoon honey
1 cup (259 g) store-bought roasted salsa verde
1 large yellow onion, thinly sliced
2 poblano peppers, deseeded and cut into thin strips
1/2 cup (12 g) roughly chopped fresh coriander leaves (cilantro)
8 small corn or flour tortillas, warmed
Lime wedges, for serving
Hot sauce, for serving (if desired)

Toppings
4–5 small radishes, trimmed and thinly sliced
Crumbled cotija cheese
Diced avocado
Fresh coriander leaves (cilantro)

COOK'S NOTE
You can substitute ancho chili powder with 1 tablespoon regular chili powder mixed with 1/2 teaspoon crushed red pepper.

Heat 1 tablespoon of the oil in a large skillet over medium-high heat. Pat the chicken thighs dry and season with ancho chili powder, salt and pepper on both sides. Sear the chicken thighs skin-side down for 4–5 minutes, or until golden brown. Flip the thighs and pour the chicken stock or broth, lime juice, honey and salsa into the pan. Bring the liquid to a low simmer, cover and braise the chicken for 35–40 minutes or until fork tender.

Remove the chicken and liquid from the pan. Reserve liquid. Transfer the chicken to a cutting board.

Using forks, shred the chicken, discard bones and skin. Set aside. Wash and dry the skillet and return to the stove.

Heat the remaining 1 tablespoon oil in the skillet over medium-high heat. Add the onions and peppers and sauté for 2 minutes. Add the reserved liquid to the skillet and bring to a low boil, about 20 minutes. Cook, stirring occasionally until the liquid is reduced by half.

Reduce the heat to low. Add the shredded chicken back into the skillet and stir to combine. Add the cilantro and season to taste with salt and pepper.

Spoon the chicken mixture into the warm tortillas. Top with radish slices, cotija cheese, avocado and cilantro. Serve immediately with lime wedges and hot sauce, if using.

Asian Ginger Pork Tacos

My kids were pleading for me to make my late mother Leeann's mu shu pork recipe but I didn't have time to make Chinese pancakes or run to the Asian market so we improvised and tossed traditional mu shu filling into store-bought tortillas. My family loves this Asian twist on taco night and the soft, warm tortillas definitely do the trick. Tender, savory and gingery, these Asian pork tacos promise to be the talk of the town.

Serves 4
Prep Time: 25 minutes
Cook Time: 10 minutes

3/4 lb (350 g) pork tenderloin, cut into thin strips
1 teaspoon cornstarch, divided
$1/2$ teaspoon salt
1 teaspoon soy sauce, divided
$1/4$ teaspoon sugar
$1/4$ teaspoon white pepper
1 teaspoon cold water
1 tablespoon oil
1 teaspoon peeled and minced fresh ginger
1 clove garlic, minced
$1/2$ cup (63 g) sliced white button mushrooms
$1/2$ cup (50 g) bean sprouts, trimmed
$1/3$ cup (43 g) canned sliced bamboo shoots, drained and cut lengthwise into thin strips
4 tablespoons chicken broth or stock
1 green onion (scallion), white and green parts cut diagonally into 2-in (5-cm) pieces, divided
Small flour tortillas, steamed
Hoisin sauce, for drizzling

Toss the pork strips, $1/2$ teaspoon of the cornstarch, $1/2$ teaspoon salt, $1/2$ teaspoon of the soy sauce, the sugar and white pepper in a medium bowl. Cover and refrigerate 30 minutes.

Mix water, the remaining $1/2$ teaspoon of the cornstarch and the remaining $1/2$ teaspoon of the soy sauce. Set aside.

Heat the oil in a wok or non-stick skillet over medium-high heat. Add the ginger and garlic and pork and stir-fry 2 minutes until the meat is no longer pink. Add the mushrooms, bean sprouts and bamboo shoots. Stir-fry 1 minute. Stir in the stock or broth and cook and stir 2 minutes. Stir in the cornstarch mixture. Cook and stir 10 seconds or until thickened. Add half of the green onions and stir-fry for 30 seconds.

To serve, spoon about 2 tablespoons of the mixture onto the center of each tortilla and sprinkle with some of the remaining scallions. Drizzle with hoisin sauce and serve immediately.

Crispy Tofu with Orange Glaze

Knock knock? Who's there? Orange. Well, you know the rest and orange you glad I included this recipe? If your kids are obsessed with orange chicken like all of my friend's kids are, here is a plant-based, Meatless Monday take on this all time fave. Instead of chicken, you flash fry cubes of plant-based, protein-rich tofu to golden perfection. The crispy tofu absorbs all the glorious flavors from my signature glistening, sweet-tart orange sauce. Before you know it, your kids will be saying, "Chicken who?"

Serves 6–8
Prep Time: 30 minutes + 30 minutes resting time
Cook Time: 30 minutes

Crispy Tofu

Two 14 oz (792 g) packages firm tofu, drained, patted dry and cut into 1-inch cubes
$\frac{1}{2}$ cup (60 g) all-purpose flour
$\frac{1}{2}$ cup (64 g) cornstarch
1 teaspoon salt
Oil, for frying
Orange slices, for garnish

Orange Glaze

2 tablespoons cornstarch
2 tablespoons water
$\frac{3}{4}$ cup (150 g) sugar
$\frac{1}{2}$ cup (125 ml) chicken stock or broth, or vegetable stock
2 tablespoons orange juice concentrate
6 tablespoons unseasoned rice vinegar or white vinegar
2 teaspoons oil
2 teaspoons dark soy sauce
$\frac{1}{4}$ teaspoon salt
1 clove garlic, minced
$\frac{1}{4}$ teaspoon crushed red pepper
$\frac{1}{4}$ teaspoon orange zest

COOK'S NOTE
If using vegetable stock, add additional salt to taste.

Dry out the tofu: Line a rimmed baking sheet with paper towels. Place the tofu blocks on the paper towels and put another layer of paper towels on top of the tofu blocks. Place a cutting board on top of the paper towels and then weigh the stack down with heavy books, cast iron skillet or cans. Let is rest for 30 minutes and pat dry. Cut the tofu into 1-inch (2.5-cm) cubes.

Meanwhile, make the Orange Glaze: Combine the cornstarch and water in a small bowl. Bring the sugar, chicken stock or broth (or vegetable stock), orange juice concentrate, vinegar, oil, soy sauce, $\frac{1}{4}$ teaspoon salt, garlic, crushed red pepper and orange zest to a boil in a medium saucepan. Add the cornstarch mixture to the sauce, stirring continuously until thickened, about 10 seconds. Remove from heat.

Combine the flour, cornstarch and salt in a bowl. Toss the tofu cubes in the flour mixture. In a large wok or deep skillet, heat 2–3 inches (5–7.5 cm) of the oil to 350°F (175°C). Fry tofu for 4 minutes. Flip over tofu and fry for another 4 minutes until golden brown all over. Drain on a sheet pan lined with paper towels. Transfer the tofu cubes to a platter.

Reheat the sauce over medium-high heat and pour over the tofu. Garnish with orange slices and serve immediately.

Vegan Mac and Cheese

Most of my friends and I think Meatless Monday is a good idea but the reality is there's always the dreaded, "yuck mom, what is this?" reaction. Never fear, because Vegan Mac and Cheese is here! In my test kitchen my friend Dina Barry made this and we served it to a group of 8-year-olds without telling them it was vegan. The verdict: thumbs up all around in silence (little girls were too busy chewing)! The combination of nutritional yeast and Dijon mustard mimics the flavor of cheese and is super duper creamy. Shhhh! Just don't let the word get around (especially around Dina's house).

Serves 4
Prep Time: 25 minutes
Cook Time: 10 minutes

8 oz (227 g) dried gluten-free elbow
  macaroni or shell pasta of choice
1½ cups (225 g) raw cashews
3 tablespoons freshly squeezed lemon juice
¾ cup (185 ml) water
1½ teaspoons salt
½ teaspoon freshly ground black pepper
4 tablespoons nutritional yeast
½ teaspoon chili powder
⅛ teaspoon smoked paprika, plus more, for
  garnish
¼ teaspoon garlic powder
¼ teaspoon onion powder
Pinch of ground red pepper (cayenne)
  (optional)
½ teaspoon Dijon mustard
Chopped fresh parsley, for garnish

Topping
3 slices white gluten-free bread
2 tablespoons vegan butter or extra virgin
  olive oil
1 clove garlic

Preheat the oven to 375°F (190°C).

Prepare the pasta according to package directions. Rinse and drain and set aside.

While the pasta is cooking, combine the cashews, lemon juice, water, salt, black pepper, nutritional yeast, chili powder, smoked paprika, garlic powder, onion powder, ground red pepper (if using) and mustard in a high speed blender or food processor and blend until smooth. If the mixture is too thick, add 2–3 more tablespoons of water and blend again. Return the pasta to the pot. Pour the "cheese" mixture from the blender or food processor over the pasta and stir to combine.

Make the **Topping**: Wash and dry the blender or food processor. Break the bread into pieces and place in the blender or food processor with the butter or olive oil and garlic clove. Blend until crumbs form. Set aside.

Spoon the macaroni mixture into an ovenproof dish. Sprinkle the crumbs evenly on top. Place in the oven and cook for 20–25 minutes or until piping hot and the crumb topping is golden brown and crispy. Garnish with paprika and parsley. Serve immediately.

Tofu Mushroom Stir-fry

Some of my friends feel "meh" about tofu. They're not sure how to prepare it to make it tasty, i.e., so it doesn't taste like a big bland block. The thing about tofu is that it absorbs all of the flavors around it. This simple vegan stir-fry recipe calls for an intoxicating combo of Shaoxing wine, soy sauce and rice vinegar, ginger and shallots with a kick from crushed red pepper. When stir-fried with tofu and mushrooms, it creates a lustrous, silky and flavorful dish filled with delicious umami notes.

Serves 4–6
Prep Time: 15 minutes
Cook Time: 5 minutes

One 14-oz (396-g) block extra-firm tofu, drained, patted dry and cut into large squares
1¹/₂ teaspoons cornstarch
¹/₂ teaspoon crushed red pepper
3 tablespoons soy sauce, divided
2 tablespoons seasoned rice vinegar
2 tablespoons Shaoxing wine (Chinese rice wine) or cooking sherry
1 tablespoon sugar
2 tablespoons oil, divided, plus more
1 lb (500 g) mixed mushrooms (such as shiitake, oyster, button, baby bellas), thinly sliced
2 teaspoons finely chopped shallot
2 teaspoons peeled and minced fresh ginger
1 green onion (scallion), white and green parts, finely chopped, for garnish

Toss the tofu, cornstarch, crushed red pepper and 1 tablespoon of the soy sauce in a medium bowl.

Combine the vinegar, Shaoxing wine, the remaining 2 tablespoons of the soy sauce and the sugar in a small bowl.

Heat 1 tablespoon of the oil in a wok or large non-stick skillet over medium-high heat. Add the mushrooms, shallots and ginger and stir-fry for about 5–7 minutes. Remove from the wok or skillet and set aside.

Add the remaining 1 tablespoon of oil to the wok or non-stick skillet. Add the tofu pieces and arrange in a single layer in the wok or skillet. Cook, undisturbed, until the tofu is browned on the first side, about 2 minutes. Add a bit more oil if necessary, and then turn pieces and continue to cook, undisturbed again, until second side is browned, about a minute or two longer. Transfer the tofu pieces to a platter.

Add the vinegar mixture and mushrooms back to skillet. Stir-fry until the sauce is thickened and all the ingredients are coated, about 30 seconds. Spoon the mushroom mixture over the tofu pieces. Serve immediately with steaming hot jasmine white or brown rice and top with the green onions.

Oven Baked Eggplant Parmesan

My kids always love this Meatless Monday dish because it's oozing with cheese and it's soul-satisfying after a day of tests, dance rehearsal, baseball practice and Fortnite challenges. I'm not a huge fan of eggplant but this dish is so flavorful, and because of the "sweating" (salting) technique, it's not bitter but it is very tender, and I devour it every time. Plus, eggplant can lower high blood pressure and is loaded with fiber, potassium and vitamin C. Now, that's what I call purple pleasing power!

Serves 6
Prep Time: 20 minutes + resting time
Cook Time: 40–45 minutes

$2^{1}/_{2}$ lbs (1.25 kg) eggplant, sliced into $^{1}/_{2}$-in (1.3-cm) rounds
$2^{1}/_{4}$ teaspoons salt, divided
2 eggs
2 teaspoons water
$^{3}/_{4}$ cup (48 g) panko bread crumbs (Japanese-style bread crumbs)
$^{3}/_{4}$ cup (75 g) grated Parmesan cheese, plus 2 tablespoons for topping
1 teaspoon dried oregano
$^{1}/_{2}$ teaspoon dried basil
$^{1}/_{8}$ teaspoon freshly ground black pepper
6 cups (1.35 kg) chunky tomato sauce
$1^{1}/_{2}$ cups (170 g) shredded mozzarella cheese
Fresh basil leaves, for garnish

Preheat the oven to 375°F (190°C).

Toss the eggplant slices with 2 teaspoons of the salt in a colander set over a bowl. Let drain 30 minutes. Rinse off the salt and pat dry with paper towels. Spray 2 baking sheets evenly with cooking spray and set aside. In a medium shallow dish, whisk together the eggs and 2 tablespoons of water. In another medium shallow dish, combine panko bread crumbs, Parmesan cheese, oregano, basil, the remaining $^{1}/_{4}$ teaspoon of the salt and pepper.

Dip the eggplant slices into the egg mixture, letting the excess drip off, and then dredge in the breadcrumb mixture, coating well. Place the eggplant slices on the baking sheets. Bake until golden brown on the bottoms, about 20–25 minutes. Turn the slices over and continue baking until the slices are browned on other side, about 20–25 minutes more. Remove the slices from the oven; increase the oven heat to 400°F (200°C).

Spread 2 cups (500 ml) of the tomato sauce in a 9 x 13-inch (23 x 33-cm) baking dish. Arrange half of the eggplant in the dish; cover with 2 cups (500 ml) of the tomato sauce, and then $^{1}/_{2}$ cup (56 g) mozzarella. Repeat with remaining eggplant, sauce and mozzarella. Sprinkle with the remaining 2 tablespoons of the Parmesan cheese. Bake until the sauce is bubbling and the cheese is melted, 15–20 minutes. Let stand 5 minutes before serving. Garnish with basil leaves and serve.

COOK'S NOTE
Salting or "sweating" the eggplant makes it more tender, flavorful and eliminates its bitter taste.

Cherry Tomato & Basil Pizza on Cauliflower Crust

I'll admit I was a little reluctant to try cauliflower crust pizza with my hubby when we were out to dinner last year. Ever since he started spinning on our Peloton bike daily and cutting down on carbs to reshape his "dad bod" (which I think is adorable, BTW), he's fallen in love with cauliflower anything. I have to say I was pleasantly surprised at how thin and crisp the cauliflower crust was, and tasty at that. I tested several different ways to recreate our fave pizza joint's version of cauliflower crust and I think I nailed it. I hope you think so too!

Serves 4
Prep Time: 30 minutes
Cook Time: 20 minutes

Crust

1 head cauliflower, stem removed
1/2 cup (50 g) shredded mozzarella cheese
4 tablespoons grated Parmesan cheese
1/2 teaspoon dried oregano
1/2 teaspoon salt
1/4 teaspoon garlic powder
2 eggs, lightly beaten

Topping

2 tablespoons extra virgin olive oil
Fresh basil leaves, cleaned and patted
  dry
1 1/2 cups (150 g) shredded mozzarella
  cheese
1 small red onion, thinly sliced
8 cherry tomatoes, sliced
1/2 teaspoon salt
1/4 teaspoon freshly ground black pepper

> **COOK'S NOTE**
> **Try adding slices of prosciutto for a boost of flavor and protein!**

Preheat the oven to 400°F (200°C)

Make the **Crust:** Line a baking sheet with parchment paper. Break the cauliflower into florets and pulse in a food processor until rice-consistency fine. Line a steamer basket with a kitchen towel (not terrycloth). Set in a saucepan with 2 inches (5 cm) of boiling water. Add the cauliflower, cover and cook 5 minutes. Drain well, and then wring dry in the towel to remove the excess moisture. Let cool.

In a bowl, combine the cauliflower with the mozzarella, Parmesan cheese, oregano, 1/2 teaspoon salt, the garlic powder and eggs. Transfer to the center of the baking sheet and spread into a 10-inch circle to make a pizza crust. Bake until golden, about 20 minutes. Remove from oven.

Make the **Topping:** Brush the crust with extra virgin olive oil. Place a layer of basil leaves onto the crust and then top with shredded cheese, red onion and cherry tomatoes. Sprinkle evenly with salt and pepper. Bake 10 minutes longer or until cheese is melted. Cut into slices and serve immediately.

Pepperoni Arugula Sheet Pan Pizza

I didn't have time to make fresh pizza dough the other day so my sister Laura suggested I use refrigerated pizza crust from a can. I was skeptical at first but was pleasantly surprised to discover it makes for a crispy and fluffy crust and that takes just a few minutes. This simple, yet delicious recipe combines our family's faves—pepperoni, mushrooms and olives—but feel free to improvise with your favorite toppings. It's so much less expensive than delivery pizza and you can control how much cheese and toppings go onto the pizza. Best of all, it's a way to get your kids in on the act and off their screens!

Serves 4
Prep Time: 30 minutes
Cook Time: 20 minutes

One 13.8-oz (391-g) can store-bought refrigerated pizza crust
4 tablespoons extra virgin olive oil, divided
1/2 cup (114 g) store-bought pizza sauce
1 1/2 cups (150 g) shredded mozzarella, divided
1/2 cup (230 g) grated Parmesan cheese, divided
1/2 cup (69 g) pepperoni slices
1/2 cup (63 g) sliced white button mushrooms
1/4 cup (45 g) sliced black olives
1 cup (20 g) arugula

COOK'S NOTE
Swap out the tomato sauce with pesto for a green version of this pizza, or with ricotta for a white version.

Preheat the oven to 425°F (220°C). Spray a baking sheet with cooking spray. Unroll dough onto the baking sheet. Starting at the center, press out dough with your hands to form 12 x 8-inch (30 x 20-cm) rectangle.

Brush the dough with 2 tablespoons of extra virgin olive oil and bake for 5–6 minutes. Remove the crust from the oven and set aside.

Spread the pizza sauce in an even layer all over the crust. Sprinkle 1 cup (100 g) of the mozzarella cheese and 4 tablespoons of Parmesan cheese evenly on top of the sauce. Distribute the pepperoni, mushrooms and olives evenly on the pizza.

Add the remaining 1/2 cup (50 g) of the mozzarella cheese and 4 tablespoons of the Parmesan cheese to the top.

Place the pizza in the oven and bake until the cheese is melted and the edges are lightly browned.

When the pizza comes out of the oven, sprinkle the arugula all over the top, slice and serve immediately.

Chicken Tikka Masala Pizza

This recipe was inspired by my friends Greg and Brad who tried my Chicken Tikka Masala recipe (see the recipe on page 106) one day. They called to tell me how delicious it was and it got me craving it, but at the same time I was craving pizza and.... TA-DAH! Chicken Tikka Masala Pizza was born! Enjoy all the authentic flavors of cumin, turmeric and garam masala in this popular Indian dish married with gooey cheese and a fluffy and crispy flatbread crust.

Serves 4
Prep Time: 20 minutes + marinating time
Cook Time: 30 minutes

1 whole boneless, skinless chicken breast
4 tablespoons plain yogurt
1¼ teaspoons turmeric, divided
1¼ teaspoons cumin, divided
2 teaspoons garam masala, divided
Salt and freshly ground black pepper
One 14.5-oz (411-g) can diced tomatoes, drained
2 teaspoons extra virgin olive oil
1 tablespoon butter
1 teaspoon peeled and minced fresh ginger
3 cloves garlic, minced
½ teaspoon salt
2 tablespoons heavy whipping cream
1 store-bought flatbread pizza crust or store-bought naan
½ small red onion, thinly sliced
1 cup (100 g) shredded mozzarella cheese
2 tablespoons fresh coriander leaves (cilantro)

Preheat the broiler.

Cut the chicken breast in half lengthwise and pound it to flatten the thick part so the chicken is of consistent thickness. In a medium bowl, combine the chicken, yogurt, ¼ teaspoon turmeric, ¼ teaspoon cumin and ½ teaspoon garam masala. Cover and refrigerate for 10 minutes.

Place the chicken pieces on a foil-lined baking sheet coated with cooking spray. Sprinkle with salt and pepper. Insert the pan so the chicken breast are 4–5 inches from the heat. Broil 12–15 minutes, turning the chicken over about halfway through the cooking time. Remove the chicken.

Preheat the oven to 375°F (190°C). Cut the chicken into ¾-inch (1.9-cm) cubes and set aside.

Place the tomatoes in a mini chopper or food processor; pulse until almost puréed. Set aside.

Heat the oil and butter in a large non-stick skillet over medium-high heat. Add the ginger and garlic and sauté until fragrant, about 30 seconds. Add 1½ teaspoons of the garam masala, the remaining 1 teaspoon cumin, the remaining 1 teaspoon turmeric and sauté for 1 minute. Stir in the reserve tomatoes. Reduce heat and simmer for 4 minutes. Stir in ½ teaspoon salt and the cream and cook for 1 minute. Add the chicken cubes to pan and stir to combine.

Remove from heat. Spread the chicken mixture on the pizza crust. Top with the onion and cheese. Transfer to a baking sheet and bake 10–12 minutes, until crust is golden. Sprinkle with cilantro and serve.

Thai-style Pizza

When I created the recipe for Thai Peanut Sauce I knew it would be great tossed with noodles or as a dipping sauce for satay or other grilled meats but I didn't realize how delicious it would taste on a pizza until I tested it for some friends and they all said in unison, "OMG...amazing!" Gracing the yummy sauce are fresh veggies like bean sprouts and carrots along with crunchy peanuts and aromatic cilantro leaves. Along with tender cubes of broiled chicken, this recipe will have you telling everyone, "*Thai* it—you'll like it!"

Serves 4
Prep Time: 25 minutes
Cook Time: 22–25 minutes

Thai Peanut Sauce (page 34)

Pizza
1 whole boneless, skinless chicken breast
Salt and freshly ground black pepper
1 store bought flatbread pizza crust
1 cup (100 g) shredded mozzarella cheese, divided
1 green onion (scallion), white and green parts, slivered diagonally
4 tablespoons shredded carrot
4 tablespoons bean sprouts, trimmed
2 tablespoons chopped roasted peanuts
2 tablespoons chopped fresh coriander leaves (cilantro)

Preheat the broiler.

Cut the chicken breast in half lengthwise and pound it to flatten the thick part so the chicken is of consistent thickness. Season the chicken breast with salt and pepper. Insert the pan so the chicken breasts are 4–5 inches from the heat. Broil 12–15 minutes, turning the chicken over about halfway through the cooking time. Remove the chicken. Preheat the oven to 375°F (190°C). Cut the chicken into $3/4$-inch (1.9-cm) cubes and set aside.

While chicken is broiling, make the Thai Peanut Sauce as directed on page 34.

Spread $1/2$ cup (125 ml) of the Thai Peanut Sauce evenly on the pizza crust. Sprinkle $3/4$ cup (75 g) of the mozzarella cheese over the sauce. Place the chicken on top of the cheese followed by the green onions, carrots and bean sprouts. Top with remaining 4 tablespoons of mozzarella cheese and the peanuts. Bake 8–10 minutes, until crust is golden. Sprinkle with cilantro and serve.

COOK'S NOTE
The Thai Peanut Sauce recipe makes approximately 1 cup (250 ml). You can store leftover peanut sauce covered in the refrigerator for up to 5 days. Use it as a dipping sauce, stir-fry sauce or salad dressing.

Honey BBQ Pork Bao Sliders

Pillowy soft bao buns encase succulent and juicy honey BBQ pork slices in these delicious sliders! Bao buns can be intimidating to make but here's an easy recipe you can make with refrigerated biscuit dough (*Pssst!*—BTW, it's also totally okay to buy store-bought bao buns available at Asian markets). If you're feeling adventurous, try this method as it only takes a few minutes and you'll be glad you did. This honey BBQ pork recipe is my late mom Leeann's signature pork dish and once you try it, you'll know why. Although this recipe takes some time, it's quite easy and your friends will be asking you to take a BAO!

Serves 8–10
Prep Time: 20 minutes
Cook Time: 80–90 minutes

Honey BBQ Pork
1½ lbs (680 g) boneless pork butt or
  shoulder, trimmed of fat

Marinade
2 tablespoons ketchup
1 teaspoon salt
2 teaspoons sugar
1 clove garlic, minced
1 teaspoon brandy
½ teaspoon five spice powder
4 tablespoons honey
Hoisin sauce, for serving
Shredded green onions (scallions), for garnish
Lettuce leaves, for garnish
Slivered carrots, for garnish

Bao Buns
2 tablespoons all-purpose flour for
  dusting work surface
Two 7.5-oz (212-g) cans store-bought
  refrigerated biscuit dough
16–18 parchment squares (about 4 x 4-in
  / 10 x 10-cm each)

Preheat the oven to 425°F (220°C).

Make the **Marinade:** In a small bowl, combine the ketchup, salt, sugar, garlic, brandy, 5 spice powder and honey. Rub this mixture on the pork pieces, covering all sides. Marinate the pork in the refrigerator, covered, for 2 hours or longer.

Place the pork on a rack in a roasting pan and cook for 20 minutes. Turn the pork and cook for an additional 20 minutes. Reduce the heat to 350°F (175°C) and cook for an additional 20 minutes, until the pork reaches an internal temperature of 170°F (77°C). Remove from the oven.

While the pork is roasting, make the **Bao Buns:** dust the work surface with flour. Open the cans of dough and separate out the biscuits into 16–18 pieces total. Keep the dough covered loosely with a kitchen towel. Roll each piece of dough into an oval shape and fold it in half. Place on each folded oval on a parchment square. Keep the buns covered until ready to steam.

Steam the buns in batches (do not overcrowd) for 12 minutes at a time. Transfer steamed buns to a platter.

When the pork is cool enough to handle, cut across the grain into pieces that are ¼-inch (6.3-mm) thick, and then cut cross-wise if necessary to fit in bao buns. Brush any remaining cooking sauce over the sliced pork slices.

To serve, carefully open each bun and add a slice or two of pork. Top with a bit of hoisin sauce and some green onion strips. Serve immediately with lettuce and slivered carrots.

COOK'S NOTE
Honey BBQ Pork is also delicious served room temperature so it's a perfect dish for entertaining.

Salmon Sliders with Chipotle Mayo

My sister Jeanie used to live on Bainbridge Island near Seattle and she'd treat me to her delicious salmon recipes all the time. I was reminiscing about those rainy Seattle trips and came up with this recipe. My favorite part of this recipe is the chipotle mayo because it's smoky with just the right amount of kick. Just because you don't live in Seattle doesn't mean you can take a bite out of the Pacific Northwest with these yummy sliders.

Serves 4
Prep Time: 25 Minutes
Cook Time: 20 Minutes

Chipotle Mayo
1 chipotle pepper in adobo sauce
$1/2$ cup (116 g) mayonnaise
Juice of $1/2$ lemon
$1/2$ teaspoon adobo seasoning

$3/4$ lb (350 g) salmon fillet, skin removed, cut into 1-in (2.5-cm) pieces
$1/2$ red bell pepper, coarsely chopped
1 green onion (scallion), green and white parts, coarsely chopped
2 tablespoons mayonnaise
$3/4$ cup (48 g) panko bread crumbs
1 tablespoon freshly squeezed lemon juice
$1/8$ teaspoon salt
$1/8$ teaspoon freshly ground black pepper
3 tablespoons canola oil
8 slider rolls of your choice
8 small lettuce leaves
Red onion slices, for serving

COOK'S NOTE
Swap out the mayonnaise with Greek yogurt for a lighter version of this recipe.

Make the **Chipotle Mayo:** Place all of the chipotle mayo ingredients in a food processor and combine until blended. Transfer to a bowl. Clean and dry the food processor bowl.

Place the salmon, red pepper, green onion, bread crumbs, 2 tablespoons mayonnaise, lemon juice, salt and black pepper in the food processor bowl. Pulse until just combined. Form into 8 patties, about a scant 4 tablespoons each. Place the patties on a greased baking sheet.

Heat the oil in a large non-stick skillet over medium-high heat. Cook the patties in batches, adding more oil as needed, for 2–3 minutes per side, until browned and cooked through.

Place the patties on rolls, top with lettuce and spread about $1\frac{1}{2}$ teaspoons chipotle mayonnaise over each. Top with red onion slices and serve immediately.

Korean Fried Chicken Sliders

I love putting an Asian twist on comfort food classics. Whenever I'm craving fried chicken but don't want to feel weighed down, this is my go-to recipe. I get my fix but with loads more flavor. And the oven-fried method yields crispy results without all the extra calories from deep-frying. The sauce is sweet, savory and sublimely smoky and you'll be singing, "It's finger-licking gochujang good!"

Serves 4
Prep Time: 30 minutes
Cook Time: 25 minutes

Korean Slaw
1/4 small head purple cabbage, shredded
  into thin strips
1 green onion (scallion) white and green parts,
  finely chopped
2 tablespoons shredded carrot
1 clove garlic, minced
2 teaspoons light soy sauce
2 teaspoons seasoned rice vinegar
1 teaspoon toasted sesame oil
2 teaspoons sugar
2 teaspoons toasted sesame seeds
Salt and freshly ground black pepper, to taste

Chicken
2 eggs, beaten
1 cup (50 g) panko bread crumbs
1 cup (120 g) all-purpose flour
4 whole boneless, skinless chicken breasts, cut
  in half
Salt and freshly ground black pepper
4 small Hawaiian sweet rolls
Gochujang Sauce (page 33)

Preheat oven to 375°F (190°C).

Make the **Korean Slaw**: Place all of the slaw ingredients in a medium bowl and toss to combine. Set aside and allow the flavors to meld.

Put the beaten eggs, panko and flour in 3 shallow bowls. Season the chicken thigh with salt and pepper. Dust the chicken with the flour, then dip it in the egg, and finally in the panko, pressing to help the bread crumbs adhere.

Place the chicken breasts on a baking sheet lined with parchment paper. Bake the chicken breasts for about 25 minutes until an internal thermometer registers 165°F/75°C and they are golden brown and crispy, turning halfway through.

Separate the rolls and slice them in half horizontally. Place the chicken pieces onto the bottom half of rolls. Top each chicken piece with slaw. Drizzle with Gochujang Sauce. Place the tops onto the sliders and serve immediately.

COOK'S NOTE
The Gochujang Sauce will yield approximately 3/4 cup (185 ml) so halve the recipe for sliders or store the remainder covered in your fridge to drizzle on your favorite meat.

Cuban Sliders

My sister Jeanie and I saw the movie "Chef" starring Jon Favreau together. Spoiler alert: In the film, he reinvents himself by launching a Cuban Midnight Sandwich Food Truck which becomes an overnight sensation. It inspired me to create this recipe which is a riff on a Cuban Midnight Sandwich but you don't have to wait until midnight to enjoy them. It's also quick and easy and it doesn't require a sandwich press. I love the cilantro butter which gets drizzled on top for a garlicky and glistening finish. Just the thing for your next movie night!

Serves 6
Prep Time: 25 minutes
Cook Time: 15–20 minutes

12 poppy seed rolls or other roll of choice
1 1/2 tablespoons Dijon mustard
1/3 cup (80 g) mayonnaise
3/4 lb (350 g) thinly sliced roast pork, cut into fourths
3/4 lb (350 g) thinly sliced ham, cut into fourths
3 slices Swiss cheese, cut into fourths
24 dill pickle slices
6 tablespoons butter, melted
1 tablespoon chopped fresh coriander leaves (cilantro)
1 clove garlic, minced

Preheat the oven to 350°F (175°C).

Separate the rolls and slice them in half horizontally. Arrange the bottom halves of rolls in a 13 x 9-inch (33 x 23-cm) baking pan.

Mix the mustard and mayonnaise together in a small bowl. Spread half of the mustard-mayonnaise mixture liberally onto the bottom halves. Layer roll bottoms with roasted pork. Add sliced ham and pickles. Top with Swiss cheese.

Spread the rest of the mustard-mayonnaise mixture over the cut side of the roll tops. Carefully turn the roll tops over the cheese, cut side down.

In a small bowl, combine the melted butter, cilantro and garlic. Spoon the butter mixture over the roll tops.

Cover the baking pan with foil and bake for 15 minutes. Remove the foil and bake for 5 to 6 minutes longer, or until the cheese is melted and rolls are lightly brown. Serve immediately.

RISE & SHINE

My son Dylan is always up before the alarm clock goes off while my daughter Becca needs all the beauty sleep she can get. The thing they have in common is their love of breakfast! I'm lucky because they're always ready to throw down a big breakfast and I'm not worried about them losing energy before lunch. I like to shake things up so they don't lose interest in the most important meal of the day. Speaking of shaking up, I surprised them the other day with **African Eggs Poached in Tomato Sauce (*Shakshuka*)** and they loved the luscious sauce they got to dip some crusty bread into. They also loved helping me put an unexpected spin on classics like **Coconut Pancakes with Mango Lime Purée** or the **German Pancake (Dutch Baby).** Another favorite of mine (after a long night of karaoke) is the **Mexicali Breakfast Skillet**, which is hearty— and the extra dose of hot sauce always does wonders when you're a little bleary eyed. When you feel like treating yourself, try the **Brioche French Toast.** It is simply magnifique!

Mexicali Breakfast Skillet

I know this may sound strange, but after I cater a big party of my gourmet Asian specialties, I often crave Mexican food (my friend DJ Cathy Michele always eats a burrito after spinning, too). Maybe I just eat too much of my Asian appetizer catering inventory and need a change of pace the next day. This mouthwatering Mexicali Breakfast Skillet hits the spot every time. Its savory combination of chorizo sausage, shredded cheese and potatoes gives me energy all day and the kick of green chili peppers (and the hot sauce I like to add) is a much needed wake-me-up after a long night of cooking. By dinnertime, I'm craving Asian food again.

Serves 4
Prep Time: 15 minutes
Cook Time: 20 minutes

6 oz (175 g) Mexican chorizo sausage,
  casing removed
1 red bell pepper, chopped
1 small yellow onion, chopped
1 clove garlic, minced
1 tablespoon oil
1/2 lb (250 g) baby yellow potatoes, diced
One 4-oz (113-g) can chopped green chilis,
  drained
Salt and freshly ground black pepper, to taste
4 eggs
3/4 cup (75 g) shredded Mexican blend cheese
1 avocado, sliced, for topping
1 tablespoon fresh coriander leaves (cilantro)
  finely chopped, for topping
Salsa, for topping
Hot sauce (optional)
Warm tortillas

Heat a large skillet (preferably cast iron) over medium-high heat. Add the chorizo, breaking up to crumble, and cook for about 3 minutes or until browned. Add the bell pepper, onion and garlic and cook for 3 minutes, stirring occasionally. Remove from the pan and set aside.

Heat the oil in the skillet. Add the potatoes and cook for 6–8 minutes until potatoes are browned and crispy. Stir in the reserve sausage mixture. Add the chopped green chilis and cook for 1 more minute. Season to taste with salt and pepper. Make 4 egg-size depressions in the mixture with a spoon. Crack 1 egg into each well. Top with the cheese and cover and cook 4 minutes or until egg yolks are slightly set.

Top with avocado, cilantro and salsa and serve immediately with hot sauce (if desired) and tortillas.

Po Po's Chinese Rice Porridge Congee

To me, *congee* or *jook* is the ultimate Chinese comfort food. It's enjoyed all over China for breakfast and some say it's the true Breakfast of Champions. At dim sum restaurants, you will see servers wheeling around carts of congee to be ladled out for lucky patrons. My late mom Leeann (or Po Po to my twins, which means "grandma" in Cantonese) made this for my brother and sisters and I growing up in Minnesota and made it for the twins when they were toddlers. It's like Asian risotto, creamy and savory, nurturing and warming. It's just a few simple ingredients and while it takes a while to cook, it's definitely worth the wait.

Serves 8
Prep Time: 10 minutes
Cook Time: 1³/₄ hours

1¹/₂ cups (300 g) long-grain white rice
Four 1-in (2.5-cm) slices peeled fresh ginger
8 cups (1.75 liters) chicken broth or stock
5¹/₂ cups (1.5 liters) water
2 cups (250 g) shredded rotisserie chicken
2 green onions (scallions), white and green
  parts, finely chopped
Store-bought crispy garlic, for garnish
Soy sauce, for drizzling
Dark sesame oil, for drizzling

Fill a large heavy pot with the rice and cool water. Swirl the water around with your hands and "wash" the rice by rubbing it gently between your fingers, and then drain. Repeat this process until the water runs clear, about 5 or 6 times. After the last rinse, carefully drain all the water from the pot.

Add the ginger, chicken broth or stock and water to the pot. Bring to a boil and stir. Reduce the heat to low and simmer, covered until the mixture achieves the consistency of oatmeal, about 1³/₄ hours, stirring frequently during last ¹/₂ hour of cooking. (Congee will continue to thicken as it stands. Thin with water if necessary.)

Divide the porridge into bowls. Top it with shredded chicken, green onions and crispy garlic, and drizzle with soy sauce and sesame oil before serving.

COOK'S NOTE
Try making this recipe in your rice cooker if it has a porridge setting. Simply halve the recipe, place the first 4 ingredients in the rice cooker bowl, press the porridge setting and you'll have steaming, hot jook once the cycle completes. Feel free to top with any kind of cooked meat, and you can even top with crispy wonton strips for some crunch.

African Eggs Poached in Tomato Sauce Shakshuka

Out of Africa and into my skillet with this luscious and exotic dish. You'll want to soak up every bit of its delicious sauce with a handful of crusty bread after you devour the delicately cooked and perfectly runny eggs bathing in the sauce. Easy enough to serve at your next brunch and definitely more memorable than the quiche recipe you have taped to your fridge. (No offense to your quiche or your fridge—but trust me here!)

Serves 6
Prep Time: 15 minutes
Cook Time: 30 minutes

1 tablespoon extra virgin olive oil, plus more, for drizzling
1/2 yellow onion, diced
1 clove garlic, minced
1 red bell pepper, diced
1 1/2 teaspoons store-bought harissa paste
1 teaspoon mild chili powder
1 teaspoon cumin
1 teaspoon smoked paprika
Pinch of ground red pepper (cayenne)
2 tablespoons tomato paste
Two 14-oz (396-g) cans diced tomatoes (including liquid)
1 teaspoon sugar
Salt and freshly ground black pepper, to taste
6 eggs
2 teaspoons chopped fresh parsley
Crusty bread

Heat the oil in a large non-stick skillet over medium-high heat. Add the onions and sauté until soft and translucent, 5–7 minutes. Add the garlic and red bell pepper and sauté for 1–2 minutes. Add the harissa paste, chili powder, cumin, smoked paprika and cayenne pepper. Cook for another 2 minutes. Stir in the tomato paste, followed by the diced tomatoes and their liquid and the sugar. Reduce heat to a simmer until slightly thickened, about 10 minutes. Season to taste with salt and pepper.

Make 6 little wells in the sauce and crack in the eggs. Cover and simmer until the egg whites are set but the yolks are still runny, about 8–10 minutes. Remove from heat, drizzle with extra virgin olive oil and sprinkle the eggs with more salt and pepper. Top with parsley. Serve immediately from the skillet with crusty bread.

COOK'S NOTE

Harissa (ha-RISS-uh) paste is a North African blend of dried chili peppers, fresh herbs, garlic, citrus juice, tomato and spices. It's spicy and sublimely delicious. Use less if making this for young kids and more if you like it hot! You can find it at gourmet specialty stores as well as Trader Joe's and online.

Coconut Pancakes with Mango Lime Purée

Love pancakes but don't love the carb-heavy feeling that comes with a stack attack? Well, lighten up with these light, fluffy, low-carb coconut pancakes made with coconut flour. Full of coconutty flavor, these pancakes are topped with a sweet-tart and bright mango lime coulis. These pancakes are a fun and easy way to put a tropical twist on your morning routine.

Serves 3–4
Prep Time: 20 minutes
Cook Time: 30 minutes

Mango Lime Purée
2 cups (186 g) thawed frozen mango chunks
4 tablespoons sugar
3 tablespoons water
1 tablespoon freshly squeezed lime juice

Pancakes
4 eggs
1/2 cup (60 g) softened cream cheese
6 tablespoons coconut flour
4 tablespoons half and half
2 tablespoons sugar
1 teaspoon baking powder
1 teaspoon vanilla extract (optional)

Butter, for frying
Toasted sweetened coconut flakes, for topping
Fresh mango slices, for topping

Make the **Mango Lime Purée:** bring the mango chunks, sugar, and water to a boil in a medium saucepan, stirring until the sugar is dissolved. Reduce the heat and simmer, covered, stirring occasionally, until the mangoes are very soft, about 20 minutes. Stir in the lime juice. Using an immersion blender (alternatively, place mixture in a food processor), purée until smooth. Set aside. If using a food processor, remove the mixture to a bowl and set aside, and then wash and dry the food processor.

Make the **Pancakes:** While the sauce is cooling, purée all of the pancake ingredients in a food processor or blender until smooth.

Heat a griddle or large non-stick skillet over medium heat. Add a pat of butter and allow it to melt. Swirl to coat. Pour a small scoop (about 2 tablespoons) of the batter onto the griddle. Cook on one side until bubbles begin to form, about 2 minutes. Then, turn the pancakes with a spatula and cook the other side until golden brown, about 1 1/2 to 2 minutes. Turn over only once. Top with toasted coconut flakes and fresh mango slices. Serve immediately with the Mango Lime Purée.

COOK'S NOTE
These pancakes are light and delicate, so handle with care when flipping.

Berry Quinoa Breakfast Bowl

I'm not the biggest breakfast person because I'm not starving when I wake up. But if I don't eat something I'm ravenous by 10:30 AM and my "hangry" fangs and attitude start to show. Not pretty (just ask my hubby). I love this nurturing, healthy and plant-protein-based bowl because it gives me the energy I need from the quinoa and almond milk without weighing me down. The berries and bananas lend just the right amount of sweet.

Serves 4
Prep Time: 10 minutes
Cook Time: 25 minutes

1/2 cup (85 g) tri-color quinoa, rinsed and drained
1 cup (250 ml) sweetened almond milk
1 teaspoon cinnamon
1 teaspoon vanilla extract
2 bananas, sliced
12 strawberries, hulled and sliced
1 cup (150 g) blueberries
4 teaspoons pepitas or sliced almonds
4 teaspoons honey, for drizzling
1/2 cup (125 ml) warm sweetened almond milk, for drizzling
Ground cinnamon and nutmeg for dusting (optional)

Combine the quinoa, 1 cup of the almond milk, 1 teaspoon of the cinnamon and the vanilla extract in a medium saucepan and bring to a boil over medium heat.

Reduce the heat to a simmer and cover and cook on low until the liquid evaporates, about 20–25 minutes. Fluff with a fork.

Divide the hot quinoa into 4 bowls, and top each with the sliced fruit and pepitas or almonds, drizzle with honey and add the warm almond milk. Dust with ground cinnamon and nutmeg, if desired.

Brioche French Toast

Brioche has similar ingredients to regular bread but is made with a lot more butter and eggs, so it's lighter and fluffier—like biting into a croissant. This recipe is like adding a little je ne sais quoi to your French toast and you'll never turn back. But the piece de resistance in this dish is the browned butter sauce which is simply manifique! Don't get burned: brown butter can burn easily, so it's important to keep an eye on it while cooking.

Serves 6
Prep Time: 10 minutes
Cook Time: 10 minutes

$1/2$ cup (125 ml) whole milk
4 eggs
1 teaspoon vanilla extract
1 teaspoon sugar
$1/4$ teaspoon cinnamon
$1/4$ teaspoon ground ginger
$1/2$ teaspoon ground nutmeg
1 pinch salt
2 tablespoons butter, plus more if needed
Six 1-in (2.5-cm) thick slices day-old dry brioche bread or challah

Topping
4 tablespoons butter
6 tablespoons maple syrup
Confectioners' sugar

Whisk the milk, eggs, vanilla extract, sugar, cinnamon, ginger, nutmeg and salt together in a bowl. Heat 2 teaspoons butter in a large non-stick skillet over medium heat. Working in batches, dip each slice of brioche bread in the egg mixture and cook until golden, 2–3 minutes per side, adding more butter as needed. Transfer to a platter.

Make the **Topping**: Melt the 4 tablespoons butter in the skillet over medium-low heat, stirring frequently. Once melted, the butter will foam up a bit, and then subside. Watch carefully for lightly browned specks that will form at the bottom of the pan. Smell the butter: it should have a nutty aroma. Transfer the browned butter to a small bowl.

Drizzle the browned butter over the French toast and top each slice with 1 tablespoon of the maple syrup. Dust with confectioners' sugar and serve.

COOK'S NOTE
Challah is similar to brioche and is a fine substitute (hey, Jewish friends—it's a great way to use a leftover challah on Saturday mornings after your Shabbat dinner).

Breakfast Quinoa Bowl with Chicken Apple Sausage

Here's a delicious, healthy and satisfying breakfast bowl that's chock full of protein and nutrition. Experiment with other veggies, swap out the sausages with a vegan alternative, or replace the quinoa with brown rice.

Serves 4
Prep Time: 20 minutes
Cook Time: 10 minutes

2 tablespoons extra virgin olive oil, divided
1/2 teaspoon red wine vinegar
Pinch of salt
12 grape tomatoes, halved
4 eggs
1 small shallot, minced
4 pre-cooked smoked chicken apple sausages, sliced into rounds
1 bunch Swiss chard, stems removed and coarsely chopped
Salt and freshly ground black pepper, to taste
3 cups (555 g) cooked tri-color quinoa
Finely chopped parsley, for serving

Whisk together 1 teaspoon of the olive oil, the red wine vinegar and pinch of salt. Add the tomatoes and toss to coat. Set aside.

Heat a large non-stick skillet over medium heat. Add 2 teaspoons of the extra virgin olive oil and swirl to coat. Crack the eggs, one at a time, into the pan. Cover, and cook until the whites are set and the yolk is still runny, about 2–3 minutes. Remove and set aside.

Add the remaining 1 tablespoon of the extra virgin olive oil to the skillet and swirl to coat. Add the shallot and sauté until fragrant, about 30 seconds. Add the sausages and pan-fry until browned, about 4–5 minutes. Add the Swiss chard and cook until tender, about 2 minutes. Salt and pepper to taste.

Divide the quinoa evenly among 4 bowls. Top each bowl evenly with the sausages and Swiss chard. Evenly distribute the tomatoes to the side of each bowl. Top each bowl with a fried egg. Garnish with parsley. Serve immediately.

> ### COOK'S NOTE
> For added flavor, steam the quinoa with chicken stock or vegetable stock.

Margaret's Salsa Sunrise Eggs Benedict

Hollandaise Sauce is one of my friend Margaret's most delicious childhood taste memories. Each weekend, her dad would make Eggs Benedict with homemade hollandaise sauce. Margaret was also fortunate enough to visit with renowned chef Anne Willan for her *Kitchen Chat* podcast. Ann taught Margaret all about essential sauces from her book *Secrets from the La Varenne Kitchen*. In honor of her father and in appreciation of her friend, Anne Willan, she brings us this easy and delicious recipe.

Serves: 4
Prep Time: 20 minutes
Cook Time: 15 minutes

Hollandaise Sauce
4 egg yolks
2 tablespoons water
2 tablespoons freshly squeezed lemon juice
Pinch of ground red pepper (cayenne)
Pinch of salt
3/4 cup (172 g) unsalted butter, melted
Pinch of freshly ground black pepper

Salsa
4 tablespoons finely chopped coriander leaves (cilantro)
2 tomatoes, deseeded and finely chopped
1/2 small white onion, finely chopped
1 jalapeño pepper, deseeded and finely chopped
1 tablespoon freshly squeezed lime juice

8 eggs
8 slices store-bought mini naan bread
8 slices smoked Gouda cheese
Avocado slices

Make the **Hollandaise Sauce:** Whisk together the egg yolks, water, lemon juice, cayenne pepper and salt in the top of a double boiler or a metal bowl over simmering water. Cook until the mixture reaches 160°F (72°C) or until the mixture is thick enough to coat a metal spoon. Remove from the heat.

Drizzle the melted butter into the mixture, whisking constantly. Add the pepper and whisk. Transfer to a small bowl. Place the bowl in a larger bowl filled with warm water, stirring occasionally.

Poach the eggs: Bring 2–3 inches (5–8 cm) of water to a boil in a large saucepan or high-sided skillet. Reduce to a simmer. Break 1 egg into a small bowl. Gently slip the egg into the water. Repeat with 3 more eggs. Cook, uncovered, 2–4 minutes or until whites are completely set and yolks just begin to thicken. Using a slotted spoon, remove the eggs from the water. Repeat with the remaining eggs.

Top the mini naan with the cheese slices. Toast in a toaster oven until melted. Meanwhile, make the **Salsa:** combine the cilantro, tomatoes, onion, jalapeño pepper and lime juice in a small bowl.

Remove the naan from the toaster oven. Top each naan with avocado slices, salsa and a poached egg. Drizzle with reserved hollandaise sauce and serve immediately.

German Pancake Dutch Baby

My daughter Becca is on a dance team with her friend Laurel. One day, Laurel's mom Maureen (Mo) and I were frantically getting them ready for a dance competition at 6 AM at her house. We looked at the hair instructions and it said "Space Buns" and we both screamed (Mo and I aren't the best make-up-and-hair dance moms!). I was beginning to worry that the girls would be super cranky if they didn't eat something when a steaming skillet with a puffy German pancake (aka Dutch Baby) "magically" appeared from Mo's oven. This pancake is light, fluffy and buttery, and is packed with tons of protein from the eggs for all-day dance stamina. The girls inhaled their slices on the spot. Both Becca and Laurel's hairdos—and these pancakes—were out of this world!

Serves 6–8
Prep Time: 10 minutes
Cook Time: 25 minutes

6 tablespoons butter
3 large eggs
1¹/₂ tablespoons sugar
Pinch of salt
³/₄ cup (185 ml) milk, warmed for 30
   seconds in microwave
2 teaspoons vanilla extract
³/₄ cup (90 g) all-purpose flour
2 tablespoons butter
Confectioners' sugar, for serving
Sliced strawberries, for serving

Preheat the oven to 400°F (200°C).

Put the butter in a large, ovenproof skillet and place it in the oven until the butter has melted.

Meanwhile, in a blender or food processor, combine the eggs, sugar, salt, milk and vanilla extract and blend or process until well blended. Transfer the batter to a bowl.

Carefully remove the hot skillet from the oven. Swirl the butter around the pan to coat completely. Pour the melted butter into the batter and whisk vigorously to remove lumps. Pour the batter into the hot skillet and return the it to the oven. Cook until the pancake is puffed in the center and golden brown along the edges, 20–25 minutes.

Using a spatula, remove the entire Dutch baby from the pan and place it on a cooling rack for a few minutes to allow the steam to escape without condensing along the bottom and rendering the pancake soggy. Dust with confectioners' sugar when cooled slightly and top with sliced strawberries. Slice the pancake into 8 wedges on a serving platter or cutting board.

GET THE PARTY STARTED!
Finger Food & Small Bites

My name is Katie and I am party-throwing addict. I'm not planning to quit anytime soon (shhhh, don't tell my hubby) because throwing parties simply sparks joy for me (decluttering my home does not). I truly believe that food is an expression of love and cooking is a wonderful way to show your friends you adore them. Show them you heart them with this fabulous collection of appetizers and small bites that is guaranteed to get your party started! Why settle on a one-note flavor theme when you can treat your guests to a symphony of global flavors from classics like **Spanish Tapas-style Meatballs** and **Mini Chicken Samosas with Cilantro Mint Sauce** to modern fusion twists such as **Bacon, Date & Goat Cheese Potstickers** and **Greek-style Nachos**. I also included recipes for **Deviled Eggs Four Ways** in this chapter, because who doesn't love deviled eggs? And, who doesn't want to try some creative takes on the classic like **Miso Deviled Eggs** or **Niçoise Deviled Eggs**? Yep, the devil made me do it! And the cocktails included in this book— **Tipsy Thai Basil Lemon Soda** (page 212) and **Ginger Beer Sangria** (page 213)—go great with these small bites!

Potato Beef Empanadas

My friend Liset hails from Ecuador and I knew she'd be able to swing by and show me and the twins Dylan and Becca how to expertly fold and crimp empanadas. This recipe is very easy to make and you will likely have most ingredients on hand in your pantry (except for maybe the annatto or achiote powder, which you can substitute with equal parts paprika and turmeric). Seasoned with authentic spices, ginger, onion and cilantro, these savory and delicious empanadas are loved by kids (of all ages) and they love getting to help make them in the kitchen.

Serves 8 as an appetizer
Prep Time: 30 minutes
Cook Time: 20 minutes

Filling

2 tablespoons oil
2 cloves garlic, crushed
1 small white onion, diced
2 teaspoons dried oregano
2 teaspoons cumin
1 teaspoon annatto or achiote powder
1/2 large baking potato, peeled and diced
1 green bell pepper, diced
1 lb (500 g) ground beef
1/2 small bunch coriander leaves (cilantro), finely chopped
2 plum tomatoes, deseeded and chopped
Salt and freshly ground black pepper, to taste

1 package refrigerated pie crust (2 rolls)
1 egg
2 tablespoons milk

Preheat oven to 375°F (190°C).

Heat the oil in a non-stick skillet over medium-high heat. Add the garlic, onion, oregano, cumin and annatto or achiote powder and sauté for 2 minutes. Add the potato and green pepper and cook for 8–10 more minutes or until potato is cooked through. Add the beef, cilantro and tomatoes and continue cooking until the meat is browned, about 8–10 minutes. Add the salt and pepper to taste. Remove from heat and set aside.

Using a bowl or large circle cutter, cut out 3-inch (7.5-cm) circles from the pie crust. Fill each circle with 1 tablespoon of the filling and fold the extra dough over the top. Crimp the edges with a fork and place the empanadas on a baking sheet lined with parchment paper.

Whisk together the egg and milk. Brush the tops of the assembled empanadas with this mixture. Bake for 20–25 minutes. Remove from oven and cool slightly before eating.

Pizza Wontons

The Los Angeles school district went on strike a while back. Instead of crossing the picket line, I invited six of Becca's then 10-year-old friends over for a cooking class. We were going to make homemade pizzas followed by dumplings but it dawned on me that we could put the pizza in the dumplings! This recipe is so fast and easy and the girls squealed with delight at being able to make their own signature mini pizza wontons filled with cheesy pepperoni goodness. Becca's friend Jordan is a vegetarian so she skipped the pepperoni and added extra mushrooms. Word spread quickly—so much so that six of Dylan's friends arrived the next day for Pizza Wonton class. Now, that's what I call "School of Wok!"

Serves 6 as an appetizer
Prep Time: 15 minutes
Cook Time: 5 minutes

1 package square wonton wrappers
1 egg
1 teaspoon water
1 cup (228 g) store-bought pizza sauce
1 cup (100 g) shredded mozzarella cheese
Pizza toppings of your choice, such as:
  pepperoni, crumbled sausage, mushrooms
  and olives, chopped into small pieces
Oil, for frying

Lay the wonton wrappers flat on a cutting board.

Whisk the egg with the water in a small bowl.

Place a small scoop of pizza sauce in the center of the wrapper. Then, add cheese and toppings.

Lightly brush outside edges of the wonton with the egg mixture and fold it over to make a triangle.

Press gently on the edges to make sure they are sealed.

In a large wok or deep skillet, heat 2–3 inches (5–7.5 cm) of the oil to 350°F (175°C). Gently drop 6 to 8 wontons at a time into the hot oil and fry for 1–2 minutes or until golden brown.

Remove from oil and place on a baking sheet lined with paper towels. Serve with a little extra pizza sauce on the side.

COOK'S NOTE
Make sure you don't overstuff your wontons with so much filling that they ooze from their sides. Make sure you are able to firmly seal the edges.

Greek-style Nachos

I'm a lover of all things Greek. Just ask my Greek besties—Christos, Kristin, Greg and Martina! Not only do I love the fresh ingredients and flavors found in Greek cuisine, I also love how clean and healthy they are. With feta cheese, Kalamata olives, red onion, tomatoes and dill, this is a twist on a classic Chopped Greek Salad that you can make in minutes. You'll feel like you're experiencing a taste of the Greek Isles with every bite!

Serves 4–6 as an appetizer
Prep Time: 15 minutes
Cook Time: 13–15 minutes

6 pitas
3 tablespoons extra virgin olive oil
Salt
1/2 cup (143 g) plain Greek yogurt
2 tablespoons finely chopped fresh dill
Juice of 1 large lemon
4 tablespoons pitted and chopped Kalamata olives
1 cucumber, peeled, deseeded and finely chopped
8 grape tomatoes, quartered
1/2 small red onion, finely chopped
Crumbled feta cheese, for topping

Preheat the oven to 375°F (190°C).

Brush the pitas with the extra virgin olive oil and cut each into 6 triangles. Spread the triangles in a single layer on a baking sheet, sprinkle with salt and cook until they are crunchy, 8–10 minutes (rotate the sheet halfway through cooking).

In a medium bowl, combine the Greek yogurt, dill and lemon juice. Add the olives, cucumbers, tomatoes and red onions, and stir to combine.

Spoon the yogurt sauce over the pita chips and sprinkle with feta cheese. Serve immediately.

Mini Chicken Samosas with Cilantro Mint Sauce

Because of their triangular shape, samosas were originally named Samsa after the pyramids in Central Asia. This Indian favorite is traditionally made with homemade dough, but to save time I use store-bought wonton wrappers. Samosas have gained so much popularity over the history that they've been elevated from being cooked over campfires to being blessed by Indian royalty. I hope you enjoy this easy and delicious recipe that's fit for a king or queen!

Serves 8–10 as an appetizer
Prep Time: 30 minutes
Cook Time: 15 minutes

Filling

$1/2$ cup (78 g) frozen spinach
2 tablespoons oil
$1/2$ small onion, finely chopped
1 clove garlic, minced
1 teaspoon peeled and minced fresh ginger
1 teaspoon ground cumin
$1/2$ teaspoon ground chili powder
$1/4$ teaspoon cinnamon
2 tablespoons curry powder
$1/2$ lb (250 g) ground chicken
1 small potato, peeled, boiled and mashed
$1/2$ teaspoon salt
$1/4$ teaspoon freshly ground black pepper

Cilantro Mint Sauce

3 cloves garlic
One 1-in (2.5-cm) piece fresh ginger, peeled
1 bunch fresh mint leaves
1 bunch fresh coriander leaves (cilantro)
1 jalapeño pepper, seeds and stem removed
1 teaspoon sugar
2 tablespoons freshly squeezed lime juice
1 tablespoon water
1 tablespoon extra virgin olive oil
Salt and freshly ground black pepper, to taste

20 square wonton wrappers
1 egg, beaten with a splash of water
Oil, for frying

Make the Filling: Thaw the frozen spinach in a colander and squeeze it with your hands to get as much moisture out as possible. Set aside.

Heat the oil in a large non-stick skillet over medium-high heat. Add the onion, garlic and ginger, and stir-fry until fragrant, about 30 seconds. Add the cumin, chili powder, cinnamon and curry powder and sauté for 1 minute. Add the ground chicken and sauté for 6–7 minutes until cooked through. Add the potato, reserved spinach and salt and pepper, and stir-fry for 3–4 minutes. Remove from the heat and let cool to room temperature.

Make the Cilantro Mint Sauce: Place the garlic and ginger in a food processor and pulse until finely chopped. Add the mint, cilantro, jalapeño, sugar, lime juice and water, and purée until blended. With the motor running, pour the extra virgin olive oil slowly into the mixture until combined. Add salt and pepper to taste.

Spoon $1^1/2$ teaspoons of the filling into the middle of each wonton skin. Brush the edges of the wonton skin with egg wash. Bring the edges together and seal to form a pouch.

In a large wok or deep skillet, heat 2–3 inches (5–7.5 cm) of the oil to 350°F (175°C). Fry the samosas, a few at a time, until golden brown. Drain the samosas on a sheet pan lined with paper towels. Serve immediately with Cilantro Mint Sauce.

Charred Shishito Peppers

Burn baby, burn! My friends are always asking how to make this restaurant fave and it couldn't be simpler to make. Most recipes don't call for charring and burning, but this appetizer wouldn't be the same without its signature blackened and blistered skin. Served with a spicy Sriracha Mayo Dipping Sauce, this easy and delicious appetizer is destined to become a go-to for your family and friends.

Serves 4–6 as an appetizer
Prep Time: 5 minutes
Cook Time: 6 minutes + pan-heating time

Sriracha Mayo Dipping Sauce
4 tablespoons mayonnaise
1 teaspoon freshly squeezed lemon juice
1 tablespoon sriracha sauce

8 oz (250 g) shishito peppers
1 teaspoon oil
1/8 teaspoon coarse sea salt

Make the Sriracha Mayo Dipping Sauce: Combine the three ingredients in a small bowl and set aside.

In a medium bowl, combine the peppers and oil and toss to coat.

Heat a large skillet (preferably cast iron or non-stick) over high heat for 5 minutes.

Arrange peppers in a single layer in the pan. Cook without moving them for 3 minutes or until the skins are blistered or slightly blackened. Turn the peppers over and cook for 3 more minutes or until charred all over. Sprinkle with sea salt and serve immediately with the dipping sauce.

COOK'S NOTE
To keep peppers from exploding, puncture each pepper once with a toothpick or knife tip.

Spanish Tapas-style Meatballs Albondigas

These meatballs were inspired by a trip my hubby and I took to Spain many moons ago. On the way to the hotel, we stumbled upon a huge open air food hall where we found a tapas stall serving the most delicious and tender albondigas. I think I've come pretty close to recreating them and my kids just gobble them up too. I love serving these with a pitcher of Ginger Beer Sangria (see page 213) and along with some marcona almonds and chunks of manchego cheese.

Serves 6–8 as an appetizer
Prep Time: 20 Minutes + marinating time
Cook Time: 15 Minutes

Meatballs
1 slice white or brown bread (crust removed), soaked in 1/2 cup (125 ml) milk
1/2 lb (250 g) ground beef
1/2 lb (250 g) ground chorizo
1/2 teaspoon salt
1/8 teaspoon freshly ground black pepper
4 cloves garlic, minced
1 small onion, finely chopped
1 tablespoon chopped parsley
1 egg, beaten
1 cup (90 g) bread crumbs
4 tablespoons extra virgin olive oil

Sauce
1 tablespoon extra virgin olive oil
2 cloves garlic, minced
4 large tomatoes, quartered and deseeded
1/2 cup (115 g) tomato paste
1/4 teaspoon smoked paprika
1/2 teaspoon cumin
1/4 teaspoon crushed red pepper
1/2 teaspoon dried thyme
1 tablespoon honey
1/2 teaspoon salt
1/8 teaspoon freshly ground black pepper
Crusty bread (optional)

> ### COOK'S NOTE
> Swap out the beef and chorizo with ground turkey or chicken, if you wish.

Make the **Meatballs**: Squeeze the milk from the bread slice and set aside. In a large bowl, combine the ground beef, ground chorizo, salt, black pepper, garlic, onion, parsley, bread and egg until blended. Cover with plastic wrap and refrigerate for 30 minutes. Place the bread crumbs in a shallow dish.

Shape the mixture into ping-pong-ball sized meatballs. Roll the meatballs in the bread crumbs one at a time until evenly coated.

Heat the 4 tablespoons extra virgin olive oil in a large non-stick skillet over medium-high heat. Working in batches, add meatballs and fry until brown and slightly crisp, 5–6 minutes. Be careful not to crowd the pan. Turn and brown the other sides, about 5 minutes more. Transfer the cooked meatballs to a paper towel-lined baking sheet.

Make the **Sauce**: Heat the 1 tablespoon extra virgin olive oil in a dutch oven or large pot over medium heat. Add the garlic and sauté until fragrant, about 30 seconds. Add the tomatoes and sauté until softened, about 2 minutes. Using an immersion blender, purée the mixture until smooth. Add the tomato paste, smoked paprika, cumin, crushed red pepper, thyme, honey, salt and pepper, and stir until combined.

Transfer the meatballs to the pot. Reduce heat and simmer for 8–10 minutes. Serve immediately with crusty bread, if desired.

Chinese BBQ Bite-size Spare Ribs

These bite-size ribs remind me of our family friend Uncle Jack's Cantonese restaurant in Hopkins Minnesota. We used to go there every Friday night when my dad had a side hustle as a host. This is one of those classic Chinese restaurant appetizers that you'd never imagine you could make at home but are surprisingly easy to make. Great to make ahead for a party as they can be served at room temperature. Be forewarned, they tend to fly off the platter so consider doubling the recipe for a hungry gang.

Serves 8–10 as an appetizer
Prep Time: 15 minutes + marinating time
Cook Time: 60 minutes

$2^1/_2$–3-lb (1.25–1.5 kg) rack pork ribs, cut across bones into halves
$^1/_2$ cup (117 g) ketchup
2 tablespoons sugar
2 tablespoons hoisin sauce
1 tablespoon dry white wine
2 teaspoons salt
2 cloves garlic, minced
Chinese hot mustard, for serving (optional)

Heat the oven to 400°F (200°C).

Trim the fat and remove the membranes from the ribs. Place the ribs in a shallow dish. Combine the remaining ingredients in a small bowl. Pour the mixture over the ribs and turn to coat. Cover and refrigerate for at least 2 hours but no longer than 24 hours.

Place the ribs in a single layer on the rack in a roasting pan and brush them with the sauce. Bake the ribs uncovered for 30 minutes. Turn the ribs and brush them with sauce. Continue to bake uncovered until done, about 30 minutes longer (reduce the temperature to 375°F [190°C] if the ribs are thin). Cut between each rib to separate them and serve with hot mustard, if desired.

COOK'S NOTE
Many Asian markets sell pork ribs already cut for this style of preparation. If you're at a regular grocery store, ask the butcher to cut the ribs for you.

Bacon, Date & Goat Cheese Potstickers

My friend, Bob Mandler (founder of the famed Chin Chin restaurant chain in Los Angeles), just opened a new restaurant called My Little Dumpling in West Hollywood. It's known for its innovative dim sum fare like Reuben Eggrolls and Cream Cheese Wontons with Lox. I was lucky enough to serve on the R & D team for this concept. It inspired me to create this potsticker based on the beloved appetizer—Goat Cheese Stuffed Dates wrapped in Bacon. I mean, who doesn't love this classic combo? And now you get to enjoy it wrapped up as a cute dumpling! Salty-sweet and oozing with creamy goat cheese and crispy bits of bacon in every bite, this one is a little dumpling winner. Make it a date!

Serves 6 as an appetizer
Prep Time: 15 minutes
Cook Time: 10 minutes

1/2 cup (115 g) fresh goat cheese
4 tablespoons chopped pitted dates
3 slices cooked bacon, chopped
1 package round dumpling wrappers
Oil, for pan-frying
2–3 fresh basil leaves cut into thin ribbons (optional)
Balsamic vinegar, for drizzling

Combine the goat cheese, dates and bacon in a small bowl.

Lay dumpling wrappers flat on a cutting board. Brush the top edge of the wrappers with a bit of water. Place 1 1/2 teaspoons of the goat cheese mixture in the center of each wrapper. Lift up the edges of the circle and pinch several pleats to create a pouch encasing the mixture. Pinch the top together. Repeat with the remaining wrappers and filling.

Heat 1 tablespoon of oil in a wok or large non-stick skillet over medium-high heat. Place 12 dumplings in a single layer in the wok and fry for 2 minutes, or until the bottoms are golden brown.

Add 1/2 cup (125 ml) water. Cover and cook 6–7 minutes or until the water is absorbed. Repeat with the remaining dumplings. Top with basil ribbons (if using) and drizzle with balsamic vinegar. Serve immediately.

COOK'S NOTE
To chiffonade basil, stack the leaves on top of each other, gently roll them into a cigar, and then use a sharp knife to slice them into thin ribbons.

Honey Sriracha Turkey Lollipops

Looking for a way to spice up your next party? Well, hop on board the good ship Honey Sriracha Turkey Lollipop! I created this delicious honey-sriracha glaze for a chicken wing recipe and decided to toss some turkey meatballs seasoned with lime juice, ginger, cilantro and scallions with it. The result is a honey-sriracha masterpiece. Each juicy meatball is a mouthful of tender, succulent, flavorful deliciousness that will have your guests coming back for more...and more. My friend Amy requests these every year on her birthday. Trust me, they are worth growing old for!

Serves: 6–8 as an appetizer
Prep Time: 30 minutes
Cook Time: 18 minutes

Turkey Lollipops

1 lb (500 g) ground turkey
2/3 cup (42 g) panko bread crumbs, plus more
  if needed
4 tablespoons finely chopped green onion
  (scallion), white and green parts
4 tablespoons finely chopped fresh coriander
  leaves (cilantro)
1 tablespoon freshly squeezed lime juice
1 egg
1 teaspoon peeled and minced fresh ginger
1 teaspoon salt
1/4 teaspoon freshly ground black pepper

Honey Sriracha Glaze

6 tablespoons butter
1/3 cup (113 g) honey
4 tablespoons sriracha sauce
1 tablespoon soy sauce
Juice of 1 lime

Preheat the oven to 375°F (190°C).

Combine all of the Turkey Lollipop ingredients in a large bowl until blended. Shape the mixture into ping-pong-ball sized meatballs. Place the lollipops onto a parchment paper-lined baking sheet and bake for 18 minutes.

While the meatballs are baking, make the Honey Sriracha Glaze: Heat the butter in a medium saucepan over medium heat until melted. Add the remaining glaze ingredients, stir and bring to a boil. Let the glaze mixture boil for 1 minute. Lower heat and simmer for 10 minutes.

Add the baked meatballs to the sauce and toss to combine. Serve immediately with a bamboo skewer placed in each one.

COOK'S NOTE
Try ground beef, chicken or pork instead of turkey. Make ahead tip: Bake a large batch of meatballs, let them cool and then freeze—a life-saver for last minute entertaining!

Galina's Russian Meatballs

This recipe for authentic Russian meatballs was given to me by my friend Rita Drucker's mother Galina, who grew up in Kiev, Russia. Rita told me her mother would make these to comfort her when she was feeling homesick after they immigrated from Russia to Los Angeles. This is an easy and delicious recipe that I love to make when I have leftover white rice. It's excellent for entertaining as you can make it in advance and then heat it up and pop it into a chafing dish just as your guests arrive.

Makes 36 meatballs
Prep Time: 30 minutes
Cook Time: 45 minutes

2 tablespoons extra virgin olive oil, divided
1 cup (150 g) finely chopped onion
$^1/_2$ cup (75 g) cooked long-grain white rice, chilled
1 lb (500 g) ground turkey (preferably dark meat)
1 lb (500 g) ground round
1 teaspoon salt
$^1/_4$ teaspoon freshly ground black pepper
1 tablespoon butter

Sauce
Two 8-oz (227-g) cans tomato sauce
3 tablespoons ketchup
1 teaspoon brown sugar
$^1/_2$ teaspoon Tabasco sauce
4 tablespoons water

COOK'S NOTE
Use 1 lb (500 g) of ground veal instead of ground round for a richer meatball experience.

Heat 1 tablespoon of the olive oil in a large non-stick skillet over medium-high heat. Add the onion and sauté until softened, about 3 minutes. Transfer to a bowl and allow to cool.

In a large mixing bowl, combine the cooked rice, reserve onions, ground turkey, ground round, salt and pepper. Using wet hands, form mixture into 1$^1/_2$-inch (3.8-cm) meatballs. Heat the remaining 1 tablespoon extra virgin olive oil and 1 tablespoon butter and allow butter to melt. Add the meatballs in batches, browning on all sides. Remove the meatballs from the pan.

Make the **Sauce**: Bring the tomato sauce, ketchup, brown sugar, Tabasco sauce and water to a boil in a large non-stick skillet. Add the reserved meatballs. Reduce the heat and simmer for 30–40 minutes, until the meatballs are no longer pink inside.

Transfer to a chafing dish and serve with toothpicks.

Lemongrass Beef Skewers

If you're unfamiliar with lemongrass, I like to call it "ginger's frisky cousin." It's woodsy, earthy, citrusy and extremely fragrant. It makes for an intoxicating marinade for beef skewers when combined with shallots, ginger, brown sugar, fish sauce and lime juice. I made these for the annual New Orleans Wine & Food Experience with my sous chef, Stacy, who was in charge of grilling over 200 of these babies for the crowd. They were so tender, flavorful and juicy that there were none left for me! Pro tip: keep a few stashed away for yourself before guests arrive.

Serves 8–10 as an appetizer
Prep Time: 20 minutes + marinating time
Cook Time: 20 minutes

10-in (25-cm) wooden skewers
Thai Peanut Sauce (page 34)

Marinade
2 cloves garlic, minced
2 tablespoons finely chopped shallots
2 teaspoons peeled and minced fresh ginger
3 tablespoons minced lemongrass
1 tablespoon palm sugar or brown sugar
3 tablespoons fish sauce (*nam pla*)
1¹/₂ tablespoons freshly squeezed lime juice
2 teaspoons oil

1¹/₂ lbs (750 g) top sirloin steak, cut into thin strips against the grain
2 tablespoons crushed roasted peanuts, for garnish
2 tablespoons finely chopped fresh cilantro, for garnish

Soak the wooden skewers for at least 30 minutes.

Make the **Marinade**: Whisk together the marinade ingredients in a large mixing bowl. Place the beef in a large resealable plastic food storage bag. Pour the marinade mixture over the beef. Refrigerate for 2 hours.

Meanwhile, make the Thai Peanut Sauce on page 34. Transfer the sauce to a small bowl, garnish with peanuts and set aside. Cover and refrigerate any remaining sauce for future use.

Insert the wooden skewers through the meat. Preheat a grill. Grill for 2–3 minutes on each side or until desired tenderness. Remove the skewers from the grill and garnish them with peanuts and fresh cilantro. Serve immediately with Thai Peanut Sauce.

COOK'S NOTE
You can store remaining peanut sauce covered in the refrigerator for up to 5 days. Use it as a dipping sauce, stir-fry sauce or salad dressing.

Touchdown Chili Garlic Chicken Wings

Spicy, sweet and sticky, these easy-to-make wings will add a fabulous Asian twist to your Super Bowl or birthday party! (Or "Thank God It's Friday and I Made It Through Another Week" Party!) The wings are tossed in flour seasoned with five spice powder, deep fried until golden brown and then tossed in a yummy sweet and savory chili-garlic sauce. Whatever the occasion, you'll score extra points when you serve these wings to your hungry crowd!

Serves 4 as an appetizer
Prep Time: 20 minutes
Cook Time: 45–60 minutes

1/2 cup (60 g) all-purpose flour
1/2 teaspoon Chinese five spice
  powder
1/2 teaspoon salt
2 lbs (1 kg) chicken wings, cut into
  drummettes and flats
1/2 cup (113 g) butter, melted
1 tablespoon minced garlic
1 tablespoon peeled and minced fresh
  ginger
2 teaspoons fish sauce (*nam pla*)
4 tablespoons store-bought sweet
  Thai chili sauce plus more for
  brushing
3 tablespoons sriracha sauce
Oil, for frying

Preheat the oven to 375°F (190°C).

In a small bowl, mix together the flour, five spice powder and salt.

Place the chicken wings in a large bowl. Add the flour mixture and toss until they are evenly coated.

Meanwhile, combine the butter, garlic, ginger, fish sauce, sweet chili sauce and sriracha sauce in a small bowl.

In a large wok or deep skillet, heat 3-inches (7.5-cm) of the oil to 350°F (175°C). Fry the wings in batched for 12–15 minutes until golden brown. Do no overcrowd. Drain on a sheet pan lined with paper towels.

Transfer the wings to a large bowl. Pour the sauce over the wings and toss to coat.

Place the wings on a non-stick baking sheet and bake for 15 minutes. Brush the wings with more sweet chili sauce before serving.

Tess's Lumpia Spring Rolls

I was exposed to Filipino cuisine when I moved to LA in the late '80s and it changed my world! This *lumpia prito* (meaning "fried lumpia") recipe was given to me by my Filipino bestie and Fortune Cookie Divas partner Ann's mom, Tess. Ann remembers helping her mom and grandma make these for big family parties, and they were her son Dylan's first solid food that he'd gnaw on as a toddler. These highly addictive little finger foods are perfect for parties, lunch boxes and picnics, and they're served with a unique vinegar and black pepper sauce.

Serves 6–8 as an appetizer
Prep Time: 30 minutes + draining time
Cook Time: 17 minutes

Dipping Sauce
1/2 cup (125 ml) white vinegar
2 teaspoons crushed garlic
Freshly ground black pepper, to taste

Lumpia
4 tablespoons oil
3 cloves garlic, minced
1 lb (500 g) ground lean pork
1 large white onion, finely chopped
1 teaspoon salt
1/4 teaspoon freshly ground black pepper
2 cups (300 g) peeled and grated sweet potato
2 cups (300 g) peeled and grated red potato
2 cups (300 g) julienned green beans
2 cups (100 g) peeled and grated carrots
2 cups (140 g) grated cabbage
4 tablespoons chicken stock or broth
Salt and freshly ground black pepper, to taste
Lumpia wrappers or spring roll wrappers
1 egg, beaten with a splash of water
Oil, for frying

Make the **Dipping Sauce**: Whisk the Dipping Sauce ingredients together in a small bowl. Set aside.

Make the **Lumpia**: Heat the 4 tablespoons oil in a wok or large, deep non-stick skillet over medium-high heat. Add the garlic and stir-fry until fragrant, about 30 seconds. Add the pork and onions and stir-fry until the pork is tender, about 5 minutes. Add the salt, pepper, sweet and red potatoes, and stir-fry for about 3 minutes. Add the green beans, carrots and cabbage and stir-fry for 2 minutes. Add the chicken stock or broth and stir to combine and continue cooking until the vegetables are tender, about 3 minutes. Add salt and pepper, to taste. Remove from the heat and drain the mixture in a colander until cool.

Place 1/2 cup (50 g) of the lumpia filling slightly below center of a spring roll skin (cover remaining skins with a dampened towel to keep them pliable). Fold the corner of the lumpia wrapper closest to the filling over of the filling, tucking the point underneath. Fold in and overlap the two opposite corners. Brush the fourth corner with the egg mixture and roll up to seal, enclosing the filling. Repeat with the remaining eggroll wrappers and filling.

In a wok or deep skillet, heat 2–3 inches (5–7.5 cm) of the oil to 350°F (175°C). Fry 4 or 5 eggrolls at a time until golden brown, about 2–3 minutes per side, turning 2–3 times. Drain on a sheet pan lined with paper towels. Serve immediately with the Dipping Sauce.

COOK'S NOTES
Vietnamese lumpia wrappers can be found in the freezer section of your local Asian market (but Chinese spring roll wrappers can also be used).

Store-bought sweet and sour sauce also goes great with lumpia.

Spicy Ahi Tuna Tartare on Wonton Chips

This appetizer is so easy to make, yet feels *très bougie* when you serve it. It's also easy to handle one of these babies while holding a glass of bubbly in your other hand. I made these for a fundraiser I was catering for Kyle Richards (*Real Housewives of Beverly Hills*) and they were a hit! The crispness of the wonton chip along with the tender and fresh coolness of the ahi tuna are a dynamic duo and an instant crowd pleaser! This couldn't be simpler to make and it's really quick to whip together. Plus, a little tuna goes a long way. Impress all your friends with this sophisticated appetizer.

Serves 8–10 as an appetizer
Prep Time: 20 minutes
Cook Time: 5 minutes

Oil, for frying
10 square wonton wrappers, cut into
    quarters
1 tablespoon mayonnaise
$3/4$ teaspoon low-sodium soy sauce
1 teaspoon dark sesame oil
$1/2$ teaspoon sriracha sauce
Freshly squeezed lemon juice, to
    taste
8 oz (250 g) sushi grade ahi tuna, cut
    into $1/4$-in (6-mm) dice
Sesame seeds, for garnish

Heat oil in a deep skillet or wok to 375°F (190°C). Fry wonton wrappers until golden brown. Drain on a paper towel-lined baking sheet.

Whisk together the mayonnaise, soy sauce, sesame oil and sriracha sauce. Add freshly squeezed lemon juice, to taste. Add the tuna and toss to coat.

Spoon the tuna mixture onto wonton crisps and garnish with sesame seeds.

California Rolls Makizushi

Who doesn't love the classic California roll? Once you do it yourself, you'll realize that it's so easy, you can even get the kids involved. I break out my sushi mat and put Dylan and his sister Becca to work all the time. Not only is this a great healthy dinner or snack, but kids also have so much fun making their own creations. You just need to know the basics and a few simple tips, then you can let your creativity fly free on an adventure with other ingredients! Remember that squeezing some lemon juice on the avocado after it's been cut will prevent it from browning; and if you want to splurge, fresh lump crab meat is delicious, but "crab sticks" are fine for everyday snacking.

Serves 4 as an appetizer
Prep Time: 25 minutes
Cook Time: 10 minutes

Sushi Rice
1 cup (200 g) sushi or short grain rice
1 cup (250 ml) water
1 tablespoon rice vinegar
1 tablespoon sugar
1 teaspoon salt

4 sheets nori
1/3 cup (40 g) black and white toasted sesame
  seeds
1 small cucumber, peeled, deseeded, and cut
  into matchsticks
1 medium avocado, peeled, pitted, and sliced
  into 1/4-in (6-mm) thick pieces

4 crab sticks, torn into pieces
Pickled ginger, for serving
Wasabi, for serving
Soy sauce, for serving

Make the **Sushi Rice**: Place the rice into a mixing bowl and cover with cool water. Let soak for 20 minutes. Swirl the rice in the water, pour off the cloudy water, and repeat 2–3 times or until the water clears.

Place the rice and 1 cup (250 ml) of water into a medium saucepan and place over high heat. Bring to a boil, uncovered. Once it begins to boil, reduce the heat to the lowest setting and cover. Cook for 15 minutes. Remove from the heat and let stand, covered, for 10 minutes.

Combine the rice vinegar, sugar and salt in a small bowl and heat in the microwave on high for 30–45 seconds or bring the mixture to a simmer in a saucepan. Transfer the rice into a large wooden or glass mixing bowl and

add the vinegar mixture. Fold thoroughly to combine and coat each grain of rice with the mixture. Allow to cool to room temperature.

Cover a bamboo rolling mat with plastic wrap. Cut the nori sheets in half crosswise. Lay 1 sheet of nori, shiny side down, on the plastic covered mat. Wet your fingers with water and spread about 1/2 cup (125 g) of the rice evenly onto the nori. Sprinkle the rice with sesame seeds.

Turn the sheet of nori over so that the rice side is down. Place 1/8 of the cucumber, avocado and crab sticks in the center of the sheet. Grab the edge of the mat closest to you, keeping the fillings in place with your fingers, and roll it into a tight cylinder, using the mat to shape the cylinder. Pull the mat and plastic wrap away and set aside. Repeat until all rolls are completed. Slice each roll into six pieces using a wet serrated knife. Serve with ginger, wasabi and soy sauce.

Coconut Shrimp with Pineapple Yogurt Sauce

I brought the twins to Minneapolis for a family reunion a couple of summers ago. Between kayaking, roller-coastering at the Mall of America and a trip to the emergency room after a crazy allergic reaction to a bee sting, we squeezed in a fun dinner party with friends Laura Keller and Andrea Stein. It was balmy and humid that night and I got the urge to whip up some tropical cocktails and these sweet, crunchy and succulent coconut shrimp. I mean, who doesn't love coconut shrimp? The shrimp are served with a luscious pineapple yogurt sauce. Next time you feel like bringing some "Tiki" to your table, try this easy and delicious recipe and take your taste buds on a trip to the Tropics. No passport required.

Serves 6–8 as an appetizer
Prep Time: 20 minutes
Cook Time: 12–15 minutes

Pineapple Yogurt Sauce
²/₃ cup (220 g) pineapple marmalade
¹/₂ cup (143 g) plain Greek yogurt
2 tablespoons flaked, sweetened coconut
1–2 tablespoons coconut milk
Chopped fresh mint, for garnish

Coconut Shrimp
3 egg whites
¹/₃ cup (80 ml) lager beer
¹/₃ cup (40 g) cornstarch
1 teaspoon salt
2 cups (200 g) flaked, sweetened coconut

1 lb (500 g) peeled and deveined large shrimp with tails intact
Oil, for frying

Make the Pineapple Yogurt Sauce: Place all of the sauce ingredients except the mint in a small bowl and stir to combine. Cover and place in the refrigerator.

Beat the egg whites and beer until frothy in a medium bowl. Mix the cornstarch and salt in a separate shallow bowl. Place the coconut flakes in a separate shallow bowl.

Working with one shrimp at a time, dredge in the cornstarch mixture, and then dip it in the egg white and beer mixture, and then roll it in the coconut flakes, making sure to coat the shrimp well.

In a large wok or deep skillet, heat 2–3 inches (5–7.5 cm) of the oil to 350°F (175°C). Fry the shrimp in batches until golden brown, about 3 minutes, turning once. Drain on a sheet pan lined with paper towels. Serve immediately with dipping sauce garnished with the mint.

The Devil Made Me Do It—Deviled Eggs Four Ways

Indian-style Deviled Eggs

Garam Masala is a spice used in many Indian recipes that can be found in most grocery stores. It's actually a blend of spices such as clove, cinnamon, cardamom and cumin. It's exotic and incredibly flavorful, adding an Indian twist to anything it touches. Keep a tin on hand for this easy recipe. These are definitely not your grandmother's deviled eggs! They're a great way to bring a little Bombay spice to your next potluck.

Serves 6 as an appetizer
Prep Time: 15 minutes + cooling time
Cook Time: 12 minutes

6 large eggs
2 tablespoons butter
4 tablespoons finely chopped onion
2 cloves garlic, minced
1 tablespoon garam masala
3 tablespoons mayonnaise
1 tablespoon Dijon mustard
Smoked paprika, for garnish
Finely chopped coriander leaves (cilantro), for garnish

COOK'S NOTES

If you don't have a piping bag you can use a large resealable plastic food storage bag. Snip off the corner to pipe the filling into the egg white halves.

Place the eggs in a single layer in a large saucepan; add enough cold water to cover by 1 inch (2.5 cm). Cover and quickly bring to a boil. Remove from the heat. Let stand for 15 minutes. Rinse the eggs in cold water and then place them in ice water until completely cooled. Drain and peel.

Slice the eggs in half lengthwise. Remove the yolks into a medium bowl. Set the cooked egg white halves aside.

Melt the butter in a non-stick skillet over medium-high heat. Add the chopped onions and sauté until dark brown, about 3–4 minutes. Add the garlic and sauté until fragrant, about 1 minute. Add the garam masala and sauté for 1 minute. Remove the mixture from the heat and transfer it to a food processor and purée for 1–2 minutes. Allow to cool to room temperature in the food processor.

Add the reserved yolks to the cooled onion mixture in the food processor. Add the mayonnaise and mustard and purée for 1–2 minutes.

Place the mixture into a piping bag and pipe it into the egg white halves. Sprinkle with smoked paprika and chopped cilantro and serve immediately.

Niçoise Deviled Eggs

C'est manifique! This was my friend Amy's reaction to this recipe. It's like basking in the Provence sunshine with every bite. If you're a lover of salade niçoise you will simply adore this dish. We felt so inspired enjoying this fresh and colorful appetizer that we cracked open a bottle of champagne and blasted Edith Piaf in the background. Talk about adding a little oh la la to an otherwise ordinary afternoon.

Serves 6 as an appetizer
Prep Time: 20 minutes
Cook Time: 11 minutes

6 large eggs
One 7-oz (198-g) can solid white albacore tuna
    packed in water, drained
2 tablespoons mayonnaise
2 teaspoons Dijon mustard
1 tablespoon white wine vinegar
2 tablespoons pitted and finely chopped Kalamata
    olives
1 teaspoon capers, finely chopped
1 teaspoon finely chopped shallot
Salt and freshly ground black pepper, to taste
3 steamed green beans, cut into 1-in (2.5-cm) pieces
3 grape tomatoes, cut into quarters, for garnish
12 whole capers, for garnish
12 fresh tarragon leaves, for garnish

Place the eggs in a single layer in a large saucepan; add enough cold water to cover by 1-inch (2.5 cm). Cover and quickly bring to a boil. Remove from the heat. Let stand for 15 minutes. Rinse the eggs in cold water and then place them in ice water until completely cooled. Drain and peel.

Slice the eggs in half lengthwise. Remove the yolks into a medium bowl. Set the cooked egg white halves aside.

Mash the yolks with a fork and add the tuna, mayonnaise, mustard, vinegar, olives, capers and shallots. Gently combine the mixture with a fork. Salt and pepper to taste. Place the yolk mixture into the egg whites using the back of a spoon.

Garnish each egg with a piece of green bean, a slice of tomato and a caper. Garnish with tarragon and serve.

Miso Deviled Eggs

Miso tired of making miso puns but never tired of making these Miso Deviled Eggs! Heh heh. Miso drops an umami bomb on these savory, salty and creamy Japanese-inspired deviled eggs. Made with other classic deviled egg ingredients like mayo and Dijon mustard, this creamy sensation is sure to be a hit at your next potluck or gathering. Your friends will never look at deviled eggs the same way again and neither will you. You little devil, you.

Serves 8 as an appetizer
Prep Time: 10 minutes + resting time
Cook Time: 10 minutes

8 large eggs
1/3 cup (76 g) mayonnaise
1 tablespoon Dijon mustard
1 teaspoon low-sodium soy sauce
1 tablespoon white or yellow miso paste
1 teaspoon sriracha sauce
Pinch of freshly ground black pepper
Toasted black sesame seeds, for garnish
Finely chopped green onions (scallions), white and green parts, for garnish

Place the eggs in a single layer in a large saucepan; add enough cold water to cover by 1 inch (2.5 cm). Cover and quickly bring to a boil. Remove from the heat. Let stand for 15 minutes. Rinse the eggs in cold water and then place them in ice water until completely cooled. Drain and peel.

Slice the eggs in half lengthwise. Remove the yolks into a medium bowl. Set the cooked egg white halves aside.

Mash the yolks with a fork, and then add the mayonnaise, mustard, soy sauce, miso paste, sriracha and pepper. Gently combine the mixture with the fork.

Place the mixture into a piping bag and pipe it into the egg white halves. Refrigerate until set, about 20 minutes. Garnish with sesame seeds and green onions before serving.

COOK'S NOTE
If you don't have a piping bag you can use a large resealable plastic food storage bag. Snip off the corner to pipe the filling into the egg white halves.

Mexican-style Deviled Eggs

Sometimes when I'm craving tacos I make this recipe instead as it's low-carb, protein-packed and a quick and easy way to satisfy my craving. It's a great after-school snack too because I can make a batch earlier in the day and pop them into the fridge. My friend Ann and I recently whipped some up to keep the twins and her kids Dylan and Sofia satisfied until dinnertime, and it was a welcome alternative to chips and sweets. Luckily, we got to enjoy the leftovers with some margaritas at sundown. Ole!

Serves 6 as an appetizer
Prep Time: 10 minutes
Cook Time: 15 minutes

6 large eggs
1/4 ripe avocado, mashed
2 tablespoons store-bought pico de gallo
1/8 teaspoon salt
1 1/2 teaspoons store-bought taco seasoning plus more, for garnish
2 tablespoons shredded Mexican blend cheese
Finely chopped coriander leaves (cilantro) for garnish

Place the eggs in a single layer in a large saucepan; add enough cold water to cover by 1 inch (2.5 cm). Cover and quickly bring to a boil. Remove from the heat. Let stand for 15 minutes. Rinse the eggs in cold water and then place them in ice water until completely cooled. Drain and peel.

Slice the eggs in half lengthwise. Remove the yolks into a medium bowl. Set the cooked egg white halves aside.

Mash the yolks with a fork. Add the mashed avocado, pico de gallo, salt and taco seasoning. Gently combine the mixture with the fork.

Place the yolk mixture into the egg white halves using the back of a spoon.

Using a fine mesh strainer, sprinkle the top of the eggs with more taco seasoning. Top with shredded cheese and garnish with cilantro. Serve immediately.

Thai-Inspired Poutine French Fries

Here's a fabulous Asian fusion creation that marries sweet, salty, sour and hot Thai flavors with the ingredients of the Canadian classic, poutine. Replacing the usual brown gravy is spicy Thai peanut sauce drizzled over crispy fries and layered with fresh herbs and crunchy carrots, bean sprouts and crushed peanuts. This appetizer is a match made in heaven that's sure to be a hands-down keeper in your Far-East-fusion file!

Serves 4 as an appetizer
Prep Time: 20 minutes
Cook Time: 30 minutes

1 lb (500 g) frozen shoestring french fries
1 tablespoon oil
1 teaspoon salt
$1/4$ teaspoon freshly ground black pepper
2 teaspoons dried coriander leaves (cilantro)
  (optional)
Thai Peanut Sauce (page 34)
$1/2$ cup (50 g) bean sprouts, trimmed
$1/2$ cup (25 g) shredded carrots
4 tablespoons finely chopped fresh coriander
  leaves (cilantro)
4 tablespoons finely chopped Thai basil or
  Italian basil leaves
4 tablespoons roasted chopped peanuts, plus
  more, for garnish
1 green onion (scallion), white and green parts,
  finely chopped
Sriracha sauce (optional)

Toss the frozen french fries with the oil, salt and pepper and dried coriander leaves (cilantro) if using. Place the fries on a baking sheet and cook according to the package directions. Transfer to a platter.

While fries are cooking, make the Thai Peanut Sauce (page 34).

Layer the bean sprouts and carrots on top of the fries. Top with cilantro and basil. Drizzle $1/2$ cup (125 ml) of the Thai Peanut Sauce on top. Sprinkle with chopped peanuts, green onions and sriracha sauce, if desired. Serve immediately.

> ### COOK'S NOTE
> The Thai Peanut Sauce recipe makes approximately 1 cup (250 ml). You can store remaining peanut sauce covered in the refrigerator for up to 5 days. Use it as a dipping sauce, stir-fry sauce or salad dressing.

SIMMERING SOUPS & SASSY SALADS

Prepared soups and salad bars are appealing because of their variety and on-the-go convenience, but why not make some delicious soul-warming soups and crisp, fresh salads from scratch? Now that you've got these flavorful, out-of-the-ordinary recipes in your arsenal, they'll be a snap to prepare! Besides the cost savings, it's a lot healthier because you control exactly what you're putting in your soup (restaurant soups are often loaded with sodium) or salad (you're in control of how much dressing you use). I think the best salads are made from the freshest ingredients selected at the peak of their season (remember to eat the rainbow, folks), so I encourage you to hit your local farmers' market. The collection of flavorful soups in this chapter are fast and easy too, like **30-Minute Chicken Pozole** and **Quick Udon Noodle Soup**, and although simple to make, they're brimming with complex flavors from miso to citrus. The salads range from the rustic and exotic **Vietnamese Glass Noodle Salad with Crab** to the sunny, bright and light **Melon & Peach Salad with Prosciutto & Mozzarella** and the classic **Chopped Greek Salad**.

Mediterranean Bulgur Salad Tabbouleh

This recipe puts the "Oooh" In "Tabbouleh!" A Mediterranean favorite, this dish brings a bright, fresh, clean and healthy addition to any get together. The longer it rests, the more flavorful it becomes so it's an ideal recipe for a potluck or picnic that you can make in the morning or the evening before. I like to serve it with romaine lettuce leaves that guests can fill and enjoy. You could also fill endive cups.

COOK'S NOTE
The flavor will improve if you allow the tabbouleh to sit for several hours in your fridge before eating.

Serves: 4–6
Prep Time: 20 minutes + resting time

1 cup (225 g) bulgur wheat
1 1/2 cups (375 ml) boiling water
4 tablespoons freshly squeezed lemon juice
4 tablespoons extra virgin olive oil
1 1/2 teaspoons salt, divided
1 bunch green onions (scallions), white and green parts, finely chopped
1 cup (25 g) finely chopped fresh mint leaves
1 cup (25 g) finely chopped flat-leaf parsley
1 English cucumber, peeled, deseeded and diced
2 firm Roma tomatoes, deseeded and diced
1 teaspoon freshly ground black pepper
Romaine lettuce leaves (optional)

Place the bulgur wheat in a large bowl, pour in the boiling water, and add the lemon juice, extra virgin olive oil and 1/2 teaspoon of the salt. Stir, and then allow to stand at room temperature for about 1 hour.

Add the green onions, mint, parsley, cucumber, tomatoes, the remaining 1 teaspoon of the salt and the pepper; mix well. Season, to taste, and serve or cover and refrigerate at least one hour. Serve in lettuce leaves, if desired.

Monica's Norwegian Salmon Soup

My friend Monica Danielsen and her husband Øystein live in Norway, but luckily for me they visit Los Angeles often. I felt an immediate kinship with Monica when I first met her, probably because I grew up in Minnesota and our family belonged to the Sons of Norway (there were no Chinese clubs at the time!) Monica and her hubby love to cook together as a couple, and they were kind enough to share this seafood soup recipe brimming with chunks of salmon and shrimp. Sautéing the shrimp shells and simmering them adds a boost of flavor to this creamy broth. They make it so often that it has become a signature go-to recipe in their home.

Serves 4
Prep Time: 20 minutes
Cook Time: 30–33 minutes

$1\frac{1}{2}$ lbs (750 g) small shrimp in shells
2 tablespoons extra virgin olive oil, divided
3 tablespoons canned tomato sauce
$3\frac{1}{2}$ cups (875 ml) store-bought fish stock or water
6 tablespoons dry white wine
$\frac{1}{2}$ teaspoon salt
1 leek, white part only, washed and thinly sliced
3 medium carrots, peeled and thinly sliced on the diagonal
Pinch of ground red pepper (cayenne)
2 teaspoon cornstarch
2 teaspoons water
6 tablespoons heavy cream
Pinch of saffron
Salt and freshly ground black pepper, to taste
1 tablespoon white wine vinegar
$1\frac{1}{4}$ lbs (600 g) salmon fillet, skin removed, cut into large chunks
1–2 tablespoons chopped fresh dill
1 baguette, sliced

Peel the shrimp. Retain the shells and set the shrimp meat aside. Heat 1 tablespoon of the extra virgin olive oil in a dutch oven or pot over medium-high heat. Sauté the shells for 1–2 minutes. Add the tomato sauce and cook, while stirring, for 1 minute. Add the stock or water, the wine and $\frac{1}{2}$ teaspoon salt and bring to a boil. Reduce the heat and let the mixture simmer for 10 minutes.

Strain the liquid over a bowl to remove the shrimp shells, or remove them with tongs. Discard the shells. Clean and dry the dutch oven or pot. Heat the remaining 1 tablespoon of olive oil over medium-high heat. Add the leek slices and sauté until softened, about 4–5 minutes. Add the liquid back in the dutch oven or pot. Add the carrot slices and cayenne and bring to boil. Reduce the heat and simmer, covered, for 10 minutes.

While the soup is simmering, combine the cornstarch and water in a small bowl to form a slurry.

Add the cream and saffron to the dutch oven or pot and stir to combine. Add salt and pepper, to taste. Whisk in the cornstarch slurry until thickened. Add the vinegar and stir to combine. Bring the mixture to a boil and add the salmon chunks. Reduce heat and bring to a simmer.

Add the shrimp and chopped dill and simmer for 3–5 minutes, until the shrimp is cooked through.

Serve immediately with the baguette.

> ### COOK'S NOTE
> You may substitute the heavy cream with soy cream or coconut cream.

30-Minute Chicken Pozole

Pozole means "hominy" in Spanish, and it is a traditional dish served on New Year's Day. This flavorful recipe can be made in 30 minutes and it is chock-full of flavor from the wonderful blend of spices which are probably sitting on your spice rack right now. This is a warm and hearty soup that is perfect on a chilly day, and who doesn't love a new idea for using up that rotisserie chicken sitting in your fridge?

Serves: 4
Prep Time: 10 minutes
Cook Time: 20 minutes

2 tablespoons oil
1 small yellow onion, diced
2 tablespoons all-purpose flour
2 teaspoons chili powder
2 cups (500 ml) water
5 tablespoons tomato paste
$1/2$ teaspoon cumin
$1/2$ teaspoon garlic powder
$1/4$ teaspoon ground red pepper (cayenne)
$1/2$ teaspoon oregano
$1/2$ teaspoon smoked paprika
$3/4$ teaspoon salt
3 cups (750 ml) chicken stock or broth
$1 1/2$ cups (300 g) store-bought shredded rotisserie chicken
One 4-oz (113-g) can chopped green chilis
One 15-oz (425-g) can hominy, drained
$1/2$ bunch fresh coriander leaves (cilantro), roughly chopped
1 fresh lime, cut in wedges, for serving
Store-bought red and green salsa (optional)

Heat the oil in a large non-stick skillet over medium-high heat. Add the onions and sauté for 3 minutes until tender and transparent. Add the flour and chili powder and sauté for 2 minutes more, stirring continuously.

Add the water, tomato paste, cumin, garlic powder, cayenne pepper, oregano, smoked paprika and salt. Whisk the ingredients together until the tomato paste is dissolved. Reduce heat to a simmer and allow to thicken, about 5 minutes.

Add the chicken stock or broth, shredded chicken, diced chilis and hominy. Stir to combine and then heat through, about 10 minutes.

Top each bowl with chopped cilantro and a wedge of lime to squeeze over top. Serve immediately with red and green salsa on the side, if desired.

Easy Beef Pho Soup

Ever since we served the Vietnamese classic soup, pho, to Dylan and Becca when they were 3 years old, they simply cannot get enough of it. They love slurping up the slippery noodles in a rich beef broth topped with crunchy bean sprouts and cooling herbs. And when they're sick, it's all about the pho (when it used to be all about the chicken noodle soup). Here's an easy way to recreate the pho from your favorite Vietnamese restaurant without requiring hours to make the bone broth (hint: use store-bought beef stock!). Trust me, even Becca says it's PHObulous!

Serves 4–6
Prep Time: 15 minutes
Cook Time: 30 minutes

8 cups (1.75 liters) store-bought beef stock
2 cups (500 ml) water
Three 1/4-in (6-mm) thick slices fresh ginger
1 small white onion, thinly sliced
2 cloves garlic, thinly sliced
2 pods star anise
1 cinnamon stick, lightly bruised
1 1/2 tablespoons sugar
4 tablespoons fish sauce (*nam pla*)
14 oz (410 g) flat dried rice noodles
3/4 lb (350 g) beef tenderloin, very thinly
   sliced against the grain
1 cup (100 g) bean sprouts, trimmed
1 fresh hot red or green chili pepper
   (preferably Thai), deseeded if you prefer less
   heat, thinly sliced
1/3 cup (8 g) fresh Thai basil leaves, for
   serving
1/3 cup (8 g) fresh mint leaves, for serving
1/3 cup (8 g) fresh coriander leaves (cilantro),
   for serving
Lime wedges, for serving

Place the stock, water, ginger, onion, garlic, star anise, cinnamon, sugar and fish sauce in a large pot. Bring to a boil, and then reduce the heat to low. Cover and simmer for 20 minutes. Using a fine mesh strainer, remove the ginger, onion, garlic, star anise and cinnamon. Continue simmering.

While the soup is simmering, bring a pot of water to a boil. Turn off heat and add the rice noodles. Let sit for 10 minutes. Drain and rinse well.

Divide the noodles among warmed soup bowls, and then top with the sliced beef. Pour the hot soup mixture over the beef slices (the heat will gently cook the meat). Top with the bean sprouts, chili pepper and fresh herbs. Serve immediately with lime wedges.

> ### COOK'S NOTE
> Look for rice noodles that are labeled "pho." If you can't find rice noodles you can use fettuccine pasta as a substitute.

Chopped Greek Salad

My friends complain that it's hard to eat healthy with their busy lives and I can totally relate. Whenever I'm scratching my head at 4 PM trying to whip up a healthy dinner for my family I luckily remember this classic gem. Add some chopped up grilled chicken for added protein and pan-fry some shrimp to serve alongside it. Double the dressing and keep a jar handy in your fridge for easy weeknight Greek!

Serves 4–6
Prep Time: 20 minutes

Dressing
Juice of one lemon
1 teaspoon dried oregano
1 clove garlic, minced
1 teaspoon dried basil
2 tablespoons red wine vinegar
$1/4$ teaspoon salt
$1/4$ teaspoon sugar
4 tablespoons extra virgin olive oil

Salad
2 cups (266 g) deseeded and diced
  English cucumber
1 cup (175 g) diced red or yellow bell
  pepper
$1^1/2$ cups (262 g) halved cherry tomatoes
12 pitted Kalamata olives, halved
4 tablespoons finely chopped red onion
4 tablespoons finely chopped parsley
$1/2$ cup (75 g) crumbled feta cheese

Make the **Dressing**: Whisk all of the ingredients except the extra virgin olive oil in a medium bowl. Gradually whisk in the extra virgin olive oil. Set aside.

In a large serving bowl, combine the cucumbers, bell pepper, cherry tomatoes, olives, onion and parsley. Add the reserved Dressing and toss to coat. Sprinkle the feta cheese over the top and serve immediately.

COOK'S NOTE
You may store the dressing in a jar with a lid for up to 3 weeks in the fridge.

Citrusy Cuban Black Bean Soup

This is a fast and easy soup that is loaded with plant-based protein from the black beans. It's satisfying yet light, and layered with bright and fresh citrusy notes compliments of the freshly squeezed orange juice and zest. This is a fun soup you can make ahead and serve at a party where your guests can choose their own toppings. My kids even crush Goldfish crackers to put on top for some added cheesy crunch and I'm all for it if it gets them to clean their soup bowl!

Serves: 4
Prep Time: 10 minutes
Cook Time: 10 minutes

2 tablespoons extra virgin olive oil
1 medium onion, finely chopped
1 clove garlic, minced
1 teaspoon ground cumin
1/2 teaspoon dried paprika
1/2 teaspoon dried oregano
Two 15-oz (425-g) cans black beans, rinsed and drained
1/2 cup (125 ml) freshly squeezed orange juice
1 teaspoon orange zest
1 cup (250 ml) chicken stock or broth
4 tablespoons plain Greek yogurt
Salt and freshly ground black pepper, to taste
Lime wedges, for serving

Optional Toppings
Finely chopped coriander leaves (cilantro)
Finely chopped green onions (scallions)
Diced avocados
Crushed tortilla strips

Heat the oil in a large pot over medium-high heat. Add the onion and sauté until slightly browned, about 3–4 minutes. Add the garlic, cumin, paprika and oregano, and sauté for 1 minute. Add the beans, orange juice and zest, chicken stock or broth and yogurt, and cook while stirring for 5 minutes.

Remove half of the bean mixture. Using an immersion blender, purée the remaining beans in the pot. Add the reserved beans to the pot and heat until hot. Season with salt and pepper, to taste. Serve immediately with lime wedges and garnished with the desired toppings.

COOK'S NOTE
For a vegan version of this recipe, omit the yogurt and use vegetable stock. Add 1 tablespoon of soy sauce for enhanced flavor.

Chinese Chicken Salad

I got to make this delicious salad on the *Home & Family Show* on the Hallmark Channel and the on-set guests went gaga over it. They loved how light and healthy this salad is, and how it's filled with amazing textures, from the red cabbage (loaded with vitamins, nutrients and anti-oxidants, by the way) and carrots to the sliced almonds and crunchy wonton chips tossed in a yummy ginger sesame dressing. They especially enjoyed eating it in a cute red Chinese take-out container with chopsticks—a fun and colorful way to serve this salad up at your next luncheon!

Serves 4
Prep Time: 25 minutes

Dressing
- 1/3 cup (80 ml) unseasoned rice vinegar or white vinegar
- 1 clove garlic, minced
- 1 teaspoon peeled and minced fresh ginger
- 2 tablespoons brown sugar
- 1 1/2 teaspoons chili garlic sauce or *sambal oelek*
- 2 tablespoons extra-virgin olive oil or canola oil
- 1 teaspoon dark sesame oil

Salad
- 6 cups (300 g) bite-sized pieces torn romaine lettuce
- 1/4 head red cabbage, shredded
- 1 large carrot, shredded
- 2 green onions (scallions), green and white parts, finely chopped
- 1/2 cup (50 g) sliced almonds, plus more, for garnish
- One 11-oz (312-g) can mandarin oranges in water, drained
- 2 cups (300 g) shredded store-bought rotisserie chicken
- 1/2 cup (20 g) fried wonton strips, plus more, for garnish
- 2 tablespoons toasted sesame seeds, plus more, for garnish

Make the **Dressing**: In a small bowl, whisk together the Dressing ingredients. Gradually whisk in the olive or canola oil and sesame oil.

In a large bowl, combine the romaine lettuce, red cabbage, carrot, green onion, sliced almonds, mandarin oranges, shredded chicken, wonton strips and sesame seeds. Add the Dressing and toss to combine. Garnish with additional almonds and sesame seeds. Serve immediately.

Shoyu Ramen with Chicken

If you're like me and you're craving ramen, you just gotta have it. I'm not always in the mood to go out or we simply don't always have the time with our crazy schedules. With this easy recipe, my family and I can get our fix in under 30 minutes. Plus, it's healthier and cheaper to make this yummy recipe at home. By the way, *shoyu* simply means "soy sauce" in Japanese, in case you were wondering. I included nutrient rich kale in this recipe for a boost of antioxidants but feel free to swap out with spinach or another veggie.

Serves 4
Prep Time: 25 minutes
Cook Time: 10 minutes

2 teaspoons toasted sesame oil
2 cloves garlic, minced
1 tablespoon peeled and grated fresh ginger
4 cups (1 liter) chicken stock or broth
4 oz (100 g) sliced fresh shiitake mushrooms
1 teaspoons salt
1 teaspoon sugar
1 tablespoon sake (optional)
1 tablespoon soy sauce
1¹/₂ cups (100 g) chopped kale
1 cup (50 g) shredded carrots
Three 5.6-oz (158-g) packages refrigerated yaki-soba noodles, seasoning packets discarded
2 cups (400 g) store-bought shredded rotisserie chicken
Finely chopped green onions (scallions), for topping

Other toppings (optional):
Nori (dried seaweed)
Menma (fermented bamboo shoots)
Soft-boiled egg
Slices of *naruto* (fish cake)
La-Yu (Japanese chili oil)
Corn kernels
Crispy garlic

Heat sesame oil over medium-high heat in a medium pot. Add the garlic and ginger and sauté until fragrant, about 30 seconds. Increase heat to high and add the chicken stock or broth, mushrooms, sugar, salt, sake (if using) and soy sauce and bring to a boil. Reduce heat and bring to a simmer. Add the chopped kale, carrots and the yaki-soba noodles and stir until the noodles are loosened and cooked through, about 3 minutes.

Divide ramen into four bowls. Top with shredded chicken, green onions and other toppings, if desired. Serve immediately.

COOK'S NOTE
You can substitute the fresh yaki-soba noodles with three small packages of dried ramen noodles, if you prefer. Simply discard the seasoning packets and follow the package instructions to cook the noodles. Divide the cooked noodles into the bowls before pouring the stock and other ingredients on top.

Orzo, Mozzarella & Sugar Snap Pea Salad

Orzo is a form of pasta that is shaped like a large grain of rice. In this recipe, tender, pillowy soft chunks of mozzarella are married with tender-crisp sugar snap peas and the orzo in a light lemony dressing which allows the fresh herbs to shine through. Delicate and cute (just like the perfect summer dress), I think orzo is a great choice for this easy breezy pasta salad.

Serves 4
Prep Time: 20 minutes

1 cup (100 g) dried orzo
3 tablespoons extra virgin olive oil
2 teaspoons grated lemon zest
2 tablespoons freshly squeezed lemon juice
2 cloves garlic, minced
$1/2$ teaspoon salt
$1/2$ teaspoon freshly ground black pepper
6 red cherry tomatoes, halved
6 yellow cherry tomatoes, halved
1 cup (85 g) halved snap peas with strings removed

8 oz (250 g) fresh mozzarella cheese, cut into chunks
4 tablespoons finely chopped fresh dill
4 tablespoons finely chopped fresh chives
4 tablespoons finely chopped fresh chopped tarragon

Cook the orzo according to the package directions. Drain and let cool.

Whisk together the extra virgin olive oil, lemon zest, lemon juice, garlic and salt and pepper in a medium bowl. Add the cherry tomatoes, snap peas, mozzarella cheese, herbs and orzo, and toss to combine. Serve immediately.

Sour Spicy Thai Shrimp Shooters

Who doesn't love Thai soups? Fragrant lemongrass, kaffir lime leaf and ginger comingled with fish sauce and lime juice just makes me swoon. I wanted to bring all of these delicious flavors to a recent cocktail party I was throwing, but I also wanted to enable my guests to have a hand free to carry a glass of wine or martini. And voila! That's how the Sour Spicy Thai Shrimp Shooter was born!

Serves 8–10
Prep Time: 10 minutes
Cook Time: 10 minutes

3 cups (750 ml) water
4 kaffir lime leaves, torn in half (optional)
Six $1/4$-in (6-mm) thick slices fresh ginger
2 stalks lemongrass, cut into 2-in (5-cm) long pieces and bruised
3 tablespoons fish sauce (*nam pla*)
2 tablespoons freshly squeezed lime juice
1 fresh hot red or green chili pepper (preferably Thai), deseeded if you prefer less heat, thinly sliced
16–20 cooked bay shrimp, peeled and deveined
1 tablespoon store-bought roasted red chili paste (optional)
Finely chopped fresh coriander leaves (cilantro), for garnish

Bring the water, kaffir lime leaves, ginger and lemongrass to a boil over medium heat. Add the fish sauce and lime juice. Cook uncovered for 5 minutes. Do not stir. Add the chili peppers and cook for 5 more minutes. Remove from the heat. Remove the lime leaves, lemongrass and ginger slices. Add the shrimp and chili paste (if using), and stir to combine. Let sit for 1 minute.

Divide the soup into small shooter glasses. Garnish with cilantro. Serve immediately.

> **COOK'S NOTE**
> If you don't have fresh chili peppers on hand you can use a teaspoon or two of sriracha sauce.

Quick Udon Noodle Soup

Here's a quick and soul satisfying soup you can make in under 15 minutes. It's made with healing chicken stock (aka Jewish Penicillin!), rich miso paste and yummy veggies. Whether you're nursing a cold or just want a quick and delicious lunch, this soup is for you! You can add some cubes of tofu or your favorite chopped up meat for added protein in this soup. If you don't have fresh udon noodles, you can substitute with dried udon or another type of noodle.

Serves 4
Prep Time: 20 minutes
Cook Time: 5 minutes

One 12-oz (340-g) package fresh udon noodles
4 cups (1 liter) chicken stock or broth
1/2 cup (25 g) thinly sliced carrots
1/2 cup (49 g) snow peas, sliced on the diagonal
1/2 cup (40 g) sliced fresh shiitake mushrooms
2 tablespoons white or yellow miso paste
2 teaspoons soy sauce
1 teaspoon dark sesame oil
Finely chopped green onions (scallions), for garnish
2 hard boiled eggs, halved (optional)

Cook the noodles according to the package directions, rinse, drain and set aside.

In a large saucepan, bring the broth or stock to a boil. Lower the heat to medium and add the carrots and cook until the carrots are tender, about 1 minute. Add the snow peas and cook for about 1 minute. Add the mushrooms, cook for 30 seconds and remove from the heat.

Stir in the miso paste, soy sauce and sesame oil. Keep stirring until the miso paste or concentrate is blended into the soup. Add the reserved udon noodles and cook until heated through, about 1 minute. Transfer the soup into 4 serving bowls. Garnish with green onions and top each bowl with 1/2 of a hard boiled egg, if desired. Serve immediately.

COOK'S NOTE
You can use 4 tablespoons Marukome's Miso & Easy Miso Broth Concentrate in place of miso paste.

Vietnamese Glass Noodle Salad with Crab

Crab is prevalent all over Vietnam and this is a popular dish filled with sweet, sour, spicy, hot flavors and slippery, translucent glass noodles that you can easily recreate in your own home kitchen. "Glass" noodles aka cellophane noodles are often confused with rice noodles, but they are made with mung beans so they are also gluten-free. Just when you thought it couldn't get any better, it's topped with shallots, fried to golden perfection.

Serves 4
Prep Time: 30 minutes
Cook Time: 30–60 seconds

Dressing

2 cloves garlic, minced
2 teaspoons peeled and minced fresh ginger
1 Thai chili, thinly sliced (and deseeded if you prefer less heat)
2 teaspoons brown sugar
2 tablespoons freshly squeezed lime juice
2 tablespoons fish sauce (*nam pla*)
4 tablespoons oil
1 teaspoon dark sesame oil

Fried Shallot Garnish

2 small shallots, thinly sliced
1/2 teaspoon all-purpose flour
Oil, for frying

Salad

6 oz (170 g) dried glass noodles (bean thread noodles)
8 oz (227 g) lump crab meat, picked over for shells
4 oz (100 g) shredded red cabbage
1 carrot, cut into matchsticks
4 oz (113 g) bean sprouts, trimmed
2 green onions (scallions), finely chopped
4 tablespoons finely chopped fresh coriander leaves (cilantro)
4 tablespoons finely chopped fresh mint leaves

Make the **Dressing**: Whisk together the dressing ingredients and set aside.

Make the **Fried Shallot Garnish**: Heat oil in a wok or deep skillet to 350°F (175°C). Toss shallots with the flour and shake to remove excess flour. Fry the shallots until crispy and golden brown, about 30 seconds. Drain on a paper towel-lined baking sheet. Set aside.

Bring a large pot of water to a boil. Remove from heat. Immerse the noodles in hot water and let stand for 3–5 minutes, stirring occasionally until they are al dente. Drain. Rinse with cool water and drain again.

In a large bowl, combine the crab, glass noodles, red cabbage, carrot, bean sprouts, green onions, cilantro and mint. Add the dressing and toss to combine.

Garnish with fried shallots and serve immediately.

> **COOK'S NOTE**
> If making this dish for young children, omit the Thai chili pepper.

Quinoa, Roasted Corn & Edamame Salad

Sneak a little quinoa into your life with this deceptively delicious, healthy salad! Quinoa cooks up light and fluffy, and its nutty flavor complements the sweet roasted corn, cilantro, mint and red onion in this dish. Just a spoonful of sugar does help the medicine go down, my kids can always attest to the wisdom of Mary Poppins, especially when it's mixed with cilantro, mint and lime!

Serves 4–6
Prep Time: 25 minutes
Cook Time: 45 minutes

Dressing
1 clove garlic, smashed
1 bunch fresh coriander (cilantro), including stems
2 tablespoons packed fresh mint leaves
2 teaspoons packed brown sugar
2 tablespoons rice vinegar
1 tablespoon freshly squeezed lime juice
4 tablespoons extra virgin olive oil

Salad
3 ears corn, husked
3 tablespoons water
Melted butter
3 cups (555 g) cooked quinoa, cooled
1 cup (155 g) frozen shelled edamame, cooked
1/2 red onion, finely chopped
1/2 cup (87 g) diced red bell pepper
1/4 cup (13 g) shredded carrots
Salt and freshly ground black pepper
Finely chopped fresh coriander leaves (cilantro), for topping
Finely chopped mint, for topping

Make the Dressing: In a blender or food processor, purée the garlic, cilantro, mint, brown sugar, vinegar and lime juice until smooth. With the motor running, slowly pour in the extra virgin olive oil and blend until smooth.

Make the Salad: Place each corn cob on a sheet of heavy-duty foil. Drizzle with 1 tablespoon water and spread evenly with butter. Wrap very tightly, so the packages will not leak. Place over unlit side of barbecue and grill for 45 minutes or until tender.

Let cool, then cut off kernels and place them into a large bowl. Add the quinoa, edamame, red onion, red pepper and shredded carrots to the corn. Toss to combine.

Add dressing to the quinoa mixture and toss well to combine. Season to taste with salt and pepper. Transfer to a serving platter and sprinkle with cilantro and mint.

COOK'S NOTE
For a non-roasted corn variation, substitute fresh corn with thawed frozen corn kernels.

Melon & Peach Salad with Prosciutto & Mozzarella

This salad reminds me of a trip I took to Italy when I studied acting in a castle (long story and obviously pre-kids. LOL). Using the freshest and purest ingredients, this combo of juicy and ripe fruit and fresh mozzarella and herbs feels like you're basking under the Tuscan Sun. Now, that's Amore!

Serves 4
Prep Time: 30 minutes

1 honeydew melon, cut into chunks
2 ripe peaches, sliced
1 tablespoon extra virgin olive oil
2 teaspoons balsamic vinegar
Salt and freshly ground black pepper, to taste
2 tablespoons finely chopped basil
2 tablespoons finely chopped marjoram
8 oz (226 g) fresh mozzarella, cut into chunks
8 thin slices of prosciutto

In a bowl, toss the melon and peach with the extra virgin olive oil and balsamic vinegar. Season with salt and pepper. Let stand for 5 minutes. Stir in the herbs and cheese. Transfer to a platter. Top with the prosciutto slices and serve immediately.

COOK'S NOTE
If you can't find fresh marjoram you can substitute with fresh oregano.

Asian Pear and Gorgonzola Salad

This recipe features crisp and fragrant Asian pear with the soft, crumbly Gorgonzola cheese and crunchy pistachio nuts but it also stars (drum roll, please)....pomegranate, a superfood! I developed this recipe for City of Hope, a leading cancer research hospital in Southern California, when I was their Culinary Ambassador for their Superfoods initiative. Not only is this salad delicious and filled with wonderful texture and flavors, it has super anti-oxidant cancer-fighting pomegranate power! Here's to your health!

Serves 6–8
Prep Time: 15 minutes

Vinaigrette
2 tablespoons fresh pomegranate arils
3 tablespoons red wine vinegar
$1/2$ teaspoon sugar
2 shallots, thinly sliced
$1/2$ cup (125 ml) extra virgin olive oil
Salt and freshly ground black pepper, to taste

Salad
8 cups (600 g) mixed baby greens
2 small Asian Pears, thinly sliced
$1/3$ cup (90 g) fresh pomegranate arils
$1/2$ cup (100 g) crumbled Gorgonzola cheese
$1/3$ cup (30 g) pistachio nuts, roughly chopped

Make the **Vinaigrette**: In a small bowl, crush the pomegranate arils to release their juices. Add the vinegar, sugar, shallots and extra virgin olive oil and whisk until blended. Season to taste with salt and pepper.

Arrange the greens onto a large platter. Place the pear slices over the greens and sprinkle the pomegranate arils, Gorgonzola and pistachios on top. Drizzle the Vinaigrette over the salad and serve immediately.

SOMETHING FOWL

What's a chicken's favorite dance? The srira-cha-cha! Get it? Sorry but I'm subjected to a barrage of 7th grade humor every day. Truth is, we all know poultry can get boring, especially when it's 4pm and you have no idea what to do with the frozen chicken you moved to the fridge in the morning to thaw in time for dinner. Well, here is an amazing assortment of globally infused chicken dishes to get your toes tapping and your taste buds a-jumpin'. Make dinner go from ho-hum to "how fun!" with these easy and delicious recipes I've hatched like **Moroccan Chicken** and **Spanish Chicken and Rice** to **Duck with Marsala Orange Sauce** and **Teriyaki Chicken**. I've also included **Roast Chicken Four Ways** in this chapter, as we're all looking for yummy twists on this classic preparation. Let me show you how to spice things up and the make the most out of your whole roast chicken with Peruvian, Indian, Thai and Jamaican Jerk inspired versions.

Sweet & Sticky Asian Chicken Thighs

Prep this Asian-inspired chicken recipe in just a few minutes, brown the chicken and toss it into the oven for a sweet, sticky, savory and satisfying supper. I keep bone-in chicken thighs in my freezer so I can whip this up with ingredients I have on hand. Brown sugar provides the perfect amount of caramelization and stickiness balanced with umami soy notes and tart acidity. I promise your family will proclaim this dish "finger-lickin' good" (without the deep-fried grease)!

COOK'S NOTE
Delicious served on a bed of sautéed spinach with garlic!

Serves 4–6
Prep Time: 20 minutes
Cook Time: 40 minutes

Marinade
1/2 cup (125 ml) plus 2 tablespoons soy sauce
1/2 cup (125 ml) plus 2 tablespoons store-bought sweet Thai chili sauce
1/2 teaspoon crushed red pepper
1 tablespoon peeled and minced fresh ginger
2 teaspoons brown sugar
2 teaspoons rice wine vinegar
2 cloves garlic, minced

8 bone-in, skin-on chicken thighs
Toasted sesame seeds, for garnish
Finely chopped coriander leaves (cilantro), for garnish

Preheat the oven to 400°F (200°C).

Make the **Marinade:** In a small bowl, whisk together the Marinade ingredients. Place the chicken thighs in a large resealable plastic food storage bag. Pour half of the marinade over the chicken thighs. Place it in the refrigerator for at least 30 minutes or up to overnight.

Transfer the chicken thighs to a baking sheet, "skin-side up," and cook for 20 minutes or until an internal thermometer registers 165°F (75°C).

While the chicken is cooking, place the remaining Marinade in a small saucepan over medium-high heat. Bring to a boil, and then reduce the heat to medium-low and simmer for about 10 minutes.

Pour the Marinade over the chicken and garnish with sesame seeds and cilantro. Serve immediately with steaming hot jasmine rice.

Spanish Chicken and Rice Arroz con Pollo

Shake it, don't break it! The secret to this recipe is the shaking of the chicken with spices before browning it. It's a modern day take on Shake n' Bake if you will. By coating the chicken with this aromatic spice mix, it creates next-level deliciousness for this one-pot meal favorite—especially when simmered with classic arroz con pollo ingredients like saffron, peas, onion, tomatoes, garlic and bell pepper.

Serves 4
Prep Time: 20 minutes
Cook Time: 60 minutes

2 teaspoons salt
1 teaspoon garlic powder
1/2 teaspoon dried cumin
1/4 teaspoon freshly ground black pepper
1/4 teaspoon ground red pepper (cayenne)
4 bone-in, skin-on chicken thighs
4 chicken drumsticks
Salt and freshly ground black pepper
3 tablespoons extra virgin olive oil
1 small onion, chopped
2 cloves garlic, minced
1 teaspoon paprika
3/4 teaspoon saffron threads
1 red bell pepper, chopped
1 3/4 cups (396 g) canned whole tomatoes, drained and chopped
1 tablespoon tomato paste
1 1/2 cups (375 ml) chicken stock or broth
1/2 cup (125 ml) white wine
1 cup (130 g) thawed frozen peas
1 3/4 teaspoons salt
1/4 teaspoon freshly ground black pepper
1 cup (175 g) long-grain white rice
1/2 cup (90 g) coarsely chopped pimiento-stuffed green olives
2 tablespoons finely chopped fresh parsley

> **COOK'S NOTE**
> Throw in a handful of cooked shrimp 5 minutes before the end of cooking for variety.

Combine the salt, garlic powder, cumin, black pepper and cayenne in a large resealable plastic food storage bag. Seal the bag and shake until the mixture is well combined.

Pat the chicken dry and place in the bag with the spice mixture. Shake the bag, making sure the chicken is well coated.

Remove the chicken from the bag and season it with salt and freshly ground black pepper. Heat the oil in a dutch oven or large, deep non-stick skillet over medium-high heat. Brown the chicken on all sides, about 8 minutes in total. Using tongs, move the chicken from the pan to a platter. Pour off all but 2 tablespoons of the accumulated fat from the pan.

Add the onion, garlic, paprika and saffron to the pan and cook, stirring occasionally, until the onion starts to soften, about 2 minutes. Add the bell peppers and cook for 3 minutes.

Add the tomatoes, tomato paste, chicken stock or broth, wine, peas and the 1 3/4 teaspoons salt and 1/4 teaspoon black pepper. Bring to a simmer. Stir in the rice and add the chicken in an even layer. Sprinkle the olives over the chicken. Simmer, partially covered, until the chicken and rice are cooked, about 20–25 minutes. Garnish with parsley and serve immediately.

Chicken Tikka Masala

I learned to make this delicious Tikka Masala dish from one of my college roommates who made it for me when our clothes were drying in our not-so-beautiful launderette in our dorm.

"Tikka" means grilled or broiled chicken "chunks" that are then served in a spicy, creamy sauce. Although I ate Chinese food almost every day growing up, I had never tried Indian food until I was a sophomore at Boston University. I couldn't believe how complex the spices were and how the heat was so sublimely tempered by the cooling yogurt in the marinade. I know Tikka Masala may at first seem complicated, but it's actually quite easy as long as you have all of your ingredients prepped and organized. This recipes takes longer than most of the recipes in this book, but trust me, it's totally worth the effort!

Serves 3–4
Prep Time: 30 minutes + marinating time
Cook Time: 1 hour 20 minutes

Marinade
1 cup (245 g) plain low-fat yogurt
2 cloves garlic, minced
1 tablespoon freshly squeezed lemon juice
1 tablespoon peeled and minced fresh ginger
1 teaspoon ground coriander
$1/4$ teaspoon ground cardamom
1 teaspoon ground cinnamon
$1/4$ teaspoon ground red pepper (cayenne)
$1/4$ teaspoon ground turmeric
1 teaspoon freshly ground black pepper
1 teaspoon salt

6 boneless, skinless chicken thighs
Salt and freshly ground black pepper

Saffron Rice
$1/8$ teaspoon powdered saffron
2 cups (500 ml) boiling water, divided
2 tablespoons butter
1 cup (180 g) uncooked long-grain white rice, not rinsed
1 teaspoon salt

Sauce
1 tablespoon butter
1 small medium onion, finely chopped
2 cloves garlic, minced
1 teaspoon peeled and minced fresh ginger
1 tablespoon garam masala
1 teaspoon chili powder
$1/4$ teaspoon ground red pepper (cayenne)
One 14.5-oz (411-g) can whole peeled tomatoes, finely chopped, with juice
1 cup (250 ml) heavy cream
1 cup (130 g) thawed frozen peas
Salt and freshly ground black pepper, to taste
4 tablespoons finely chopped coriander leaves (cilantro)

Combine all of the Marinade ingredients in a large glass bowl.

Make a few shallow cuts in each chicken thigh with a sharp knife. Place the chicken thighs in a large resealable plastic food storage bag. Pour the Marinade over the chicken. Seal and refrigerate for 2 hours or up to overnight.

Preheat the broiler. Wipe away as much marinade as possible from the chicken thighs. Season with salt and pepper. Broil for 12 minutes, turning once or twice, until just cooked through. Transfer to a cutting board and cut into bite-sized pieces.

While the chicken is broiling, make the Saffron Rice: Steep the saffron in $1/2$ cup (125 ml) boiling water. In a large non-stick skillet that can be tightly covered, melt the butter over medium high heat. Stir in the rice and salt. Cook, stirring constantly until the rice absorbs the butter and becomes opaque, about 5 minutes, being careful not to brown the rice. Quickly pour in the remaining $1 1/2$ cups (375 ml) water along with the saffron water. Cover immediately, reduce heat to low and cook for 20 minutes or until all of the liquid is absorbed. Remove from the heat and set aside, covered.

Make the Sauce: Heat a large skillet over medium high heat. Add the butter and swirl until it melts. Add the onion, garlic and ginger and sauté until the onion is translucent, about 1 minute. Add the garam masala, chili powder and cayenne pepper, and sauté for 1 more minute. Add the tomatoes and their juices and stir until combined. Reduce heat to medium and cook for about 20 minutes stirring occasionally, until the sauce is thickened. Add the cream and peas. Reduce heat to low and simmer for 10 minutes. Stir in the reserved chicken and let simmer for 10 more minutes, stirring occasionally. Season with salt and pepper to taste. Garnish with chopped cilantro and serve immediately over the saffron rice.

> **COOK'S NOTE**
> All of the spices you need, including garam masala, can be found in most well-stocked supermarkets or local Indian grocery stores.

Thai Chicken with Mint & Chili Peppers

This recipe was inspired by my husband's and my honeymoon trip to Thailand. Everyone I know just loves this dish but is completely mystified about how to cook it at home, so I felt it deserved an encore. This recipe couldn't be easier or faster to make. If you don't have time or don't have an Asian market nearby simply omit the kaffir lime leaf and use Italian basil instead of Thai basil. Everything else you can get at the your regular grocery store. Ditch the take-out and make this restaurant fave in under 20 minutes!

Serves 4
Prep Time: 10 minutes
Cook Time: 8 minutes

1¹/₄ lbs (600 g) skinless, boneless chicken breast or chicken thigh, thinly sliced crosswise into ¹/₂-in (1.2-cm) wide strips
1 teaspoon cornstarch
¹/₂ teaspoon salt
Pinch of white pepper
3 tablespoons oil, divided
2 cloves garlic, minced
1 large shallot, thinly sliced
1–2 fresh hot red or green chili peppers (preferably Thai), deseeded if you prefer less heat, thinly sliced
4 kaffir lime leaves, finely sliced (optional)
1 tablespoon soy sauce
1 tablespoon fish sauce (*nam pla*)
1 tablespoon sugar
1 cup (30 g) fresh Thai or Italian basil leaves
1 cup (30 g) fresh mint leaves

COOK'S NOTE
Swap out the chicken with tofu for a lighter version of this dish.

Toss the chicken with the cornstarch, salt and white pepper in small bowl. Cover and refrigerate for 10 minutes.

Heat ¹/₂ of the oil in a wok or skillet over medium-high heat. Add the chicken and stir-fry until the meat turns white. Remove the chicken from the pan and set aside.

Heat the remaining oil in the wok or skillet over medium-high heat. Add the garlic, shallots and chili peppers to the wok or skillet and stir-fry until fragrant, about 1 minute. Add the reserved chicken, kaffir lime leaves (if using), soy sauce, fish sauce and sugar and stir-fry for 2 minutes or until the chicken is cooked through. Add the basil and mint and stir-fry for about 30 seconds or until the basil is wilted. Dish out and serve immediately with jasmine rice.

Moroccan Chicken Tagine

Tagine is a dish that dates back centuries and is traditionally cooked in a conical clay tagine vessel. It's a savory stew made with chicken, pork or beef, dried fruits, spices and aromatics. My version doesn't require a tagine for ease and convenience, but it still captures the unique and exotic flavors this famous dish is known for. My friend Amy made this for her kids Duncan and Heidi, and she said they gobbled it right up. Turn the usual weeknight dinner into an Arabian feast for your family's senses with this easy and delicious Middle Eastern favorite.

Serves: 6
Prep Time: 20 minutes + marinating time
Cook Time: 45 minutes

1 tablespoon harissa paste
3–3½-lb (1.5–1.6-kg) cut-up whole chicken
1 tablespoon extra virgin olive oil
1 medium onion, sliced
2 cloves garlic, minced
4 tablespoons finely chopped fresh coriander leaves (cilantro)
1 teaspoon ground cumin
1 teaspoon ground turmeric
1 teaspoon ground ginger
1 teaspoon salt
1 cinnamon stick
1 cup (250 ml) chicken stock or broth
One 14.5-oz (411-g) can diced tomatoes, undrained
1 cup (175 g) prunes, cut into bite-size pieces
½ cup (125 g) pitted whole green olives
1 small lemon, cut into thick slices
2 tablespoons minced fresh mint leaves for garnish
2 tablespoons minced fresh parsley, for garnish
Greek style plain yogurt, for serving
Lemon wedges, for serving

COOK'S NOTE
You can find harissa paste at specialty stores and online. Use less harissa paste if cooking for young kids.

Spread the harissa paste over the chicken pieces. Place in a large resealable plastic food storage bag, seal and refrigerate for two hours.

Heat the oil in a 4-quart dutch oven over medium-high heat. Add the onion and garlic and sauté for 1 minute until fragrant. Add the chicken skin-side down and cook for 5–9 minutes, turning chicken occasionally, until chicken is brown on all sides.

Reduce heat to medium. Sprinkle cilantro, cumin, turmeric, ginger and salt over chicken. Add the cinnamon stick and pour the stock or broth and tomatoes over the chicken. Turn the chicken several times to coat it evenly. Add the prunes, olives and lemon, pressing them into the liquid. Reduce heat to low. Cover and simmer about 30 minutes or until the juice of the chicken is clear and when the internal temperature reaches 170°F (77°C).

Remove the chicken to a deep serving platter and cover to keep it warm. Increase the heat to high and boil the sauce uncovered for about 5 minutes, stirring occasionally, until thickened. Pour the sauce over the chicken. Garnish with mint and parsley. Serve over couscous with additional lemon wedges and yogurt on the side.

Chimichurri Chicken Burgers with Provolone

Everyone gets bored with the same old burger routine, so why not liven and lighten things up with chicken burgers made with chimichurri's tantalizing twist of flavors? My yummy and simple recipe for Chimichurri Sauce (see recipe on page 32) is mixed into chicken patties which are pan-fried and then topped with provolone cheese. The sauce is also tossed with fresh and crunchy broccoli slaw and placed on top of the cheese slices along with other toppings. This chicken burger is a full force of flavor that your whole family will love.

Serves: 4
Prep Time: 20 minutes
Cook Time: 12 minutes

Chimichurri Sauce (page 32)

Burgers
1 1/4 lbs (600 g) ground chicken
1 teaspoon salt
1/8 teaspoon freshly ground black pepper
4 slices provolone cheese

4 hamburger buns
1 cup (70 g) store-bought shredded broccoli slaw mix

Toppings
Tomato slices
Red onion slices
Avocado slices

Place the ground chicken in a bowl with the salt and pepper. Add half of the Chimichurri Sauce and mix to combine. Form chicken mixture into 4 patties.

Heat a large non-stick skillet over medium-high heat. Add the patties and cook for 6 minutes. Flip and cook for 6 minutes more on the other side. Add Provolone slices and them allow to melt.

While the patties are cooking, toss the broccoli slaw with the remaining sauce.

Place the cooked burgers on the buns and place a spoonful of slaw on top of each burger. Top with tomato, red onion and avocado slices. Serve immediately.

> **COOK'S NOTE**
> Use vegan cheese if you're avoiding dairy and use gluten-free buns if you're avoiding gluten.

Kimlai's Asian Stuffed Bell Peppers

This creative recipe was given to me by my dear friend and culinary personality Kimlai Yingling of *Eatin' Asian*. She loves it when she can use something edible to bake in and use as a serving vessel. Bell Peppers are ridiculously good for you and are such a hearty, sturdy veggie that they can hold up while being filled with a meat mixture, withstand being baked in the oven and still keep their shape and look pretty darn good being served in. This dish is the perfect balance of flavorful savory protein and fluffy grains all stuffed in a nutrient-packed red pepper.

Serves 4
Prep Time: 30 minutes
Cook Time: 25 minutes

1 tablespoon oil
1 cup (150 g) diced onions
1 tablespoon minced garlic
2 tablespoons peeled and minced fresh ginger
1 lb (500 g) ground chicken
3 tablespoons oyster sauce
2 teaspoons dark sesame oil
1 teaspoon freshly ground black pepper
1 tablespoon soy sauce

1/2 teaspoon crushed red pepper
2 cups (300 g) cooked white rice
4 red bell peppers, tops removed and deseeded
4 tablespoons cottage cheese
4 quail or small chicken eggs
Finely chopped fresh coriander leaves (cilantro)

Preheat the oven to 350°F (175°C).

Heat the oil in a wok or large non-stick pan. Stir-fry the onions, garlic and ginger until translucent, about 1 minute. Add the ground chicken and break up while cooking, about 5 minutes.

Once the chicken is no longer pink, add the oyster sauce, sesame oil, black pepper, soy sauce and crushed red pepper, and cook for 1 minute. Add the cooked rice and stir-fry for about 2 minutes until combined.

Arrange the bell peppers in a greased square baking dish. Add a few spoonfuls of the meat mixture to each, and then a tablespoon of cottage cheese, followed by additional meat mixture.

Crack an egg on top of each pepper. Roast in the oven for 20 minutes, and then broil for 5 minutes. Garnish with cilantro and serve immediately.

Duck with Marsala Orange Sauce

File this one under "I need an impressive dish that's easy and delicious." This tender duck recipe with classic Italian Marsala sauce spiked with citrus and raspberries is your new go-to when a client or in-laws come to dinner or when you want to make something special for a birthday or Valentine's Day. Your guests will be raving that it tastes just like it came from a 4-star restaurant, but they'll never know how easy it was to prepare. I promise you, your secret's safe with me! All this is not to say that you can't treat yourself after a long weekday with this rich and exquisite dish.

Serves: 2
Prep Time: 15 minutes
Cook Time: 40 minutes

2 tablespoons extra virgin olive oil
Two 8-oz (250-g) boneless duck breasts
3 tablespoons finely chopped shallots
4 tablespoons sweet Marsala wine
1 tablespoon butter
4 tablespoons freshly squeezed orange juice
2 fresh sage leaves, finely chopped
1/2 cup (62 g) fresh raspberries
Zest from 1 orange, very thinly julienned
Salt and freshly ground pepper, to taste

Heat the extra virgin olive oil in a large non-stick skillet (preferably cast iron) over high heat. Sear the duck breasts, skin side down, until deep golden brown, about 2–4 minutes. Discard the accumulated fat. Turn the breasts over and reduce the heat to medium and cook until rare or medium rare, 12–18 minutes or until internal temperature reaches 170°F (77°C). Transfer to a platter. Tent with foil to keep warm.

Reduce heat to medium. Add the shallots to the skillet and cook until soft, about 3 minutes, stirring constantly. Deglaze the skillet with the Marsala wine and the butter. When the Marsala has evaporated by half, about 3–5 minutes, add the orange juice, sage and raspberries. Cook, while stirring, until syrupy, about 7 minutes. Add the orange zest and cook 2 more minutes.

Slice the duck breasts into thin 1/8-inch (3-mm) slices and fan the sliced meat on each plate. Season with salt and pepper. Spoon the sauce over the duck and serve.

COOK'S NOTE
To julienne orange zest: use a vegetable peeler to peel long strips of orange zest (avoid peeling into the white pith, which is bitter). Cut the strips into 1/16-inch (1.6-mm) lengthwise slivers.

Clay Pot Chicken with Shiitake & Chinese Sausage

My sister Laura and I prepared this classic Cantonese dish for a show on the Cooking Channel called *Food(ology)*. Clay pot cooking has been around for centuries and results in the most tender and juicy chicken along with fluffy rice which has absorbed all the delicious flavors from the mushrooms and Chinese sausage. This is an addicting one-pot meal cooked in a vessel that doubles as a beautiful serving dish.

Serves 4
Prep Time: 30 minutes + soaking + marinating time
Cook Time: 35 minutes

6 dried shiitake mushrooms
4 boneless, skinless chicken thighs, cut into bite-sized pieces
1 teaspoon cornstarch
2 tablespoons oyster sauce
1 tablespoon Shaoxing wine (Chinese rice wine) or cooking sherry
1 tablespoon dark soy sauce
2 tablespoons low-sodium soy sauce
1 teaspoon dark sesame oil
2 teaspoons brown sugar
Pinch of salt
1/4 teaspoon white pepper
2 tablespoons oil
1 clove garlic, minced
1 *lap cheong* (Chinese sausage), sliced diagonally into 1/4-in (6-mm) pieces
1 cup (195 g) white jasmine rice, rinsed and drained
1 1/2 cups (375 ml) chicken stock or broth
2 green onions (scallions), finely chopped

Soak the mushrooms in warm water until soft, about 30 minutes. Rinse in warm water; drain. Remove and discard stems; cut caps into thin slices. Set aside.

Mix chicken pieces, cornstarch, oyster sauce, Shaoxing wine, dark and low-sodium soy sauces, sesame oil, brown sugar, salt and white pepper in a glass or plastic bowl. Cover and refrigerate for 20 minutes.

Heat the oil in a wok or large non-stick skillet over medium-high heat. Add the garlic and stir-fry until fragrant, about 30 seconds. Add the marinated chicken and stir-fry for 1 minute. Add the sausage and shiitake mushrooms and stir-fry for 30 seconds. Transfer to a platter and set aside.

Put the rice and chicken stock or broth in a clay pot. Place the lid on top and bring the mixture to a boil over medium-high heat. Reduce the heat to a simmer and allow the rice to steam for 15 minutes, covered.

Spread the chicken and sausage mixture on top of the rice. Place the lid back on top and continue to steam on low heat for 15 minutes, until chicken is cooked through. Stir thoroughly and sprinkle scallions on top. Serve immediately.

COOK'S NOTE
You can find clay pots and *lap cheong* sausage at Asian markets.
I like to stock up on lap cheong and keep it in my freezer to whip this dish up whenever I crave it (which is often once a week, it's that good!)

Kung Pao Chicken

Many people ask me, "What puts the 'Pow' in your Kung Pao, Katie?!" I tell them that it's a combination of things. When rice vinegar, sherry, soy sauce and sesame oil come together with fresh green onions, red bell peppers and peanuts, it makes a healthy and happy marriage of flavors. To add a little fire in the relationship, I sprinkle in some crushed red pepper or add sriracha sauce!

Serves 4–6
Prep Time: 10 minutes + marinating time
Cook Time: 7–8 minutes

Sauce
2 tablespoons Chinese black vinegar
2 tablespoons chicken stock or broth
1 teaspoon sugar
1½ tablespoons Shaoxing wine (Chinese rice wine) or cooking sherry
1 tablespoon hoisin sauce
2 teaspoons oyster sauce
2 teaspoons soy sauce
1 teaspoon dark sesame oil
1 teaspoon cornstarch
1 teaspoon water

12 oz (350 g) boneless, skinless chicken breast or thigh, cut into bite-sized pieces
¼ teaspoon salt
Dash of white pepper
1 teaspoon cornstarch
2 tablespoons oil, divided
1 clove garlic, minced
½ teaspoon crushed red pepper
6 dried red chili peppers or chile de árbol
1 large red bell pepper, diced
½ cup (150 g) dry roasted peanuts, plus more, for garnish
2 tablespoons finely chopped green onion (scallion), white and green parts, plus more, for garnish

> ### COOK'S NOTE
> **You may substitute Chinese black vinegar with balsamic vinegar if you wish.**

Make the **Sauce:** Combine all of the ingredients for the Sauce in a small bowl. Set aside.

Toss the chicken with the salt, white pepper and the cornstarch. Cover and refrigerate for 20 minutes.

Heat half of the oil in wok or skillet over medium-high heat. Add the chicken pieces and stir-fry until the chicken turns white, about 2 minutes. Remove the chicken from the pan and set aside. Wash and thoroughly dry the wok or skillet.

Heat the remaining oil in a wok or skillet over medium-high high heat. Add the garlic and stir-fry until fragrant, about 30 seconds. Add the crushed red pepper and dried red chili peppers and stir-fry until aromatic, about 1 minute. Add the red bell pepper and stir-fry for 1 minute. Add the reserved chicken and stir-fry for 2 minutes. Add the Sauce and stir-fry for 1 minute, until the chicken is nicely coated. Add the peanuts and green onion and stir-fry for 30 seconds. Dish out and garnish with more green onions and peanuts. Serve immediately with steaming hot rice.

Teriyaki Chicken

In Japanese, *teri* means "luster" and *yaki* means "grilled." This real-deal from scratch teriyaki glaze recipe is so easy you'll never reach for the bottled stuff again. With its sweet, savory and succulent flavor and fall-off-the-bone tenderness, you'll want to make this again and again. This is a recipe everyone in the family will dig—one that's perfect for a quick weeknight BBQ. Chicken thighs are great for grilling because they're moist, flavorful and cook quickly. Whatever the language, this dish says "YUM!"

Serves: 3–4
Prep Time: 15 minutes +
  marinating time
Cook Time: 35 minutes

Marinade
1 clove garlic, minced
1 tablespoon peeled and minced
  fresh ginger
3 tablespoons packed brown sugar
$1^1/_2$ teaspoons dry mustard
$1^1/_2$ cups (375 ml) soy sauce
$1^1/_2$ cups (375 ml) water
3 tablespoons rice vinegar

6 bone-in chicken thighs
3 tablespoons cornstarch
3 tablespoons cold water
Toasted sesame seeds, for garnish

Make the **Marinade**: In a large bowl, whisk together the garlic, ginger, brown sugar, mustard, soy sauce, $1^1/_2$ cups (375 ml) of the water and vinegar. Add chicken and turn to coat. Cover and refrigerate for 30 minutes. Remove the chicken to a plate and reserve the marinade.

Heat a grill on medium high heat. Grill the chicken thighs skin-side down for 10 minutes. Turn them over and grill another 5–10 minutes. Transfer the chicken to a plate.

Meanwhile, in a small bowl, combine the cornstarch and cold water. In a medium saucepan, bring the reserved marinade to a boil over medium-high heat. Stir in the cornstarch mixture. Reduce the heat and simmer, stirring, for about 12 minutes or until the sauce has thickened.

Brush each chicken thigh with about 1 tablespoon of sauce. Garnish with toasted sesame seeds and serve immediately with hot jasmine rice and a side of teriyaki sauce.

Roast Chicken Four Ways

Whole Roasted **Jamaica** Jerk-inspired Chicken

My hubby and I recently went on a Zumba cruise (long story and he didn't partake. LOL) to Jamaica. We decided to do the zipline excursion once we disembarked and grabbed lunch at a nearby café that was serving jerk chicken. It was so delicious and juicy that we gobbled it up in minutes with some Red Stripe Beer. Recreate the classic Jamaican flavors of this dish for roast chicken with an easy spice rub. A delicious and easy recipe sure to make you hum "Let's get together and be alright" while you're making it.

Serves 4
Prep Time: 20 minutes
Cook Time: 45 minutes to 1 hour

Spice Rub

2 teaspoons salt
2 teaspoons ground allspice
2 teaspoons packed brown sugar
2 teaspoons onion powder
1 teaspoon dried minced garlic
1 teaspoon ground nutmeg
1 teaspoon freshly ground black pepper
1 teaspoon ground ginger
1/2 teaspoon ground red pepper (cayenne)
1/2 teaspoon ground cinnamon
1/2 teaspoon dried thyme leaves

Mango Salsa

2 ripe mangoes, diced
4 tablespoons finely chopped red onions
2 tablespoons finely chopped fresh coriander leaves (cilantro)
1 teaspoon freshly squeezed lime juice

One 3–4 lb (1.5–4 kg) whole chicken
2 tablespoons extra virgin olive oil
3 tablespoons freshly squeezed lemon juice

Preheat the oven to 425°F (220°C).

Make the **Spice Rub**: Combine the Spice Rub ingredients in food processor or coffee grinder until smooth.

Rub the whole chicken with the extra virgin olive oil and lemon juice. Massage the spice rub over the whole chicken including the inside cavity and under the skin. Transfer the chicken to a roasting pan.

Roast the bird in the oven for 15 minutes. Reduce the heat to 375°F (190°C) and continue to roast for 60–70 minutes or until an internal thermometer inserted into the thickest part of the thigh registers 165°F (75°C). Allow the chicken to rest for a few minutes after you remove it from the oven.

While the bird is roasting, make the **Mango Salsa**: Whisk together all of the ingredients in a small bowl.

Carve up the chicken and serve immediately with Mango Salsa.

Whole Roasted Indian-style Chicken

My twins Dylan and Becca love Indian food but our lives are so hectic between dance and baseball practice that we rarely find time to take them out to an Indian restaurant. I wanted an easy recipe to recreate the flavors we love from our favorite Indian joint, and here it is. This roast chicken is succulent and flavorful and is served with a cooling, aromatic yogurt sauce as its sidekick. As Dylan says "Mom, this chicken is the BOM...BAY!"

Serves 4
Prep Time: 20 minutes
Cook Time: 45 minutes to 1 hour

Marinade
$^1/_2$ red onion
3 cloves garlic
$^1/_2$ teaspoon ginger powder
$^1/_2$ teaspoon cinnamon
$^1/_2$ teaspoon allspice
1 teaspoon garam masala spice
$^1/_4$ teaspoon turmeric
1 tablespoon paprika
$^1/_4$ teaspoon crushed red pepper
4 tablespoons coarsely chopped fresh mint leaves
4 tablespoons coarsely chopped fresh parsley
Juice of 1 lime
$^3/_4$ teaspoon salt
1 teaspoon freshly ground black pepper

Yogurt Sauce
1 cup (285 g) Greek yogurt
4 tablespoons cream cheese, softened
1 bunch mint leaves, finely chopped
3 tablespoons freshly squeezed lemon juice
2 cloves garlic, minced
1 teaspoon ground cumin
Salt, to taste

One 3–4 lb (1.5–4 kg) whole chicken
One lemon, quartered

Preheat the oven to 425°F (220°C).

Make the **Marinade**: Place all of the marinade ingredients in a food processor and purée into a paste. Reserve 4 tablespoons of the paste.

Make 5 or 6 slits in the chicken. Spread the paste all over the chicken, under the skin and into the slits. Slather the remaining 4 tablespoons of Marinate paste on the outside of the chicken. Place two lemon quarters inside the cavity.

Roast the bird in the oven for 15 minutes. Reduce the heat to 375°F (190°C) and continue to roast for 45 minutes or until an internal thermometer inserted into the thickest part of the thigh registers 165°F (75°C). Allow the chicken to rest for a few minutes after you remove it from the oven.

While the chicken is roasting, make the **Yogurt Sauce**: Whisk together all of the sauce ingredients in a small bowl.

Serve with warmed store-bought naan and the Yogurt Sauce.

Whole Roasted Thai-style Chicken

My friend Stella McShera loves Thailand. She was there once for its annual water festival where she had to ride around on a scooter with a plastic toy water gun so she could shoot water back at all the revelers. She even took her water gun to restaurants during her trip. She loves Thai food so much she squealed with delight when I asked her to try this recipe with her hubby Ryan. They were amazed at how easy it was to transform an everyday roast chicken into a sweet, salty, sour and hot stroke of genius. Topping it off is the Thai Peanut Sauce you can find on page 34, which is creamy, rich and fragrant with just the right amount of sweet heat. They are such a fun-loving couple, I suspect they may have attacked each other with water guns even while making this recipe in their Santa Monica home.

Serves 4
Prep Time: 30 minutes + marinating time
Cook Time: 45 minutes to 1 hour

Garlic Paste
5 cloves garlic, minced
1½ teaspoons salt, divided
1 teaspoon extra virgin olive oil

Marinade
2 tablespoons lemongrass, coarsely chopped
1 tablespoon freshly ground black pepper
4 tablespoons fish sauce (*nam pla*)
2 tablespoons cooking sherry
1 tablespoon dark sesame oil
4 tablespoons brown sugar
2 teaspoons sriracha sauce
2 tablespoons honey

Thai Peanut Sauce (page 34)
One 3–4 lb (1.5–4 kg) whole chicken
1 lime, quartered

> ## COOK'S NOTE
> The Thai Peanut Sauce recipe makes approximately 1 cup (250 ml). You can store the remaining peanut sauce covered in the refrigerator for up to 5 days. Use it as a dipping sauce, stir-fry sauce or salad dressing.

Make the **Garlic Paste**: Scrape the garlic into a small pile. Add the salt and olive oil to the pile. Hold the blunt edge of your knife with both hands, pointing it away from you at a low angle, close to the cutting board. Scrape the knife over the garlic repeatedly until it forms a paste. Occasionally scrape the garlic back into a pile and mince briefly to reduce the larger pieces.

Evenly distribute the Garlic Paste under the skin and inside the chicken cavity.

Make the **Marinade**: In a small bowl, whisk together the lemongrass, black pepper, fish sauce, cooking sherry, sesame oil, brown sugar, sriracha sauce and honey.

Place the chicken in a large resealable plastic food storage bag and pour the Marinade on top. Seal the bag and turn the bird several times to coat. Refrigerate for 4 hours or up to overnight, turning the chicken a few times while marinating.

Preheat the oven to 425°F (220°C).

Using tongs, transfer the chicken to a roasting pan. Squeeze the lime wedges into the cavity of the bird, and then place wedges into the cavity. Tie the legs together with kitchen string.

Roast for 15 minutes. Reduce heat to 375°F (190°C) and continue to roast for approximately 1 hour, until the juices of the chicken run clear when the thigh is pierced with a fork or an instant-read thermometer inserted into the thickest part of the thigh registers 165°F (75°C). Allow the chicken to rest for a few minutes after you remove it from the oven.

While the bird is roasting, make the Thai Peanut Sauce (page 34).

Carve up the chicken and serve immediately with Thai Peanut Sauce.

Whole Roasted **Peruvian**-style Chicken

This dish is inspired by the classic Peruvian *pollo a la brasa* roast chicken baked in ashes or over a roast-spit. Fresh, flavorful and garlicky, the combination of the marinade for this recipe and the cool and spicy sauce which accompanies it is divine. My friend Candace made this recently and her daughter Sabrina said, "You should cook with more spices like this all the time, Mom!" For ease and convenience, this recipe doesn't require baking the chicken in ashes. LOL. All you need is your oven and your appetite.

Serves 4
Prep Time: 20 minutes
Cook Time: 45 minutes to 1 hour

Garlic Paste

5 cloves garlic, peeled and minced
$1^1/_2$ teaspoons salt, divided
1 teaspoon extra virgin olive oil

Marinade

3 tablespoons white wine vinegar
4 tablespoons white wine
2 tablespoons extra-virgin olive oil
2 tablespoons paprika
$1^1/_2$ tablespoons ground cumin
2 teaspoons freshly ground black pepper
$^1/_2$ teaspoon dried oregano

Cilantro Sauce

$^1/_2$ cup (115 g) sour cream
$^1/_2$ jalapeño pepper, deseeded and chopped
1 clove garlic
$^1/_4$ teaspoon kosher salt
1 tablespoon freshly squeezed lime juice

One 3–4 lb (1.5–4 kg) whole chicken
2 lemon wedges

Make the Garlic Paste: Scrape the garlic into a small pile. Add the salt and olive oil to the pile. Hold the blunt edge of your knife with both hands, pointing it away from you at a low angle, close to the cutting board. Scrape the knife over the garlic repeatedly until it forms a paste. Occasionally scrape the garlic back into a pile and mince briefly to reduce the larger pieces.

Evenly distribute the Garlic Paste under the skin and inside the chicken cavity.

Make the Marinade: In a small bowl, whisk together the vinegar, wine, oil, paprika, cumin, black pepper and oregano. Set aside.

Place the chicken in a large resealable plastic food storage bag and pour the Marinade on top. Seal the bag and turn the bird several times to coat. Refrigerate for 2 hours or up to overnight, turning the chicken a few times while marinating.

Preheat the oven to 425°F (220°C).

Using tongs, transfer the chicken to a roasting pan. Squeeze the lemon wedges into the cavity of the bird, and then place wedges into the cavity. Tie the legs together with kitchen string.

Roast for 15 minutes. Reduce heat to 375°F (190°C) and continue to roast for approximately 1 hour or until the juices of the chicken run clear when the thigh is pierced with a fork or an instant-read thermometer inserted into the thickest part of the thigh registers 165°F (75°C). Allow the chicken to rest for a few minutes after you remove it from the oven.

While the bird is roasting, make the Cilantro Sauce: Place all of the sauce ingredients in a blender and purée until smooth.

Carve up the chicken and serve immediately with Cilantro Sauce.

COOK'S NOTE
You can use cut-up chicken pieces instead of a whole chicken for this recipe.

LET'S MEAT

For my family and I, it's all about moderation. We strive to integrate plant-based proteins into our meals on Meatless Mondays and eat more whole grains and veggies whenever we can, but sometimes nothing is better than sinking our teeth into a juicy, succulent steak or enjoying fall-off-the-bone short ribs. The twins are crazy active with dance and baseball so I want to make sure they're getting all the protein their growing bodies need. My husband Matthew is also a grill king so it gives me a break from cooking when he takes the BBQ reins (plus the bluetooth meat thermometer he got for Father's Day works wonders, so he can watch NASCAR on the couch while our meat is being cooked to the perfect temp—except when he falls asleep, which is another story altogether. LOL). The meat recipes in this chapter are filled with variety and interesting flavor profiles from **Weeknight Steak Frites** and **Indonesian Short Ribs Braised in Coconut** to **Ultimate Umami Burgers** and **Steak Fajitas**. These promise to satisfy the meat lovers in your family and your circle of friends.

Thai Red Curry Meatball Sub Panaeng

Talk about putting a Thai twist on a comfort food classic. This is definitely not your dad's meatball sub! These meatballs will fill your house with exotic aromas from the ginger, curry and fish sauce along with panaeng curry (which is the mildest of Thai curries). Topped with fresh herbs and crunchy peanuts and carrots, this delicious recipe is perfect anytime (and especially for game time)!

Serves 4
Prep Time: 25 minutes
Cook Time: 25 minutes

1¹/₂ lbs (750 g) lean ground beef
1¹/₂ teaspoons peeled and minced fresh ginger
³/₄ teaspoon salt
1 large egg
2 tablespoons oil
2 cups (500 ml) coconut milk
2 tablespoons panaeng curry paste or
   red curry paste
³/₄ cup (185 ml) water
1 tablespoon plus 2 teaspoons fish sauce (*nam pla*)
1 tablespoon plus 2 teaspoons brown sugar
4–6 kaffir lime leaves (optional), torn in half
Four 12-in (30-cm) soft baguettes

Toppings
Shredded carrots
Fresh coriander leaves (cilantro)
Fresh Thai basil leaves
Sliced fresh jalapeño or serrano chili peppers
Crushed roasted peanuts

Mix the ground beef with ginger, salt and egg. Shape mixture into 20 meatballs. Transfer meatballs onto a platter.

Heat the oil in a large deep non-stick skillet over medium-high heat. Add the meatballs and brown on all sides, about 3 minutes. Transfer to a plate and set aside.

Add the coconut milk to the skillet and let come a gentle simmer over medium heat for 5 minutes. Add the curry paste to the pan and cook about 3 minutes, stirring to dissolve the paste into the coconut milk. Return the meatballs and cook, turning gently to coat, 1–2 minutes.

Increase the heat to medium-high, bring to a gentle boil, and add the water, fish sauce, brown sugar and kaffir lime leaves, if using. Reduce the heat to low and simmer, stirring gently until the meatballs are cooked through, about 5 minutes.

Slice the baguettes open with serrated knife. Place cilantro, basil leaves and shredded carrots in the bottom and sides of each baguette. Using a slotted spoon, place 5 meatballs in each baguette. Drizzle curry sauce on top of the meatballs. Place chili peppers on top and garnish with crushed peanuts. Serve immediately with the remaining curry sauce on the side.

Skirt Steak with Chimichurri Sauce

Did you know that soaking meat in a solution of baking soda and water will tenderize it? This is a centuries-old technique used in Chinese cuisine. This method raises the pH which keeps the meat tender and moist when it's cooked. I decided to apply this method to the steak. The result? Tender, melt-in-your-mouth steak with a budget friendly cut. My friends are always amazed at how tender any kind of beef I make turns out and (shhhhh) now you know my secret too.

Serves 4–6
Prep Time: 20 minutes
Cook Time: 8 minutes

Chimichurri Sauce (page 32)
1 tablespoon baking soda
2 cups (500 ml) water
1½ lbs (750 g) skirt steak (about ½-in / 1.2-cm thick), cut in half crosswise against the grain
Kosher salt and freshly ground black pepper

Prepare the Chimichurri sauce (page 32.) Set aside.

In a large flat pan, dissolve the baking soda in the water. Add the beef and soak for 10 minutes. Remove the beef from the water and pat dry with paper towels. Season generously with salt and pepper.

Build a medium-hot fire in a charcoal grill, or heat a gas grill to high). Cook the beef 3–4 minutes per side until the meat is nicely charred and medium-rare.

Transfer the steak to a carving board and let it rest for 5–10 minutes. Slice thinly against grain and serve with Chimichurri sauce.

COOK'S NOTE
The Chimichurri Sauce recipe in this book makes approximately ¾ cup (185 ml). Cover and store the remainder your fridge to drizzle on your favorite meats or use as a dipping sauce.

Weeknight Steak Frites

Calling all Francophiles! Recreate classic steak frites from your favorite French bistro with this divine recipe that calls for frozen french fries for ease and convenience. Some may scoff at the idea of using frozen fries, but trust me, they turn out crisp and delicious. When tossed with olive oil and parsley they go from fries to *frites*. The herbed compound butter served with the steak is the pièce de résistance in this recipe and will have your guests shouting, "J'adore!" Bon Appétit!

COOK'S NOTE
Toss the cooked fries with truffle oil before serving for some added oh là là.

Serves 4
Prep Time: 15 minutes
Cook Time: 25 minutes

Steak

Strip steaks, about 1½ lbs (750 g) total, 1¼–1½-in (3–3.8-cm) thick, trimmed of fat
Salt and freshly ground black pepper
1 teaspoon chopped fresh rosemary

Frites

8 oz (250 g) frozen shoestring french fries
1 tablespoon extra virgin olive oil
¼ teaspoon salt
⅛ teaspoon freshly ground black pepper
1 tablespoon dried parsley

Compound Butter

1 stick salted butter, at room temperature
1 tablespoon chopped chives
1 tablespoon chopped parsley
1 clove garlic, minced

Preheat the oven to 400°F (200°C). Line a baking sheet with foil.

Bring the steaks to room temperature. Season both sides of the steak with salt and pepper. Sprinkle with chopped rosemary and set aside.

Toss the frozen french fries with the oil, salt and pepper and parsley. Place the fries on one side of the baking sheet. Partially bake the fries, turning halfway through. Cook according to the package instructions (for half of the recommended cooking time).

Remove the fries from the oven.

Turn on the broiler. Add the steak to the unoccupied side of the baking sheet and place it 4 inches (10 cm) from the heating element. Broil the steak for about 3–4 minutes on each side or until desired doneness. If the fries start to burn, remove them and continue cooking the steak. Remove the steak from the oven and let it rest for 10 minutes.

While the steak is resting, make the **Compound Butter**: In a small bowl, combine the butter, chives, parsley and garlic.

Thinly slice the steak and serve immediately with the frites and compound butter on the side.

Cuban-style Pork Shoulder

I made this recipe for some friends recently and they all raved. Pork shoulder is marinated in authentic Cuban spices like cumin and oregano along with bright citrus juices and fresh herbs and then oven roasted until tender. It was such a hit my hubby was inspired to light up Cuban cigars for everyone after dinner. Marinate the pork the night before your dinner party and you'll have all day to spend with your family. Blast some Buena Vista Social Club over dinner and you'll have one smokin' Havana night! Serve with Citrusy Cuban Black Bean Soup (see recipe on page 94) and your dinner party will really sing!

Serves: 8
Prep Time: 15 minutes + marinating time
Cook Time: 2¹/₂–3 hours

Marinade

4 cloves garlic
2 teaspoons salt
1 teaspoon freshly ground black pepper
1 teaspoon ground cumin
1 teaspoon dried oregano
1 teaspoon ground coriander
3 tablespoons freshly squeezed lime juice
3 tablespoons freshly squeezed orange juice
4 tablespoons coarsely chopped fresh oregano leaves
4 tablespoons coarsely chopped fresh mint leaves
3 tablespoons olive oil
1¹/₂ teaspoons white wine vinegar

One 4 lb (2 kg) pork shoulder roast
Lime wedges, for serving

Place all of the marinade ingredients in a food processor and purée.

Make 5 or 6 slits in the fatty side of the pork shoulder. Place the pork in a large resealable plastic food storage bag. Pour the marinade over the pork to evenly coat. Seal the bag and place it into refrigerator for 8 hours or up to overnight.

Preheat the oven to 400°F (200°C). Using tongs, transfer the pork to a roasting pan.

Roast the pork for 30 minutes, and then reduce the heat to 375°F (190°C) and continue cooking until the pork is no longer pink in the center, about 2 hours more, or until an instant-read thermometer inserted into the center registers 170°F (77°C). Remove from oven and let the pork rest for 10 minutes.

Slice and serve immediately with lime wedges and steaming hot white rice.

Persian Herb Stew Ghormeh Sabzi

This recipe was given to me by my BFF Mary Sadeghy's mom, Derakshandeh, who immigrated from Iran in 1965. Although she was a busy working mom of three and also getting her PhD, she never ceased to treat her family to the traditional Persian dishes of her heritage. Known as the "king of Persian stews," *ghormeh sabzi* is one of the most popular stews in Persian cuisine. Tender and flavorful, it combines fresh herbs with kidney beans and beef and can be prepared without beef for a vegetarian version. It is especially delicious over rice or the Persian delicacy called *tadig*, which literally translates to "the bottom of the pot" (see the recipe on page 173, also given to me by Mary's mom).

Serves 4–6
Prep Time: 30 minutes plus resting time
Cook Time: 60–90 minutes

1/2 cup (90 g) dried red kidney beans
4 tablespoons oil, divided
2 medium yellow onions, chopped
1 lb (500 g) beef stew meat, cut into 1-in (2.5-cm) cubes
1/4 teaspoon turmeric
3 cups (750 ml) water
4 dried Persian limes
1 cup (30 g) fresh spinach, coarsely chopped
1 bunch chives, finely chopped
1 bunch parsley, finely chopped
1 bunch coriander leaves (cilantro), finely chopped
3/4 cup (40 g) fresh fenugreek leaves, stemmed and chopped or 1 tablespoon dried
Juice from 1 lemon
Dash of cinnamon
Salt and freshly ground black pepper, to taste

Soak the dried kidney beans in a bowl of water for 1 hour. Drain.

Add 2 tablespoons of the oil to a pot or dutch oven over medium-high heat. Add the chopped onions and sauté until golden, about 3–4 minutes. Remove half of the onions and set aside.

Add the beef cubes and turmeric, and sauté for 5–8 minutes, until browned. Add the reserved drained beans and the water. Cook until the beans are tender and meat is cooked, about 45 minutes to an hour (depending on the tenderness of the meat).

Meanwhile, poke the Persian limes with a fork and soak in 1 cup (250 ml) of hot water for 5–10 minutes. Drain and set aside.

Heat the remaining 2 tablespoons of oil in a large non-stick skillet over medium heat. Add spinach, chives, parsley, cilantro and fenugreek leaves. Sauté for 5–10 minutes, until the herbs turn a deep green color.

Transfer the herbs to the pot (adding a bit of water if needed). Add the reserved onions, lemon juice and cinnamon and stir to combine. Season to taste with salt and pepper. Add the reserved Persian limes. Reduce heat and simmer covered for about 30–40 minutes.

Serve over Persian Rice with Crunchy Crust (*Tadig*), page 173.

COOK'S NOTE
Dried Persian limes are available in Persian grocery stores. You may substitute with 2 tablespoons freshly squeezed lemon juice if you don't have access to a Persian grocery store.

Ultimate Umami Burgers

Inquiring minds want to know: what exactly is *umami*? If you didn't know already, umami is the 5th taste sensation apart from sweet, salty, sour and bitter. It's best described as "savory" and is a flavor found in such foods as mushrooms, soy sauce, fish sauce and cheese. Many chefs combine several of these ingredients to create "umami bombs." Once you taste this addictive burger you'll want to get "umami bombed" every chance you get!

Serves 4
Prep Time: 20 minutes + chilling time
Cook Time: 20–22 minutes

Umami Ketchup
4 tablespoons ketchup
2 teaspoons Worcestershire sauce
1/2 teaspoon fish sauce (*nam pla*)
1/2 teaspoon soy sauce
2 teaspoons white miso paste
1/2 teaspoon sugar

Parmesan Discs
4 tablespoons grated Parmesan cheese

Burgers
1/2 lb (250 g) ground beef
1/2 lb (250 g) ground pork
1 egg
1 tablespoon miso paste
1 tablespoon fish sauce (*nam pla*)

1 tablespoon Dijon mustard
1 teaspoon garlic powder
1 teaspoon onion powder
1/4 teaspoon Worcestershire sauce

Browned Onion Topping
2 tablespoons oil
1 small yellow onion, sliced
1/2 cup (18 g) dried shiitake mushrooms
2 teaspoons light soy sauce

1 teaspoon oil
4 hamburger buns with sesame seeds

Preheat the oven to 400°F (200°C).

Make the **Umami Ketchup**: Combine all the ketchup ingredients in a small bowl. Set aside.

Make the **Parmesan Discs**: Pour a heaping tablespoon of Parmesan onto a silicone mat or parchment-lined baking sheet and lightly pat down. Repeat with the remaining cheese, spacing the spoonfuls about 1/2-inch (1.2-cm) apart. Bake for 3–5 minutes or until golden and crisp. Remove from the oven and let cool.

Mix all of the burger ingredients together in a medium bowl until combined. Shape into 4 patties. Cover with plastic wrap and refrigerate for 30 minutes.

Meanwhile, heat the oil in a large non-stick skillet over medium-high heat. Add the onions and cook for 5–6 minutes, until browned. Add the mushrooms and cook for 6–8 minutes. Add the soy sauce and cook until it evaporates, about 1–2 minutes. Transfer the onions and mushrooms to a bowl and set aside.

Heat 1 teaspoon of oil in the skillet. Add the burger patties, spaced evenly apart. Cook for 3–4 minutes. Flip the burgers and cook for 3–4 more minutes.

Place the cooked burgers on the buns and place a Parmesan Disc followed by a spoonful of Browned Onion Topping on top of each burger. Place a dollop of umami ketchup on top of the onions. Serve immediately.

Beef & Broccoli Udon Noodle Stir-fry

"Beef & Broccoli Udon Noodle Stir-fry!" I laugh when my friends try to say this mouthful. But, what a delicious mouthful it is. This dish features succulent beef tenderloin, a healthy serving of tender broccoli, the rich and flavor-absorbing baby bella mushroom and fresh udon noodles. This is the perfect stir-fry to spoon onto your favorite serving platter for family style dining or to plate individually as a simple one-pot entrée. Udon is a thick noodle made from wheat flour. My kids love them for their slurp-worthy slippery chewiness. Most grocers today carry udon noodles on the refrigerated shelf next to the tofu.

Serves 6
Prep Time: 20 minutes + marinating time
Cook Time: 8 minutes

3/4 lb (350 g) fresh udon noodles
1 lb (500 g) beef (tenderloin, boneless sirloin or New York strip steak), sliced diagonally across the grain into 1/4-in (6-mm) slices
1 teaspoon, plus 2 tablespoons oil, divided
1 teaspoon, plus 4 tablespoons cornstarch, divided
1 teaspoon salt
3 teaspoons sugar, divided
1 teaspoon soy sauce
Dash of white pepper
8 oz (250 g) broccoli florets
1 1/2 cups (375 ml) chicken stock or broth, divided
4 tablespoons oyster sauce
1 teaspoon peeled and minced fresh ginger
1 teaspoon minced garlic
1 cup (75 g) sliced mushrooms (such as baby bellas)
1 teaspoon salt
1/2 cup (85 g) thinly sliced red bell pepper
2 tablespoons dry white wine
Finely chopped green onions (scallions), for garnish

> **COOK'S NOTE**
> You may substitute udon noodles with gluten-free wide dried rice noodles.

Cook the udon noodles according to the package directions. Drain, rinse with cool water and set aside.

Toss the beef, oil, 1 teaspoon of the cornstarch, salt, 1 tablespoon of the sugar, soy sauce and white pepper in a medium bowl. Cover and refrigerate for 20 minutes.

Blanch the broccoli in boiling water until tender, about 1 minute. Using a slotted spoon, transfer to an ice water bath to cool, and then drain and set aside.

Mix 1/2 cup (125 ml) of the chicken stock or broth, the remaining 4 tablespoons of the cornstarch, oyster sauce and the remaining 2 teaspoons of the sugar in a small bowl until combined.

Heat the oil in a wok or large non-stick skillet over medium-high heat. Add the beef, ginger and garlic and stir-fry for 2 about minutes. Add the mushrooms and 1 teaspoon salt and stir-fry for 1 minute. Add the red bell pepper and stir-fry for 1 more minute.

Add the wine and stir-fry for 30 seconds. Stir in the remaining 1 cup (250 ml) of the chicken stock or broth and heat to boiling. Add the beef, reserved broccoli and reserved udon noodles and toss to coat. Create a well in the center of the stir-fry. Stir in the cornstarch mixture and stir-fry until thickened. Transfer to a platter and garnish with green onions. Serve immediately.

Indonesian Short Ribs Braised in Coconut

My witty and wise friend Neil has never been to Indonesia but would travel to the ends of the earth for this dish. He tested this recipe for me and especially loved the yummy coconut ginger cooking sauce. Lemongrass adds a bright and citrusy touch to this heavenly sauce. Neil loved it so much he ate the leftover sauce over some steamed rice (even though all the short ribs had been devoured the night before).

Serves 4 to 6
Prep Time: 30 minutes
Cook Time: 2.5–3 hours

3 lbs (1.5 kg) bone-in beef short ribs, cut crosswise into 2-in (5-cm) pieces
Salt and freshly ground black pepper
2 tablespoons oil
2 cloves garlic, smashed
1 small shallot, finely chopped
1 jalapeño pepper, deseeded and sliced
1 tablespoon curry powder
2 lemongrass stalks, smashed and sliced in 2-in (5-cm) pieces
One 2-in (5-cm) piece fresh ginger, peeled and sliced into coins
One 13.5-oz (400-ml) can coconut milk
2 tablespoons brown sugar
1 cup (250 ml) beef stock
1/4 teaspoon fish sauce (*nam pla*)
1 tablespoon finely chopped coriander leaves (cilantro)

Gremolata
1/3 cup (25 g) toasted coconut flakes
1 bunch coriander leaves (cilantro)
2 tablespoons freshly squeezed lime juice
Zest from 1/2 lime
Lime wedges, for serving

> ### COOK'S NOTE
> Add 1/2 cup (125 ml) of water if the braising liquid runs low.

Preheat the oven to 300°F (150°C).

Season the short ribs with salt and pepper. Heat the oil in a large dutch oven over high heat. Brown the short ribs on all sides, about 8 minutes. Transfer the short ribs to a plate.

Reduce the heat to medium-high heat. Add the garlic, shallot and jalapeño pepper, and sauté for 30 seconds. Add the curry powder and sauté for 30 more seconds. Add the lemongrass, ginger, coconut milk, brown sugar, beef stock, fish sauce and cilantro, and whisk until combined. Add the reserved short ribs. Reduce the heat and bring the mixture to a simmer. Cover and place the dutch oven in the oven for about 2 1/2 hours until fork-tender but still on the bone. Transfer the ribs to a platter. Remove the ginger and lemongrass from the braising sauce with a strainer. Spoon the sauce over the ribs.

While ribs are braising, make the **Gremolata**: Combine the gremolata ingredients in a small bowl and stir to combine.

Top the ribs with Gremolata. Serve immediately with steaming hot jasmine rice.

Steak Fajitas

As you may have read in my Skirt Steak with Chimichurri Sauce recipe, tenderizing meat with baking soda and water has been around for centuries and is widely used in Chinese cuisine. One time while I was catering for a big photo shoot, the client asked if I could serve fajitas. A light bulb went off when I realized I could use the same tenderizing techniques my mom taught me for Chinese food for fajitas. The results were melt-in-your-mouth tender and all the models went crazy for them. Marinated with authentic spices, cilantro and lime juice and sautéed with peppers and onions, these fajitas know how to work it, grrl.

Serves: 4–6
Prep Time: 20 minutes + soaking + marinating time
Cook Time: 12 minutes

2 teaspoons baking soda
1$\frac{1}{2}$ cups (375 ml) water
1 lb (500 g) flank steak or skirt steak

Marinade
Juice of 1 lime
1 teaspoon Ancho chili powder
$\frac{1}{2}$ cup (25 g) finely chopped fresh coriander leaves (cilantro)
2 tablespoons oil
2 cloves garlic, minced
$\frac{1}{2}$ teaspoon ground cumin
$\frac{1}{2}$ fresh jalapeño pepper, deseeded and finely chopped
$\frac{1}{2}$ teaspoon salt
$\frac{1}{4}$ teaspoon freshly ground black pepper

2 tablespoons oil, divided
1 yellow onion, sliced
1 red bell pepper, sliced into thin strips
1 yellow bell pepper, sliced into thin strips
1 green bell pepper, sliced into thin strips
Salt and freshly ground black pepper, to taste

For serving
Shredded cheese
Pico de gallo
Shredded iceberg lettuce
Sour cream
Guacamole
Coriander leaves (cilantro)
Warm tortillas
Lime wedges

COOK'S NOTE
Ancho chili powder has mild heat and a subtly sweet, fruity flavor. You can substitute with 1 teaspoon of regular chili powder and $\frac{1}{8}$ teaspoon crushed red pepper.

In a large flat pan, dissolve the baking soda in the water. Add the beef and let it soak for 10 minutes. Remove the beef from the water and pat it dry with paper towels.

Make the Marinade: Whisk the Marinade ingredients together in a large bowl. Place the beef in a large resealable plastic food storage bag. Pour the marinade over the beef. Seal the bag and place in the refrigerator for one hour or up to overnight. Turn the bag occasionally while the steak marinates.

Remove the steak from the bag. Wipe off excess marinade and sprinkle both sides with salt and pepper. Heat 1 tablespoon of the oil in a large skillet (preferably cast iron) over high heat. Add the steak, searing on each side for 3 minutes, or to desired doneness. Remove the steak from the pan and let it rest, tented with foil, for 5 minutes.

Add the remaining 1 tablespoon oil. Add the onions and bell peppers. Sear for 1 minute before stirring, then stir every 90 seconds, cooking for 5–6 minutes total. Salt and pepper to taste.

Slice the meat across the grain into thin slices. Serve immediately with shredded cheese, salsa, shredded lettuce, sour cream, guacamole, cilantro, warm flour tortillas and lime wedges.

Clarissa's Stuffed Corn Muffins Arepas

I recently attended a fun lunch at my Venezuelan friend Clarissa and her hubby Dan's house. Clarissa served her famous Arepas Bar and I fell in love! Slow cooked carne mechada is sautéed with sofrito in a savory sauce served in crisp-on-the-outside, tender-and-fluffy-on-the-inside arepas along with a spread of yummy toppings. She regaled us with the story of how her parents had mandatory family-and-friends Friday-night arepas feasts in order to be together at their home in Venezuela before everyone disappeared for weekend teenage fun. Clarissa has generously shared her family recipes here so you can recreate this arepas feast at home. I have a feeling if you make this for your kids, they will *never* leave the house!

Makes 18–20 arepas
Prep Time: 2 hours + resting time
Cook Time: 8 hours + 10 minutes

Carne Mechada (Make In Advance)
2 lbs (1 kg) skirt steak or flank steak cut across the grain into 2-in (5-cm) strips
2 red bell peppers, cut into quarters
2 leek stalks, white parts only
Water to the brim of the crockpot
Salt, to taste

Sofrito
1 tablespoon oil
1 large white onion, finely chopped
2 large cloves garlic, minced
1 red bell pepper, finely chopped

Sauce
1–2 tablespoons Worcestershire sauce
8 oz (227 g) tomato sauce
Salt, freshly ground black pepper and cumin, to taste

Arepas
2 cups (500 ml) warm water (plus a bit more if the dough feels too hard or dry)
1 tablespoon extra virgin olive oil
1 teaspoon salt
2 cups (300 g) pre-cooked white corn meal

Arepas Bar Toppings
Shredded gouda and white cheese (such as queso fresco or Venezuelan queso de mano)
Black beans
Sliced avocado
Sliced tomato
Venezualan cream (*nata*)
Condiments such as hot sauce, butter and guava jelly

Make the **Carne Mechada:** Place all of the carne mechada ingredients in a slow cooker pot. Cover with the lid and cook on low for 8 hours. When you're ready to serve, remove the beef with a slotted spoon and transfer it to a cutting board. Shred the beef using two forks. Set aside. Run the beef stock through a colander and discard the bits. Save the stock for other recipes.

Prepare the **Sofrito** and **Sauce:** Heat the oil in a large non-stick skillet over medium-high heat. Add the onion and garlic and sauté until onion is softened, about 3 minutes. Add the red bell pepper and sauté for 1 minute. Add the Worcestershire sauce, tomato sauce and reserved shredded beef and stir to combine. Reduce heat and simmer for 15 minutes. Season with salt and pepper, to taste.

Meanwhile, prepare the **Arepas:** Preheat the oven to 450°F (230°C). Place the warm water, extra virgin olive oil and salt in a large mixing bowl and stir to combine. Slowly pour the corn meal into the water with one hand while stirring with your other hand until a loose, moldable and moist dough forms, making sure to dissolve any clumps.

Let the dough rest, covered with a clean kitchen towel, for 5 minutes, and then check consistency. Add a bit more corn meal or water as needed.

COOK'S NOTE
Pre-cooked corn meal can be found at Latin markets. Clarissa recommends the P.A.N. brand.

Scoop the dough into portions with an ice cream scooper. Form one portion of dough into a ball. Then, press with your palms to form a 5-inch (12.5-cm) patty. Repeat with the remaining dough portions.

Heat a stove top griddle or grill pan (preferably cast iron) over medium-high heat. Grill the arepas until toasted on both sides. Remove from grill pan.

Arrange the arepas directly on the oven rack and bake for about 10 minutes, until they start to balloon. Remove them from the oven.

Split arepas in the middle and stuff them with the Carne Mechada and the toppings. You may also serve it like a tostada with the toppings on top or as a sandwich.

Drunken Pork Zucchini Noodles

Legend has it that this recipe is called "drunken" not because there's any alcohol in it but because it's perfect after a night of drinking as it's filled with garlic and heat! Whether or not you're a partier you can enjoy this delicious and flavorful dish anytime. Zoodles are all the rage these days because they're just like noodles but are low carb and loaded with fiber and nutrients. Whip these up and they're sure to be the life of the party at your next shindig!

Serves 4
Prep Time: 40–50 minutes
Cook Time: 15 minutes

Sauce
6 tablespoons oyster sauce
3 tablespoons light soy sauce
2 tablespoons dark soy sauce
4 teaspoons sugar
4 tablespoons water

4 medium zucchinis, about 6 cups spiralized
4 tablespoons oil, divided
$1^1/_2$ teaspoons salt, divided
3 cloves garlic, minced
3 small shallots, sliced
1–2 Thai or serrano chili peppers, deseeded and finely chopped
1 red bell pepper, thinly sliced
1 lb (500 g) ground pork or chicken
1 cup (35 g) Thai basil leaves (packed)
Finely chopped green onions (scallions), white and green parts, for garnish

Make the Sauce: Put the Sauce ingredients in a small bowl and stir to combine. Set aside.

Cut zucchini into zoodles using a spiralizer. Place the spiralized zucchini in a colander and toss with 1 teaspoon of salt until coated. Place the colander in a shallow bowl for 20–30 minutes while the zoodles release their moisture. Roll the zucchini in a clean, dry dish towel. Twist the dish towel to squeeze out the remaining moisture.

Heat two tablespoons of oil in a skillet over medium high heat. Add the zucchini and $^1/_2$ teaspoon salt. Stir-fry until tender, about 1 minute. Transfer to a large bowl.

Heat the remaining 2 tablespoons of oil in a wok or large non-stick skillet over medium-high heat. Add the garlic, shallots and chili peppers and cook for 30 seconds. Add the red bell pepper and stir-fry for 1 minute. Add the pork or chicken and stir-fry until cooked, around 6 minutes. Add the zoodles and reserved sauce and cook for 1 minute, tossing to coat. Add the basil leaves and toss until wilted, about 15 seconds. Garnish with green onions and serve immediately.

COOK'S NOTE
Dark soy sauce can be found at Asian markets and is sweeter and thicker than regular soy sauce as it's aged longer. Simply substitute with 2 more tablespoons regular soy sauce if you don't have dark soy sauce.

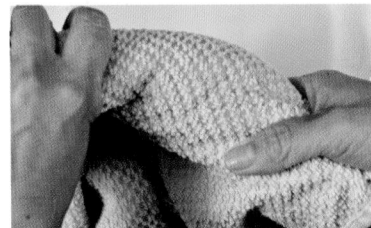

Brazilian-style Lamb Kabobs

This recipe was inspired by a trip we took to a Brazilian *churrasco* (grilled meat) restaurant in Los Angeles when my brother Bill was in town. If you haven't been to a churrasco restaurant I highly recommend it—especially if you're a meat lover. Servers magically appear with humongous metal skewers filled with deliciously marinated chunks of meat. We didn't think the night could get any better until a Carmen Miranda impersonator pulled my math professor brother onto the dance floor and the crowd went wild. All in all, a delicious night of memories. This simple and delicious Brazilian lamb recipe is paired with my fool-proof Chimichurri Sauce (page 32) for a night you'll remember too.

Serves 6
Prep Time: 20 minutes + soaking and marinating
Cook Time: 8 minutes

10-in (25-cm) bamboo skewers

Marinade
2 cups (500 ml) dry white wine
2 tablespoons lemon pepper seasoning
Juice of 1 lemon
1/2 cup (125 ml) extra virgin olive oil
1 tablespoon salt
1 bunch mint leaves, coarsely chopped

2 lbs (1 kg) trimmed leg of lamb, cut into 1-in (2.5-cm) cubes
Mint leaves, for garnish

Chimichurri Sauce (page 32)

COOK'S NOTE
Feel free to substitute with chunks of beef or pork or a combo. The chimichurri sauce recipe in this book makes approximately 3/4 cup (185 ml). Cover and store the remainder in your fridge to drizzle on your favorite meats or use as a dipping sauce.

Soak the skewers in water for at least 20 minutes.

Make the **Marinade**: Whisk together all of the marinade ingredients in a medium bowl. Place the lamb chunks in a large resealable plastic food storage bag and pour the marinade over them. Seal the bag and marinate in the refrigerator for 4 hours or up to overnight, turning the bag occasionally so the meat marinates evenly.

Thread the lamb chunks onto skewers.

Lightly coat the grill rack with cooking spray. Heat to medium-high heat. Grill, covered, turning every 1–2 minutes, until the lamb is cooked to desired doneness, 7–8 minutes for medium-rare to medium.

While the lamb is grilling, make the Chimichurri Sauce (recipe on page 32).

Garnish with mint leaves and serve immediately with Chimichurri Sauce and steaming hot rice.

FROM THE SEA

If you're a fan of The Little Mermaid you'll understand when I say you'll want the seafood recipes in this chapter to be a "part of your world." Countries all across the globe embrace the fresh seafood gracing their shores from fishing villages in Norway to Vietnam's long seacoast and many inland waterways. I'll never forget traveling with my late mom, Leeann, to her hometown of Guanghzou, China (known for its impeccable seafood dishes) for a Food Network Special. We visited a food market stall where we got to pick our prawns that had just been caught and watched the chef promptly toss them into a sizzling wok with ginger, scallions and peppers right before our eyes. You can't get any fresher than that! Whether you live in a seaport town, in a Midwestern suburb or dwell in a sprawling metropolis, I think you'll discover the recipes in this chapter—from **Teriyaki Surf & Turf Kabobs** and **Grilled Tequila Lime Shrimp** to **Mae's Spicy Sri Lankan Shrimp Curry** and **Bouillabaisse**—do justice to the diverse seafood preparations of the world and their jewels from the sea.

Mae's Spicy Sri Lankan Shrimp Curry

This recipe comes compliments of my friend Sashee's mother, Mae Chandran (a fellow cookbook author). Mae told me she brought this dish to an office holiday potluck party and didn't realize that one of the guests was judging the dishes. She won first prize and was handed a bottle of Wild Turkey Bourbon (although she doesn't even drink)! Mae is Chinese and her hubby is Sri Lankan. She uses a classic Chinese stir-fry technique and marries it with Sri Lankan curry spice for a quick, easy and flavorful dish that's always a hit with Sashee and all her friends. Bourbon, optional.

Serves 4
Prep Time: 15 minutes + marinating time
Cook Time: 7–8 minutes

1 lb (500 g) peeled (tail left intact) and deveined large shrimp
1 teaspoon salt
2 tablespoons minced garlic
2 tablespoons peeled and minced fresh ginger
1/2 teaspoon chili powder
1 tablespoon curry powder, preferably Jaffna curry powder
2 tablespoons oil
1 medium white onion, thinly sliced
3 tablespoons finely chopped fresh coriander leaves (cilantro)

In a medium bowl, mix the shrimp with the salt, garlic, ginger, chili powder and curry powder. Cover and refrigerate for at least one hour or up to overnight.

Heat the oil in a wok or large non-stick skillet over medium-high heat. Add the onion and stir-fry for 4 minutes, until the onions are lightly browned. Add the reserved shrimp and stir-fry for 5–6 minutes, until shrimp are cooked through. Add the cilantro and stir-fry for 30 seconds. Serve immediately with steaming hot jasmine rice.

COOK'S NOTE
Jaffna is the Northern part of Sri Lanka where Mae's husband hails. You may find Jaffna curry powder at Indian markets. Any curry powder you can find at a regular grocery store is a fine substitute.

Easy Seafood Paella

Paella is one of those dishes that may seem intimidating, but it's actually quite simple to make. You may think you need a special paella pan but a large skillet will do the trick. We were visiting my family over the holiday break and my brother suggested we whip up some paella as he'd spent several months in Spain recently. We concocted this easy and delicious recipe together that's loaded with shrimp, calamari and scallops in fragrant yellow-hued saffron rice. Within minutes, my sisters had the Gypsy Kings blaring and a pitcher of sangria making its rounds.

Serves: 4
Prep Time: 20 minutes
Cook Time: 40 minutes

2 tablespoons extra virgin olive oil
1 small onion, finely chopped
1 clove garlic, minced
1 red bell pepper, cut into thin strips
1 cup (200 g) Arborio rice
6 tablespoons dry white wine
1 Roma tomato, deseeded and finely chopped
1–2 pinches of saffron, soaked in 2 tablespoons water
$1/2$ teaspoon paprika
$1/4$ teaspoon crushed red pepper
Salt and freshly ground black pepper, to taste
$3/4$ cup (185 ml) store-bought chicken stock or broth
$3/4$ cup (185 ml) bottled clam juice or store-bought seafood stock
$1/4$ lb (100 g) scallops
6 peeled and deveined large shrimp
$1/4$ lb (100 g) calamari, cut into rings
6–8 mussels
$1/2$ cup (60 g) thawed frozen peas
3 slices cooked bacon, chopped
2 tablespoons finely chopped parsley, for garnish
Lemon wedges, for garnish

> **COOK'S NOTE**
> Feel free to use any seafood combination you like including chunks of your favorite fish.

Heat the extra virgin olive oil in a large deep non-stick skillet over medium-high heat. Add the onions and garlic and sauté for 1 minute. Add the red bell pepper and sauté for 1 minute. Add the rice and sauté until it begins to turn golden, about 2 minutes.

Add the wine and stir until it evaporates. Lower the heat to medium and add the tomatoes, saffron with its soaking water, paprika, crushed red pepper and salt and pepper.

Pour the chicken stock or broth and clam juice into the pan and bring the mixture to a boil. Once it begins to boil, cover the pan with a lid and simmer on low heat for 20 minutes. Uncover and add the seafood and peas. Give it a light stir. Cover and cook an additional 15 minutes or until the seafood is cooked through. Sprinkle with the chopped bacon. Garnish with parsley and lemon wedges. Serve immediately from the skillet.

Bouillabaisse

Bouillabaisse is the most famous fish stew of the Mediterranean. Its home is considered to be Marseilles but it's served in coastal towns all over Provence as well. Legend has it that Venus served Bouillabaisse to her husband Vulcan to lull him to sleep so she could consort with Mars—a tale and a recipe that are both out of this world! Loaded with fresh clams, shrimp and cod, this stew is light, flavorful and delicious, especially when served with bouillabaisse's signature accompaniment—rouille, a classic Provençal sauce.

Serves: 6
Prep Time: 30 minutes
Cook Time: 65 minutes

Rouille
1/8 teaspoon saffron threads
1/4 teaspoon hot water
2 tablespoons store-bought fish stock
4 cloves garlic, minced
1 cup (230 g) mayonnaise
1/2 teaspoon paprika
1 pinch of ground red pepper (cayenne)
1/4 teaspoon salt

Croutons
Twelve 1/2-in (1.2-cm) thick baguette slices
1 tablespoon extra virgin olive oil

Soup
4 sprigs fresh flat leaf parsley
3 sprigs fresh thyme
1 bay leaf
One 1 x 3-in (2.5 x 7.5-cm) strip orange zest
1 tablespoon extra virgin olive oil
1 yellow onion, thinly sliced
1 large fennel bulb, cored and thinly sliced
1 leek, white part only, sliced
3 cloves garlic, minced
2 tomatoes, peeled, deseeded and chopped
1 cup (250 ml) white wine
4 cups (1 liter) store-bought fish stock or
   clam juice
Salt and freshly ground black pepper, to
   taste
1 pinch saffron threads
1 1/2 lbs (750 g) cod or other white fish, cut
   into 2-in (5-cm) pieces
1 lb (500 g) small clams (such as cockles) or
   mussels, cleaned and debearded
1/2 lb (250 g) large shrimp in shells
Fresh herbs, for garnish

Make the **Rouille:** Sprinkle the saffron over the hot water in a small cup and let it stand for 1 minute. Blend the saffron mixture with the remaining Rouille ingredients in a food processor or blender until smooth. Transfer the Rouille to a bowl and set aside.

Make the **Croutons:** Put the oven rack in the middle position and preheat the oven to 250°F (120°C). Arrange the bread slices in a single layer in a shallow baking pan and brush both sides with the oil. Bake until crisp, about 30 minutes. Set aside.

Make the **Soup:** Tie together the parsley, thyme, bay leaf and orange zest with a piece of kitchen twine and set aside.

In a dutch oven or large pot, heat the extra virgin olive oil over medium heat. Add the onion, fennel and leeks, and sauté until softened, about 5 minutes. Add the garlic and tomatoes and cook for 1 minute. Turn the heat to high. Add the wine and cook for about 2 minutes or until the liquid is reduced by half.

Add the herb bundle, fish stock, salt and pepper and saffron, and bring to a boil. Reduce the heat to medium-low and simmer for 20 minutes. Remove the herb bundle and discard it.

Increase the heat to high and bring the mixture to a boil. Add the cod, clams or mussels and shrimp, and cook until the seafood is just cooked through, 5–6 minutes.

Place the Croutons at the bottom of each serving bowl. Divide the Soup evenly into the bowls. Top with 1 teaspoon of Rouille. Garnish with fresh herbs and serve immediately with extra Rouille on the side.

COOK'S NOTES
Add a splash of Pernod while adding seafood for an anise note.

Mussels and clams are purchased alive and must be kept alive. It's best to purchase them right before cooking but if you need to buy them in advance they should be kept cool and moist on ice in the refrigerator. Just before cooking, scrub them with a stiff brush under cool running water and trim off beards if they have them. If any of them are open, tap the shell. If they don't close tightly, discard them. If any don't open when cooked, discard them.

Grilled Tequila Lime Shrimp

Looking for an excuse to crack open the bottle of tequila staring at you from your liquor cabinet? Well here's a delicious recipe to jazz up some shrimp that's super fast and easy. The marinade is just a few simple ingredients: lime juice, tequila, cumin, garlic salt, extra virgin olive oil and pepper, which come together to tenderize and flavor the shrimp. Pair it with Coconut Lime Rice (recipe on page 166) and you've got a winning combo. (P.S. I won't tell if you take a shot while you're prepping. I mean, someone has to check to see if the tequila is okay. Teehee.)

Serves: 4
Prep Time: 10 minutes + soaking and marinating time
Cook Time: 7–8 minutes

10-in (25-cm) wooden skewers

Marinade
2 tablespoons freshly squeezed lime juice
2 tablespoons tequila
4 tablespoons extra virgin olive oil
Pinch of ground cumin
$1/4$ teaspoon garlic salt
$1/8$ teaspoon freshly ground black pepper

1 lb (500 g) peeled and deveined large shrimp
1 large lime, quartered, for serving

Soak the skewers in water for at least 20 minutes.

Make the **Marinade:** Whisk together the lime juice, tequila, olive oil, cumin, garlic salt and black pepper in a bowl until well blended. Place the shrimp into a large resealable plastic food storage bag.

Pour the Marinade over the shrimp. Seal the bag and turn it to coat evenly. Refrigerate for 1–4 hours, turning occasionally.

Discard the Marinade. Thread the shrimp onto the skewers, about 5–6 per skewer.

Lightly coat the grill rack with cooking spray. Heat to medium-high heat. Place the kabobs over a drip pan and grill, uncovered, for 5–7 minutes until shrimp turn pink, turning once. Serve immediately with lime wedges.

Vietnamese Salt & Pepper Crab

This is one of the most complicated recipes I've included in this book, but OH, It is SO worth all the effort! Prepping the live crabs for this dish may make some cooks squeamish, so if you'd like to view alternative methods other than putting them to sleep before chopping them, I urge you to review the instructional videos posted on YouTube. There are several videos featuring the most humane ways to prepare the crabs before dismemberment (and please disregard the one that shows the chef carrying a crab around like a purse! That's just cruel!)

Serves: 4
Prep Time: 30 minutes
Cook Time: 4–6 minutes

Salt and Pepper Seasoning
1 tablespoon salt
1 teaspoon fine white pepper
1 teaspoon sugar
$1/2$ teaspoon Chinese five spice powder

Crab
Two 14-oz (400-g) live crabs, blue swimmers or mud crabs
Oil, for frying
Potato starch, for dusting
3 shallots, finely chopped
2 cloves garlic, minced
2 green onions (scallions), trimmed and cut into thin strips, plus more, for garnish
2 Thai chili peppers, deseeded and thinly sliced crosswise on a diagonal

Make the Salt and Pepper Seasoning: In a small bowl, mix salt, white pepper, sugar and five spice pepper together.

Place the crabs in the freezer for 1 hour to put them to sleep or alternatively, place them in an ice bath using long tongs for 10–15 minutes. Remove the upper shell of the crabs, pick off the gills, which look like little fingers, and discard them. Clean the crabs under cool running water and drain.

Place each crab down right side up and chop it in half with a heavy cleaver. Chop each half into 4 pieces, chopping each piece behind each leg. Gently crack each claw with the back of the cleaver.

In a wok or skillet, heat 2–3 inches (5–7.5 cm) of frying oil to 400°F (200°C). Dust the crab pieces with potato starch, shaking off any excess. Fry the crab in batches for 3–4 minutes total, turning once, until golden brown.

Remove from the wok or skillet and place on a paper towel-lined baking sheet. Remove the oil, reserving 3 tablespoons. Clean and dry the wok or skillet.

Heat the reserved oil in the wok or skillet over medium-high heat. Add the shallots, garlic, green onions and chili peppers and stir-fry until fragrant, about 1 minute. Add the reserved crab and stir-fry for 1 more minute. Add half of the Salt and Pepper Seasoning and toss to coat. Add more salt and pepper mix, to taste, and toss again.

Garnish with scallions and serve with steaming hot jasmine rice and a finger bowl.

COOK'S NOTE
You may substitute potato starch with cornstarch if you wish. If you want a fiery version of this dish, don't deseed the chili peppers.

Steamed Mussels in Lemongrass and Basil

There's something sultry about mussels and this recipe showcases their earthiness, steamed in a combination of chicken stock, lemongrass, white wine and other southeast Asian ingredients and herbs. These mussels are soul-satisfying and exotic and fill your home with amazing aroma. The best part is that they steam in under 10 minutes! Healthy and satisfying, this dish is a sultry solution for a romantic date night at home or it can please a crowd over for the big game (just double, triple or quadruple the recipe depending on the size of your gang). I suggest pairing these mussels with a riesling or blush wine.

Serves 4
Prep Time: 20 minutes
Cook Time: 5–6 minutes

½ cup (250 ml) chicken stock or broth
2 tablespoons minced lemongrass
6 kaffir lime leaves, torn or cut in half (optional)
½ cup (125 ml) dry white wine
1 fresh hot red or green chili, preferably Thai, thinly sliced (deseeded if you prefer less heat)
2 tablespoons fish sauce (*nam pla*)
1 tablespoon palm sugar or brown sugar
½ cup (25 g) finely chopped fresh coriander leaves (cilantro)
1 lb (500 g) fresh mussels, debearded and scrubbed clean
1 clove garlic, minced
2 teaspoons cornstarch dissolved in 1 tablespoon water
Fresh basil leaves, for garnish
Fresh coriander leaves (cilantro), for garnish
Lime wedges, for serving

Pour the chicken stock or broth into a wok or large skillet. Add the lemongrass and lime leaves (if using). Bring to a boil over high heat, and then reduce to medium-high.

Add the wine, chili, fish sauce, palm sugar and cilantro. Stir to combine. When the sauce is gently boiling, add the mussels. Stir to combine and cover with a tight-fitting lid. Cook for 2–3 minutes.

Remove the lid and gently stir the mussels. If some of them still haven't opened, put the lid back on and allow to cook 1 more minute.

Reduce the heat to low and add the garlic and stir gently. Push the mussels to the side of the pan. Add the cornstarch mixture to the liquid in the pan, stirring until thickened. Once thickened, stir to combine with mussels.

Remove from the heat. Scoop or slide mussels into a large serving bowl (or individual bowls). Pour the remaining sauce on top. Garnish with cilantro. Serve immediately with lime wedges on the side.

COOK'S NOTE
Mussels are purchased alive and must be kept alive. It's best to purchase them right before cooking but if you need to buy them in advance they should be kept cool and moist on ice in the refrigerator. Just before cooking, scrub them with a stiff brush under cool running water and trim off beards if they have them. If any of them are open, tap the shell. If they don't close tightly, discard them. If any don't open when cooked, discard them.

Salmon with Sesame Ginger Glaze and Coconut Lime Rice

Ever feel like you're swimming upstream, like a salmon? You know that feeling when guests are coming over but you're stuck in traffic, have to pee, kids are whining and have nothing planned for the menu? Well, fear no more. This easy and delicious salmon (that you simply marinate and pop into the oven) will impress your guests with its notes of hoisin, soy sauce, brown sugar, citrus, crushed red pepper and garlic basking in a sesame ginger glaze that is just to die for. Served with aromatic Coconut Lime Rice flecked with cilantro, this one's definitely a catch.

Serves: 4–6
Prep Time: 15 minutes + marinating time
Cook Time: 55 minutes

Coconut Lime Rice (page 166)

Marinade

$\frac{1}{2}$ cup (85 g) brown sugar
$\frac{1}{3}$ cup (80 ml) soy sauce
2 tablespoons hoisin sauce
3 tablespoons peeled and minced fresh ginger
$\frac{1}{8}$ teaspoon crushed red pepper
1 clove garlic, minced
1 tablespoon freshly squeezed lime juice
2 teaspoons dark sesame oil
2 teaspoons toasted sesame seeds

$1\frac{1}{2}$ lbs (750 g) salmon fillet
Sliced avocado
Toasted sesame seeds, for garnish

Spinach
1 tablespoon oil
1 tablespoon minced garlic
1 lb (454 g) baby spinach leaves, cleaned
1 teaspoon salt
$\frac{1}{2}$ teaspoon freshly ground black pepper

Preheat the oven to 400°F (200°C). Make the Coconut Lime Rice (recipe on page 166).

Meanwhile, make the **Marinade:** whisk the marinade ingredients in a small bowl until blended.

Place the salmon in a shallow glass baking dish. Pour half of the marinade over the salmon, turning until covered. Cover and refrigerate for 20 minutes.

Place the remaining marinade in a small saucepan over medium-high heat. Bring to a boil, and then reduce the heat to medium-low and simmer for about 14 minutes or until the marinade forms a glaze.

Place the salmon on a baking sheet and roast it in the oven for approximately 15 minutes or until desired doneness.

Meanwhile, make the **Spinach:** In a large skillet, heat the oil over medium heat. Sauté the garlic until fragrant, about 1 minute. Add the spinach and salt and pepper and toss with the garlic and oil. Cover and cook for 2 minutes. Remove the lid, turn the burner to high heat and cook for another minute.

Remove the salmon from the oven. Transfer it to a platter and brush glaze over the salmon and garnish with more toasted sesame seeds. Serve immediately over a bed of spinach with the coconut rice and the avocado slices.

Thai Shrimp Cakes with Mango Sauce

These shrimp patties will take the cake at your next dinner party and make you look like a top chef! Jasmine rice, chopped shrimp, cilantro, green onions, fish sauce and coconut milk are shaped into petite shrimp cakes which are pan-fried and then drizzled with a delectable and fragrant mango sauce. Visually stunning and delicious, but even better... you can freeze the shrimp cakes and the sauce, and they both heat up beautifully. You'll be thanking me for the extra time saved as you are applying your final touches of mascara and getting your hair into that updo!

Serves 8–10
Prep Time: 30 minutes
Cook Time: 30 minutes

Sauce

2 tablespoons butter
2 cloves garlic, minced
1 tablespoon finely chopped green onions (white and green parts)
1 tablespoon finely chopped coriander leaves (cilantro), divided
1 tablespoon peeled and minced fresh ginger
1 tablespoon minced lemongrass
$1/2$ teaspoon salt
4 tablespoons mango purée
2 tablespoons honey
One 13.5-oz (400-ml) can coconut milk, divided
2 teaspoons sriracha sauce

Shrimp Cake

$1^1/_2$ cups (225 g) cooked and chilled white jasmine rice
1 lb (500 g) peeled and deveined cooked shrimp, chopped into $1/_2$-in (1.2-cm) pieces
1 tablespoon fish sauce (*nam pla*)
1 cup (120 g) all-purpose flour
2 teaspoons baking powder
1 teaspoon salt
4 tablespoons finely chopped green onion (white and green parts)
4 tablespoons finely chopped coriander leaves (cilantro)
4 tablespoons melted butter
3 eggs, slightly beaten

Oil, for frying

Make the **Sauce:** Melt the butter in medium saucepan over medium heat. Add the garlic, green onions, cilantro, ginger and lemongrass. Sauté for about 4 minutes or until the mixture is fragrant. Add the salt, puréed mango and honey and sauté for 2–3 minutes. Add 1 cup (250 ml) of the coconut milk and sriracha sauce and simmer, stirring occasionally, for about 5 minutes. Remove from the heat. Set aside, covered.

In a large mixing bowl, combine the rice, shrimp, fish sauce, flour, baking powder, salt, green onions and cilantro. Mix well. Add the melted butter, remaining coconut milk and beaten eggs. Stir gently to blend.

Heat a large non-stick skillet over medium-high heat. Add 2 tablespoons of oil and swirl to coat. Drop a tablespoon of shrimp mixture into the skillet, flattening slightly so that the cake is about 2 inches (5 cm) in diameter. Cook the cakes in batches, about 5 minutes on each side, or until golden brown. Add additional oil as needed. Serve warm with drizzled sauce.

Miso-glazed Cod

Whenever I make this dish it makes Miso Happy! If you've ever had miso-glazed cod at a Japanese restaurant, you know how amazingly simple and sublime this dish is. Black cod (or sablefish) isn't the most accessible fish to buy, so I use everyday cod fillet here for ease and convenience. If you can find black cod, then by all means go for it. The difference between white miso and yellow miso is that the yellow has a higher percentage of barley and is ideal for marinades and glazes, but you can substitute with white miso paste. This cod is excellent served over Wasabi Mashed Potatoes (recipe on page 161) or with steaming hot sushi rice.

Serves 4
Prep Time: 15 minutes + resting time
Cook Time: 8–10 minutes

4 tablespoons yellow miso paste
2$^1/_2$ tablespoons rice vinegar
2 tablespoons sugar
1 tablespoon soy sauce
$^1/_8$ teaspoon ground red pepper (cayenne)
2 tablespoons oil
Four 6-oz (175-g) cod fillets, each cut into 2 pieces

Preheat the broiler.

In a food processor, purée the miso, vinegar, sugar, soy sauce and cayenne pepper. With the motor running, gradually pour in the oil and blend until the mixture is smooth. Place the cod fillets in a large bowl. Pour half of the miso mixture over the fillets and toss to coat.

Transfer the cod to a rimmed baking sheet.

Broil the cod 8 inches from the heat until it begins to brown, about 3 minutes. Remove the cod from the oven and set aside.

Preheat the oven at 450°F (230°C). Roast the cod until it's opaque in the center, about 5 minutes. Divide the cod among 6 plates on top of Wasabi Mashed Potatoes (if serving). Drizzle the remaining miso mixture over the fish before serving.

COOK'S NOTE
Some miso paste contains gluten, so if you'd like to make a gluten-free version of this dish you can find gluten-free brown rice miso paste online and at some health food stores. In addition to using gluten-free miso you'll need to use tamari or Bragg's Liquid Aminos in place of the soy sauce.

Crab Tostadas with Tomatillo Salsa

We all get tired of tacos (even on Tuesdays) sometimes, so why don't switch things up with these crunchy tostadas with delicious lump crab meat bursting with fresh flavors from the cilantro, lime juice, tomatoes, jalapeño pepper and cool and creamy avocado. Best part is there is no cooking required! Served with a delicious and easy tomatillo salsa, this fresh and clean recipe will fill you up but won't weigh you down. Goes great with Mexican beer or a pitcher of margaritas.

Serves 4–6
Prep Time: 30 minutes

Tomatillo Salsa Verde
3–4 medium tomatillos, husked, rinsed and quartered
2 tablespoons finely chopped white onion
1 clove garlic
2 tablespoons fresh coriander leaves (cilantro)
2 teaspoons freshly squeezed lime juice
1/2 jalapeño pepper or serrano pepper, deseeded and chopped
Salt and freshly ground black pepper, to taste

Tostadas
1 lb (500 g) lump crab meat
3 plum tomatoes, cored, deseeded and chopped
4 tablespoons finely chopped red onion
4 tablespoons finely chopped coriander leaves (cilantro)
1 jalapeño pepper, stemmed, deseeded and finely chopped
Juice of two limes
2 teaspoons lime zest
Salt and freshly ground black pepper, to taste
1/2 cup (120 g) sour cream, for topping

One package tostadas
1 avocado, sliced, for topping
Coriander leaves (cilantro), for garnish
Lime wedges, for serving
Mexican hot sauce, for serving

Make the **Tomato Salsa Verde**: Place all of the ingredients in a food processor or blender and purée. Season with salt and pepper. Transfer to a bowl and set aside.

Make the **Tostadas**: Place the crab in a medium bowl and pick through the meat to remove any shells. Add the remaining tostada ingredients. Gently fold the ingredients to combine them. Season to taste with salt and pepper. Spoon some sour cream onto each tostada and then top with the crab mixture. Top with avocado slices. Garnish with cilantro. Serve immediately with hot sauce, Tomatillo Salsa Verde and lime wedges on the side.

Zucchini Noodles with Clam Sauce

Have you canoodled with zoodles? If you haven't, let me clue you in! Zoodles are zucchini squash that have been turned into low-carb noodles using an easily available spiralizing grater. The trick to great tasting zoodles is to remove as much water as possible by salting and squeezing the zoodles before cooking. Hopefully you have access to fresh in-the-shell clams, which give the dish an authentic Italian restaurant look when served. But if you can't find fresh clams, the dish won't suffer if you only use canned clams.

Serves 4
Prep Time: 25 minutes + resting time
Cook Time: 10 minutes

4 medium zucchinis, around 6 cups spiralized
1 teaspoon salt
2 tablespoons butter
1 tablespoon extra virgin olive oil
2 cloves garlic, minced
4 tablespoons dry white wine
4 tablespoons bottled clam juice or store-bought seafood stock
1 tablespoon fresh squeezed lemon juice
1/2 lb (250 g) small clams, scrubbed
3 oz (75 g) canned minced clams, with 1 tablespoon juice from can
6 cherry tomatoes, halved
Salt and freshly ground black pepper, to taste
4 tablespoons grated Parmesan cheese
1 tablespoon chopped fresh parsley
1 teaspoon grated lemon zest
Shaved Parmesan cheese, for garnish

Cut the zucchini into zoodles using a spiralizer. Place the spiralized zucchini in a colander and toss with the 2 teaspoons of salt until coated. Place the colander in a shallow bowl for 20–30 minutes while the zoodles release their moisture. Roll the zucchini in a clean, dry dishtowel. Twist the dishtowel to squeeze out the remaining moisture.

Heat the butter and extra virgin olive oil in a large non-stick skillet over medium-high heat. Add the garlic and sauté until fragrant, about 1 minute. Add the wine, clam juice and lemon juice and cook for 2–3 minutes until slightly reduced.

Add the canned clams and the fresh clams, cover and cook for 3–4 minutes or until all are opened (discard any that don't open). Add the cherry tomatoes and reserved zucchini noodles and toss to coat for about 1 minute, until heated through. Season to taste with salt and pepper.

Remove from the heat and stir in the Parmesan cheese, parsley and lemon zest.

Garnish with shaved Parmesan cheese and serve.

Teriyaki Surf & Turf Kabobs

My hubby Matthew and I got married in Hawaii, so whenever we're feeling nostalgic we make these Teriyaki Surf & Turf Kabobs which are sweet and savory with a lustrous, glistening glaze which is light and not goopy (like bottled teriyaki sauce can sometimes be). Loaded with succulent steak and juicy and tender shrimp, try these once and I promise you'll be saying "I do" forever.

Serves 4
Prep Time: 30 minutes +
  marinating time
Cook Time: 16 minutes

10-in (25-cm) wooden skewers

Teriyaki Marinade
1/2 cup (125 ml) water
One 6-oz (177-g) can pineapple juice
3/4 cup (150 g) packed brown sugar
4 tablespoons soy sauce
1 1/2 tablespoons honey
3 cloves garlic, minced
1 teaspoon peeled and minced
  fresh ginger
1/4 teaspoon Worcestershire sauce
1/8 teaspoon freshly ground black
  pepper

Kabobs
1 lb (500 g) beef tenderloin or top
  sirloin steak, cut into 1-in (2.5-
  cm) cubes
1 lb (500 g), peeled and deveined
  large shrimp
1 lb (500 g) whole white button
  mushrooms
1 large green bell pepper, cut into
  1-in (2.5-cm) pieces
2 medium onions, halved and
  quartered
1 pint (280–310 g) cherry tomatoes
  (about 25–30 cherry tomatoes)
2 teaspoons cornstarch
2 teaspoons water

Soak the wooden skewers in water for at least 20 minutes.

Make the **Teriyaki Marinade**: In a large bowl, whisk together the Teriyaki Marinade ingredients. Pour half of the marinade into a large resealable plastic food storage bag and the add beef chunks. Seal the bag and turn it to coat the beef; refrigerate for 8 hours or overnight, turning occasionally. Cover and refrigerate the remaining marinade.

Prepare the **Kabobs**: Thread the skewers alternately with the beef, shrimp, mushrooms, green peppers, onions and tomatoes and set aside. Discard the remaining used marinade.

Mix the cornstarch and water together to form a slurry. In a small saucepan, bring the reserved marinade to a boil. Slowly add the cornstarch slurry, stirring constantly for 1–2 minutes or until the sauce is thickened.

Spray the grill rack with cooking spray. Heat to medium-high heat. Place the kabobs over a drip pan and grill, covered, over indirect medium heat for 6 minutes, turning once. Baste with the sauce. Continue turning and basting for 8–10 minutes or until the shrimp turn pink and the beef reaches desired doneness. Serve immediately.

EAT YOUR VEGGIES
& Love Them!

So many of my friends and my kid's friends are vegetarian, vegan, pescatarian or flexitarian and others are just trying to get their kids to eat more veggies. In every scenario, we're all looking for new and interesting ways to amp up the flavor on fresh produce. Once a cameo player, veggies are taking center stage and are on a hot streak these days. I mean, who knew that cauliflower would be known as "steak" or that Tempura Green Beans would pop up on burger joint menus as a side? The wonderful world of veggies is as expansive as your imagination will allow. In this section, you'll find that marrying veggies with global flavors can be simply divine with addicting results. From **Middle Eastern Roasted Cauliflower "Steak"** and **Oven Roasted Bok Choy** to **Green Beans Tempura** and **Harissa Maple-glazed Carrots**, you'll find something for every palate in this chapter and may be pleasantly surprised to find your pickiest eater asking for seconds. They're that yummy!

Middle Eastern Roasted Cauliflower "Steak"

This recipe marries exotic shawarma spice with healthy cauliflower loaded with tons of flavor and very little fat. Who says Meatless Monday has to be boring? The shawarma spice blend is made with spices you can find at any well-stocked grocery store and you may already have most of them in your spice rack. This dish satisfies my cravings to bite into a juicy steak while feeling good about balancing our diet and keeping it healthy. In fact, did you know that cauliflower is loaded with fiber and is a good source of anti-oxidants? Now, that's using your cauliflower head!

Serves: 4
Prep Time: 20 minutes
Cook Time: 25 minutes

Shawarma Spice Blend
1/2 teaspoon ground cinnamon
1/4 teaspoon ground cardamom
1 teaspoon ground coriander
1 1/2 teaspoons ground turmeric
1/2 teaspoon ground ginger
2 teaspoon smoked paprika
2 tablespoons ground cumin
1/8 teaspoon ground red pepper (cayenne)

2 tablespoons extra virgin olive oil
2 tablespoons honey or maple syrup
2 cauliflower heads, stems trimmed and cut across into 1-in (2.5-cm) steaks
1/4 teaspoon salt

Green Chutney Sauce
1 bunch fresh coriander leaves (cilantro)
3 cloves garlic (crushed)
1/4 teaspoon salt
1/4 teaspoon pepper
Juice of 1 large lime
1 tablespoon honey or maple syrup
1/2 avocado

> **COOK'S NOTE**
> You may substitute the ground cardamom with ground cloves.

Preheat the oven to 425°F (220°C).

Make the **Shawarma Spice Blend**: Place all the spices in a small jar and shake or stir to combine.

Combine the extra virgin olive oil and honey in a small bowl. Add the spice blend and whisk to combine. Carefully brush the steaks on each side with the oil-spice mixture. Sprinkle the steaks with the salt. Place a single layer of cauliflower steaks onto a baking sheet. Roast the steaks for 15 minutes and then flip and roast for another 10 minutes or until golden.

While steaks are roasting make the **Green Chutney Sauce**: Place all the sauce ingredients in a blender or food processor and purée until creamy. Add a bit of water to thin if necessary.

Remove the cauliflower from oven and serve immediately with Green Chutney Sauce.

Dylan's Favorite Chinese-style Veggies

When my son Dylan was at a sleepover when he was 5 and asked his friend's mom to make him stir-fried veggies, I knew I was doing something right. I owe his love of vegetables to my late mother because she taught me how to blanch broccoli and other veggies (parboiling them so they stay tender-crisp while stir-frying) and to toss them in a sweet-savory combination of garlic, oyster sauce and chicken broth that my kids just gobble it up. Dylan still asks for his favorite stir-fried veggie dish all the time, and now that he's 12, I have to double the batch! This recipe is easy and fast! Keep oyster sauce in your pantry to whip this up anytime.

Serves 4
Prep Time: 10 minutes
Cook Time: 4 minutes

1 tablespoon cornstarch
1 tablespoon cold water
6 oz (100 g) broccoli florets
4 oz (100 g) snow peas
4 oz (125 g) sliced carrots
1 tablespoon oil
1 clove garlic, minced
1 small white onion, thinly sliced
1/2 red bell pepper, thinly sliced
1/4 teaspoon salt
3 tablespoons oyster sauce
1/4 cup (125 ml) chicken stock or broth

In a small bowl, mix together the cornstarch and water to form a slurry. Set aside.

Blanch the broccoli, snow peas and carrots: Place the vegetables in boiling water for 1 minute. Remove and drain. Transfer to an ice water bath to cool, and then drain and set aside.

Heat the oil in wok or skillet over medium-high heat. Add the garlic, broccoli, snow peas, carrots, onion, red bell pepper and salt and stir-fry for 1–2 minutes. Stir in the oyster sauce and chicken broth and heat to boiling. Pour in the cornstarch mixture and continue to cook, stirring constantly, until the sauce thickens and all the ingredients are nicely coated, about 30 seconds. Serve immediately with steaming hot jasmine rice.

Green Bean Tempura

Although slightly on the decadent side, this is a sure fire way to get your kids to eat green beans. Served piping hot, they're crisp, crunchy, juicy and flavorful. They're fun to eat too, kind of like veggie french fries. The Miso Mayo Dipping Sauce is an elevated treat for grown-ups but ranch dressing would be a fine accompaniment when making this for kids.

Serves 4
Prep Time: 10 minutes
Cook Time: 10 minutes

Miso Mayo Dipping Sauce
1/2 cup (220 g) mayonnaise
2 tablespoons freshly squeezed lemon juice
2 tablespoons white miso paste
1 tablespoon Cointreau or other orange liqueur
1 teaspoon *sambal oelek*
1 teaspoon finely grated orange zest

Tempura Batter
1 cup (120 g) all-purpose flour
1 tablespoon cornstarch
1½ cups (375 ml) very cold beer or club soda
1 egg, beaten
Pinch of salt

24 trimmed green beans
Oil, for frying

Make the **Miso Mayo Dipping Sauce**: Whisk together all of the sauce ingredients in a medium bowl. Set aside.

Make the **Tempura Batter**: Combine all of the batter ingredients in a medium bowl. The batter should be slightly lumpy. Place the bowl in a larger bowl lined with ice.

Rinse and pat the green beans dry with a paper towel. In a large wok or deep skillet, heat 2–3 inches (5–7.5 cm) of the oil to 350°F (175°C). Dip the beans in the batter one at a time. Fry in batches until fluffy and golden brown, being careful not to overcrowd the pan. Drain on a paper towel-lined baking sheet.

Serve immediately with the Miso Mayo Dipping Sauce.

COOK'S NOTE
Tempura batter works best when you use chilled beer in the batter. As Culinary Ambassador to the National Pediatric Cancer Foundation, I recommend using their beer, "Rising Hope," in this recipe for excellent results and to support a worthy cause.

Harissa Maple-glazed Carrots

File this one under SWEET! "Just like candy but with sweet heat," is how my friend Jodi Young described this recipe. I served them at a dinner party recently and they were scooped up in seconds flat because they were such a hit. The earthy harissa-maple syrup combo gives the carrots a gorgeous hue when roasted to caramelized glistening perfection. These sublime carrots are a boost for eyesight and a sight for sore eyes indeed.

Serves 4–6
Prep Time: 5 minutes
Cook Time: 40 minutes

1 clove garlic, minced
2 tablespoons extra virgin olive oil
2 tablespoons maple syrup
$1/2$ tablespoon harissa paste
$1/2$ teaspoon ground cumin
1 lb (500 g) baby rainbow carrots
$1/2$ lemon, thinly sliced, seeds removed
  (optional)
Salt and freshly ground black pepper

Preheat the oven to 450°F (230°C).

Whisk the garlic, oil, maple syrup, harissa paste and ground cumin together in a large bowl. Add the carrots and lemon slices and toss to coat. Transfer the carrots and lemon slices (if using) to a baking sheet in a single layer. Sprinkle with salt and pepper.

Roast until the carrots are tender and the lemons are caramelized, approximately 35–40 minutes. Serve immediately.

Kid-friendly Brussels Sprouts

After years of exile, Brussels sprouts are back as a trendy, tasty and healthful vegetable option. Unfortunately, many kids didn't get that text, but this recipe can help. With its cranberry-orange flavors, they taste just like Thanksgiving dinner, an undisputed favorite of kids everywhere. It's also super easy to make with pantry staples like dried cranberries, orange juice and pine nuts. Hopefully as kids grow up, you won't need to bribe them with sweetness to enjoy this yummy, always-available vegetable.

Serves: 4
Prep Time: 10 minutes
Cook Time: 50 minutes

1 lb (500 g) Brussels sprouts, trimmed and halved
2 tablespoons extra virgin olive oil
1/2 teaspoon salt
1/4 teaspoon freshly ground black pepper

Cranberry-Orange Glaze
2 tablespoons apple cider vinegar
1 tablespoon brown sugar
2 tablespoons freshly squeezed orange juice
Zest of one orange
Pinch of salt and freshly ground black pepper

2 tablespoons toasted pine nuts, plus more, for garnish (optional)
1 tablespoon chopped dried cranberries
Salt and freshly ground black pepper, to taste

Preheat the oven to 400°F (200°C).

In a medium bowl, combine the Brussels sprouts, extra virgin olive oil and salt and pepper until coated. Place the Brussels sprouts onto a baking sheet in a single layer and roast for 35–40 minutes, until browned and crisp. Shake the pan from time to time to brown the sprouts evenly.

While the Brussels sprouts are roasting, make the **Cranberry-Orange Glaze:** Place the apple cider vinegar, brown sugar, orange juice, orange zest and salt and pepper together in a pot. Bring to a boil over medium-high heat while stirring. Reduce heat and simmer for 5 minutes.

Remove the Brussels sprouts from oven. Add them to the pot and toss until they are covered evenly by the glaze. Add the pine nuts (if using) and cranberries and toss to combine. Season to taste with salt and pepper. Garnish with more pine nuts (if using) and serve immediately.

> **COOK'S NOTE**
> Omit the pine nuts if
> you're a nut-free home.

Oven Roasted Bok Choy

Here's a quick and simple way to roast healthy Bok Choy in your oven. Bok Choy is a nutrient-dense veggie loaded with anti-oxidants. My son Dylan's nickname used to be "Bok Choy Boy" when he was 5 because he loved this simple preparation so much. I've included an optional Miso Orange Dressing in my Cook's Note that's simply divine.

Serves 4
Prep Time: 10 minutes
Cook Time: 6 minutes

6 baby bok choy, halved lengthwise
2 teaspoons oil
1 clove garlic, minced
¼ teaspoon salt

Preheat the oven to 450°F (230°C).

Toss the bok choy, oil, garlic and salt in a medium bowl. Place the coated bok choy on a baking sheet and roast on the lowest rack, stirring twice, until wilted and tender-crisp, about 6 minutes.

While the bok choy is roasting, heat the Miso Orange Dressing (if using—see Cook's Note) in a sauce pan over medium-low heat.

Transfer the bok choy to a serving platter. Drizzle the Miso Orange Dressing (if using) over the bok choy and serve immediately.

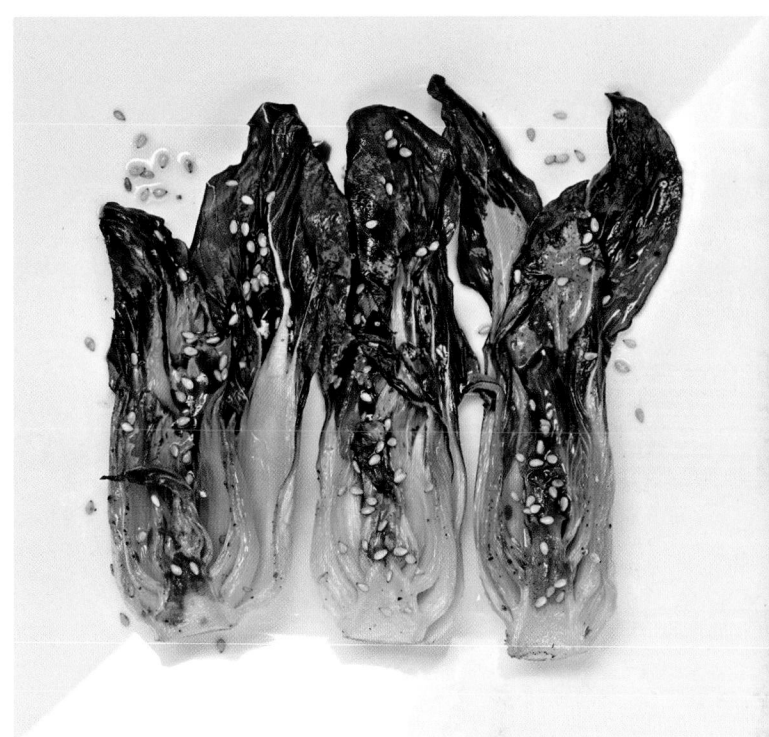

COOK'S NOTE
Make a delicious Miso Orange Dressing by combining 2 teaspoons oil, 2 tablespoons orange juice, 2 tablespoons mirin, 1 tablespoon white miso paste, 1 tablespoon honey, 2 teaspoons dark sesame oil, 1 teaspoon peeled and minced fresh ginger, 1 teaspoon orange zest and 1–2 teaspoons sriracha sauce.

Green Beans with Pancetta

My friends are always asking for tips on how to get their kids to eat more veggies and I always recommend this dish. Kids love these green beans as they soak up the yummy pancetta flavor around them and they also love the crispy texture from the panko bread crumbs. I like to blanch the green beans in the morning before I start my day. I stick them in the fridge and then simply toss them into the pan when I get home and they're ready in just a few minutes. So yummy you'll be caught in jaw-dropping amazement as your family gobbles them up. Speaking of "gobble," file this one away for Thanksgiving too!

Serves 6
Prep Time: 10 minutes
Cook Time: 16 minutes

$1^1/_4$ lbs (600 g) green beans or haricots verts, trimmed
4 tablespoons panko bread crumbs
4 oz pancetta, diced
1 tablespoon extra virgin olive oil
2 cloves garlic, minced
Salt and freshly ground black pepper, to taste
Lemon wedges, for serving

Blanch the beans in boiling water until tender-crisp, about 4–5 minutes. Using a slotted spoon, transfer them to an ice bath to cool, and then drain and set aside.

In a small sauté pan, toast the panko bread crumbs over medium heat until golden brown, about 1 minute. Remove from heat.

Heat a large non-stick skillet over medium-high heat. Add the pancetta and cook until crisp, about 8 minutes. Using a slotted spoon, transfer the pancetta to a paper towel-lined baking sheet.

Add the oil to the skillet. Once it is shimmering, add the garlic and sauté until fragrant, about 30 seconds. Add the reserved green beans and sauté for 2 minutes. Add the pancetta and panko bread crumbs and toss until combined. Season to taste with salt and pepper. Serve with lemon wedges.

Southeast Asian Vegetable Stew with Tofu

Salty, sweet, and hot and all in one pot! This hearty, soul-satisfying one-pot dish starts with not one but two kinds of the superhero-superfood mushrooms—shiitake and white button mushrooms. This is a complete one-pot meal—especially delish in the fall and winter months. Remember that when it comes to fish sauce, always go for the good stuff, unless you're a vegan—in which case you can leave out the fish sauce and substitute vegetable broth for the chicken stock.

Serves 6
Prep Time: 20 minutes
Cook Time: 20–25 minutes

One 13.5-oz (400-ml) can coconut milk
$1^1/_2$ cups (375 ml) chicken stock or broth, or vegetable stock
1 tablespoon soy sauce
1 tablespoon fish sauce (*nam pla*)
1 teaspoon sriracha sauce
$1/_2$ teaspoon salt
$1/_4$ teaspoon ground white pepper
2 sweet potatoes, peeled and cut into 2-in (5-cm) chunks
1 bunch green onions (scallions), (white and green parts) cut into 1-in (2.5-cm) pieces
1 stalk lemongrass, bottom 6-in (15-cm) only, bulb and tough outer leaves removed, bruised with a mallet
1 Thai chili pepper, deseeded and finely chopped
2 cups (280 g) chopped butternut squash (2-in/5-cm chunks)
$1/_2$ cup (40 g) halved stemmed shiitake mushrooms
$1/_2$ cup (40 g) sliced white button mushrooms
$1/_2$ cup (100 g) barley
$1/_2$ cup (124 g) diced firm tofu, blotted dry
4 tablespoons coarsely chopped fresh coriander leaves (cilantro), for garnish
4 tablespoons coarsely chopped roasted peanuts, for garnish

In a medium bowl, whisk together the coconut milk, stock, soy sauce, fish sauce and sriracha sauce. Add the salt and white pepper.

In a large pot, place the sweet potatoes, green onions, lemongrass, chili pepper, squash, mushrooms, barley and tofu. Pour the coconut milk mixture over the top. Stir to combine. Bring the mixture to a boil. Reduce heat and simmer for 20–25 minutes, until the sweet potatoes are tender and the barley is cooked through. Garnish with cilantro and peanuts and serve immediately.

Crispy Cauliflower in Gochujang Glaze

Bang a gong for Gochujang! This was my friend Stacy's hands-down favorite recipe to test. Her hubby Mark was even drizzling the leftover glaze on rice the next day for lunch because of its next-level, sweet-hot yumminess. If you haven't heard of the delicious Korean red chili paste gochujang, it's all the rage in the culinary world. Why? Because it's smoky, sweet and spicy and completely addicting. Combined with crispity, crunchity flash-fried cauliflower in a light batter, it's the best way I can think of to eat my veggies—and I think it will be yours now, too!

Serves: 4
Prep Time: 20 minutes
Cook Time: 20 minutes

Gochujang Glaze
- 1 tablespoon oil
- 1 tablespoon green onions (scallions), white parts only, finely chopped
- 1 tablespoon peeled and minced fresh ginger
- 3 cloves garlic, minced
- 4 tablespoons brown sugar
- 4 tablespoons granulated sugar
- 3 tablespoons freshly squeezed orange juice
- 1/2 cup (144 g) Korean red chili paste (*gochujang*)
- 1 1/2 tablespoons dark sesame oil
- 1 1/2 tablespoons light soy sauce
- 3 tablespoons rice vinegar
- 2 tablespoons toasted sesame seeds, plus more, for garnish

- 1/2 cup (60 g) all-purpose flour
- 1/2 cup (64 g) cornstarch
- 1/2 teaspoon salt
- 2 eggs
- Oil, for frying
- 1 head cauliflower, trimmed and cut into bite-size florets
- Finely chopped green onions (white and green parts) for garnish

> ### COOK'S NOTE
> You can find Gochujang paste at Asian markets, online and at many grocery stores as well.

Make the Gochujang Glaze: Heat the oil in a medium sized saucepan over medium-high heat. Add the green onions, ginger and garlic and sauté until fragrant, about 30 seconds. Add the sugars and the orange juice and whisk to combine. Bring to a simmer and reduce for 3–5 minutes or until large bubbles form and the mixture has some caramel color. Remove the pot from the stove and whisk in the gochujang, sesame oil, soy sauce, rice vinegar and sesame seeds.

In a large shallow bowl combine the flour, cornstarch and salt. In another bowl, whisk the eggs.

Heat 2–3 inches (5–7.5 cm) of the oil in a wok or deep skillet to 350°F (175°C). Working in batches, dip the cauliflower florets into the egg mixture and then into the flour mixture. Fry until golden, about 3 minutes per batch, being careful not to crowd the pot. Remove with a kitchen spider skimmer and transfer to paper towel-lined baking sheet.

Add the fried cauliflower florets to the saucepan and toss until evenly coated with glaze. Garnish with sesame seeds and green onions and serve immediately.

Thai Veggie Tofu Stir-fry

This simple recipe couldn't be more delicious or easier to make. The salty and sweet flavors from the fish sauce and oyster sauce come together beautifully with the heat from the chili-garlic sauce. A touch of sherry enhances the flavors and aroma in this recipe, resulting in a gorgeous dish. Served over some steaming hot jasmine rice or quinoa, it serves as a complete meal chock full of soy protein. Eliminate the *sambal oelek* if you're cooking for young kids.

Serves 2–3
Prep Time: 15 minutes
Cook Time: 5 minutes

2 tablespoons oil, divided
8 oz (250 g) firm tofu, drained, patted dry and cubed
1 clove garlic, minced
1 shallot, thinly sliced
8 oz (250 g) fresh asparagus, ends trimmed and sliced diagonally into 1-in (2.5-cm) pieces
2 teaspoons cooking sherry
4 tablespoons sliced white button mushrooms
4 tablespoons sliced fresh shiitake mushroom
2 tablespoons fish sauce (*nam pla*)
1 tablespoon oyster sauce
1½ teaspoons chili garlic sauce (*sambal oelek*)
1 tablespoon brown sugar

Heat ½ of the oil in a wok or large non-stick skillet over medium-high heat. Add the tofu pieces and stir-fry until golden brown, about 3 minutes. Remove the tofu from the pan and set aside.

Heat the remaining oil in the wok or skillet over medium-high heat. Add the garlic and shallots and stir-fry until fragrant, about 30 seconds. Add the asparagus and stir-fry for 1 minute. Add the sherry and mushrooms and stir-fry for 1 minute. Add the reserved tofu, fish sauce, oyster sauce, chili garlic sauce and brown sugar and stir-fry for 30 seconds. Dish out and serve immediately with jasmine white or brown rice.

COOK'S NOTE
Substitute the fish sauce and oyster sauce with 3 tablespoons vegetarian "oyster" sauce for a vegetarian version of this dish. Vegetarian oyster sauce is flavored with mushrooms and can be found at Asian markets and online.

Wasabi Mashed Potatoes

Achoo! If you're like me, a whiff of wasabi makes you sneeze, but I always smile when it happens to me because I know I'm about to enjoy a heaping mouthful of these yummy wasabi mashed potatoes. They make for a divine spicy, creamy pillow under Miso-glazed Cod (recipe on page 147) or a great accompaniment to any dish when you're looking for a kick-in-the-pants spin on this classic side dish.

Serves 4
Prep Time: 15 minutes
Cook Time: 20 minutes

1$\frac{1}{2}$ lbs (750 g) russet potatoes, peeled
  and cut into 2-in (5-cm) pieces
6 tablespoons whole milk
1–2 teaspoons wasabi powder
2 tablespoons butter
Salt and freshly ground black pepper, to taste

Place potatoes in large pot of cold salted water. Boil until tender, about 20 minutes. Drain. Return the potatoes to the pot; mash with a masher until lumpy. Combine the milk and the wasabi powder in small bowl, stirring to dissolve the powder. Add the milk mixture and the butter to the potatoes. Continue to mash the potatoes until smooth. Adding more milk if necessary. Season to taste with salt and pepper.

Grilled Gluten-free Miso Butter Portobellos

I created a gluten-free version of my Miso Butter Portobello Mushroom recipe for my friend Monica, who's allergic to gluten. She and my other dinner guests went bananas! I simply swapped out soy sauce for tamari and call for gluten-free oyster sauce and gluten-free brown rice miso paste for this recipe. If there had been any leftovers, I would have chopped them up and tossed them into a breakfast omelet for my husband. Instead, my friends enjoyed every little bite, we enjoyed their company, and my husband didn't even know what he was missing!

Serves 4–6
Prep Time: 20 minutes
  + **resting** + **marinating** time
Cook Time: 6–8 minutes

10-in (25-cm) wooden skewers
4 tablespoons butter
4 cloves garlic, minced
2 tablespoons minced shallot
1 green onion (scallion),
  (white and green parts)
  finely chopped, plus more,
  for garnish
4 tablespoons gluten-free
  brown rice miso paste
2 tablespoons tamari
2 tablespoons sake
2 tablespoons chicken stock
  or broth
2 teaspoons gluten-free
  oyster sauce
1 lb portobello mushroom,
  cut into 1/4-in (6-mm) slices

Soak the skewers in water for at least 20 minutes.

Heat the butter in a sauce pan over medium heat until melted. Add the garlic, shallot and green onion, and sauté for 30 seconds until fragrant. Add the miso paste, tamari, sake, chicken stock or broth and oyster sauce, and stir for 30 seconds until smooth. Allow to cool for 10 minutes.

Transfer to a medium bowl. Add the mushrooms and allow them to marinate for 30 minutes.

Thread the mushroom slices onto skewers.

Lightly coat the grill rack with cooking spray. Heat to the grill to medium-high heat. Grill the mushrooms until just tender and slightly charred, about 2–3 minutes per side. Brush them with the remaining marinade occasionally while cooking. Garnish with more green onions and serve immediately.

COOK'S NOTE
You can find gluten-free brown rice miso paste and gluten-free oyster sauce online and at specialty stores. Tamari is widely available. I recommend the San-J brand. You can also use gluten-free soy sauce or Bragg's Liquid Aminos in place of soy sauce.

Japanese-style Shrimp with Vegetables

I came up with this recipe while craving Japanese food after teaching a cooking class in Little Tokyo. I just love the combination of soy sauce, rice vinegar, mirin and sesame oil in the light glaze on this healthy and flavorful dish. I used bell peppers and bok choy, but experiment with whichever veggies you have on hand.

Serves 2–3
Prep Time: 15 minutes
Cook Time: 6–7 minutes

Stir-fry Sauce
1/3 cup (80 ml) low-sodium soy sauce
2 tablespoons rice vinegar
3 tablespoons mirin
1 tablespoon sugar
1 teaspoon dark sesame oil

2 tablespoons oil, divided
1 small white onion, diced
2 teaspoons peeled and minced fresh ginger
2 cloves garlic, minced
12 oz (350 g) peeled and deveined large shrimp
4 heads of baby bok choy, chopped
1 red bell pepper, diced
1 green bell pepper, diced
Toasted sesame seeds, for garnish

Make the **Stir-fry Sauce**: In a small bowl, combine the soy sauce, rice vinegar, mirin, sugar and sesame oil until blended and sugar is dissolved. Set aside.

Heat 1 tablespoon of the oil in a wok or large non-stick skillet over medium-high heat. Add the onion, ginger and garlic and stir-fry until fragrant, about 30 seconds.

Add the remaining 1 tablespoon of oil and add the shrimp and sauté for 2 minutes. Add the bok choy and stir-fry for 2 more minutes. Add the bell peppers and stir-fry for 1 minute. Add the Stir-fry Sauce and toss to coat for 1 minute. Garnish with sesame seeds and serve immediately with hot jasmine rice or brown rice.

Thai Cauliflower Pineapple "Fried Rice"

This "fried rice" isn't your grandmother's version of fried rice! All my paleo and keto friends have gone gaga for this cauliflower rice version of my Thai Pineapple Fried Rice recipe. Bursting with fresh herbs like mint and cilantro along with notes of fish sauce and lime juice, this dish is loaded with bright and exotic flavors and protein without any starch to weigh you down.

Serves 4–6
Prep Time: 25 minutes
Cook Time: 8

1 whole pineapple
1 medium head cauliflower, stem removed
2 large eggs
1 teaspoon salt, divided
Pinch of ground white pepper
2 tablespoons high-heat cooking oil, divided
1 clove garlic, minced
1 small shallot, finely sliced
1 fresh hot red or green chili pepper, preferably Thai
  (deseeded if you prefer less heat), finely sliced
2 tablespoons fish sauce (*nam pla*)
1 tablespoon soy sauce
1 cup (150 g) cubed cooked chicken breast
1 cup (150 g) cubed cooked shrimp
1/2 cup (37 g) fresh or thawed frozen peas
4 tablespoons finely chopped fresh coriander leaves
  (cilantro), plus more, for garnish
4 tablespoons finely chopped fresh mint

Cut the pineapple in half lengthwise and remove the fruit from the middle, leaving shell halves intact. Cut out the eyes and core. Set the shell halves aside. Dice the fruit. Dry the diced pineapple with paper towels and set aside.

Cut the cauliflower into chunks. Working in batches, pulse the cauliflower in a food processor until coarse in texture, like rice.

In a medium bowl, whisk together the eggs, 1/2 teaspoon of the salt and the pinch of white pepper.

Heat 1/2 of the oil in a wok or large non-stick skillet over medium-high heat. Cook the eggs, stirring until set but still moist. Transfer the eggs to a plate. Wash and thoroughly dry the wok or skillet.

Heat the remaining oil over medium-high heat. Add the garlic, shallots and chili pepper and stir-fry until fragrant, about 30 seconds. Add the cauliflower and stir-fry for 2–3 minutes. Add the fish sauce, soy sauce, chicken, shrimp, peas and the remaining 1/2 teaspoon salt, and stir-fry for 2–3 minutes. Add the reserved eggs, pineapple, cilantro and mint, and stir-fry for 30 seconds.

Scoop the "fried rice" into the pineapple shells and garnish with cilantro. Serve immediately.

COOK'S NOTE
Buy pre-riced cauliflower available in the frozen food section at the store to save time.

OODLES OF NOODLES & OTHER GRAINS

Noodles are slurped, twirled and savored all over the world. Basking in sensational sauces or tossed with a few simple ingredients, they are a beloved staple in most homes. Noodles come in countless shapes and sizes and are made from a variety of ingredients including rice and mung beans—allowing those on gluten-free diets to also indulge. The recipes in this chapter explore the diverse preparations I've enjoyed on my international travels, from **Greek-style Shrimp Pasta** and **Butternut Squash Ravioli in Butter Sage Sauce** to **Easy Weeknight Pad Thai** and **K-Town Chap Chae**. Let's not forget about Noodles' first cousin: Grains. I pay homage to several types of grains in this book, starting with rice. Rice has been the most important staple food for much of the world's population for more than 5,000 years. I include several fried rice recipes in this chapter, including **Leeann's Chicken Fried Rice**, **Kimchi Fried Rice** and **Indonesian Fried Rice** in addition to other rice specialties, such as the popular **Persian Rice with Crunchy Crust.** I've also included healthy options in the **Bowled Over** section of this chapter with four unique grain and noodle bowls such a **Whole Grain Veggie Burrito Bowl** and a **Quinoa Bibimbap Bowl.**

Coconut Lime Rice

This aromatic rice is so easy to make, and it turns plain white jasmine rice into something fragrant and sublime. Flecked with cilantro and bright, fresh lime juice, you'll be making this rice again and again.

Serves 4
Prep Time: 10 minutes
Cook Time: 25 minutes

1¼ cups (280 g) uncooked white jasmine rice
One 13.5-oz (400-ml) can coconut milk
¾ cup (185 ml) water
½ teaspoon salt
1 tablespoon finely chopped fresh coriander leaves (cilantro)
1 tablespoon freshly squeezed lime juice

Place the rice in a large bowl and rinse several times with cool water until the water runs clear. Drain the rice. Combine the rice with the coconut milk, water and salt in a medium saucepan. Cover and bring to a boil. Reduce to a simmer and cook until the rice is tender and the liquid has been absorbed, about 25 minutes. Stir in the chopped coriander and lime juice and fluff with a fork. Cover and keep warm until ready to serve.

Greek-style Shrimp Pasta

I love reminiscing about the trip to Mykonos for my bestie, Christos' 40th birthday. It makes me crave the classic ingredients found in Greek cuisine—feta cheese, Kalamata olives, lemon and fresh oregano. This light, healthy and easy recipe is perfect for a weeknight because you probably already have many of the ingredients in your pantry and fridge. Opa!

Serves 4
Prep Time: 15 minutes
Cook Time: 5 minutes + pasta cooking time

12 oz (350 g) dried spaghetti or linguini
4 tablespoons extra virgin olive oil
4 cloves garlic, minced
1 lb (500 g) shelled and deveined large shrimp
1½ cups (252 g) canned marinated artichoke hearts, drained and quartered
1½ cups (225 g) crumbled feta cheese
½ cup (90 g) quartered cherry tomatoes
½ cup (100 g) pitted and sliced Kalamata olives
3 tablespoons freshly squeezed lemon juice
3 tablespoons chopped fresh parsley, plus more, for garnish
2 tablespoons finely chopped fresh oregano
Salt and freshly ground black pepper, to taste

Prepare the pasta according to the package directions. Drain and rinse with cool water. Set aside.

Heat the oil in a large non-stick skillet over medium-high heat. Add the garlic and sauté for 30 seconds. Add the shrimp and sauté for 2 minutes. Add the artichokes, feta, tomatoes, olives, lemon juice, parsley and oregano, and sauté for about 2 minutes, until the shrimp have turned pink. Season with salt and pepper to taste.

Add the reserve pasta to the skillet and toss to coat.

Transfer to a platter. Garnish with more parsley and serve immediately.

COOK'S NOTE
If you don't have fresh oregano, substitute with 1½ teaspoons dried oregano.

Easy Weeknight Pad Thai

Pad Thai lovers unite! This is the Pad Thai you've been waiting for because it's so easy to make and you can find everything in this recipe at the regular grocery store. Traditional Pad Thai recipes call for tamarind concentrate which can only be found at Asian markets or online. A great way to recreate the flavors of tamarind is by using brown sugar and lime juice to mimic its sweet-tart signature taste. All the sweet, salty and sour flavors you've come to love from your favorite dish can now be whipped up within minutes on any night of the week.

Serves 4
Prep Time: 15 minutes
Cook Time: 6 minutes

8 oz (250 g) dried rice stick noodles
1/3 cup (65 g) brown sugar
4 tablespoons freshly squeezed lime juice
4 tablespoons fish sauce (*nam pla*)
3 tablespoons store-bought chicken stock or broth
3 teaspoons chili garlic sauce (*sambal oelek*)
3 teaspoons soy sauce
1 tablespoon cornstarch
2 teaspoons paprika
2 tablespoons oil
2 cloves garlic, minced
12 oz (350 g) boneless, skinless chicken thigh or breast, cut into thin strips
6 oz (170 g) firm tofu, drained, patted dry with paper towels and cubed
1 large egg, lightly beaten

Garnishes
Bean sprouts, trimmed
Carrots, cut into matchsticks
Shredded red cabbage
Crushed roasted peanuts
Finely chopped green onions (scallions)
Fresh coriander leaves (cilantro)
Lime wedges

Prepare the rice noodles according to the package directions. Rinse with cool water and drain. Set aside.

In a medium bowl, whisk together the brown sugar, lime juice, fish sauce, chicken stock or broth, chili garlic sauce, soy sauce, cornstarch and paprika. Set aside.

Heat the oil in a wok or skillet over medium-high heat. Add the garlic and stir-fry until fragrant, about 30 seconds. Add the chicken and stir-fry until the chicken turns white, about 2 minutes. Add the tofu and egg and stir-fry for 1 minute, until the egg is scrambled. Add the reserved rice noodles and sauce mixture and stir-fry for 2–3 minutes, tossing so the ingredients are evenly coated.

Transfer to a platter and garnish with small piles of bean sprouts, carrot and red cabbage on the sides of the platter. Sprinkle the peanuts, green onions and cilantro over the top. Serve immediately with lime wedges.

K-Town Noodles Chap Chae

While October 6th is officially National Noodle Day, it's always the right day to "use your noodle" and whip up this delicious and easy Korean staple! It's my go-to dish when I'm in Los Angeles' Korea Town to meet my friends for a marathon night of karaoke. Chap chae is an oh-so-flavorful anytime restaurant fave that's delicately seasoned with soy sauce, garlic, sugar, sesame oil and green onions, and now you can make it at home! You can substitute the beef with any protein you have on hand—like that roast chicken you had for dinner last night—or throw in some tofu for a vegetarian version. Chap chae is divine paired with Korean BBQ or served as a one-pot meal. K-Pop dinner soundtrack, optional.

Serves 4
Prep Time: 30 minutes
Cook Time: 6–8 minutes

8 oz (250 g) sweet potato noodles or dried cellophane noodles (also called glass noodles or Chinese vermicelli)
1 teaspoon plus 3 tablespoons dark sesame oil, divided
2 cups (60 g) baby spinach
1 carrot, peeled and cut into matchsticks
2 tablespoons oil, divided
1 small white onion, thinly sliced
2 cloves garlic, minced
8 oz (250 g) filet mignon or sirloin steak, sliced into thin strips against the grain
2 green onions (scallions), finely chopped
3 tablespoons soy sauce
2 tablespoons sugar
Toasted sesame seeds, for garnish

COOK'S NOTE
You can find dried sweet potato noodles at Korean markets and other Asian grocery stores. If not, substitute with dried cellophane or glass noodles instead.

Cook the noodles according to the package directions. Rinse and drain. Toss with 1 teaspoon of the dark sesame oil. Set aside.

Blanch the spinach in boiling water, about 30 seconds. Using tongs, transfer the spinach to an ice bath for 1 minute. Drain in a colander in the sink. Remove any remaining ice and use your hands to squeeze out the excess water from the spinach. Set aside.

Add the carrots to the boiling water and blanch for 1 minute. Using a slotted spoon, transfer the carrots to an ice bath for 1 minute. Drain in the sink using the colander. Remove any remaining ice and use your hands to squeeze out excess water from the carrots. Set aside.

Heat a wok or large non-stick skillet over medium-high heat. Add half of the oil and swirl to coat. Add the onion and garlic and stir-fry until fragrant, about 30 seconds. Add the beef and stir-fry for 1 minute.

Heat the remaining oil and add the reserved spinach and carrots, and the green onions. Stir-fry for 3–4 minutes. Add the reserved noodles, the remaining dark sesame oil, and the soy sauce and sugar. Toss for 30 seconds to coat. Dish out onto a platter and garnish with sesame seeds.

Chinese Sesame Peanut Noodles

This Chinese take-out favorite is totally delicious and oh-so-easy to make. You can serve it at room temperature or chilled, so it's a great potluck dish or fantastic when entertaining a crowd. In fact, it's been my go-to dish for the annual Spring Melt benefit for foodforward.org, which feeds LA's hungriest with surplus fruits and vegetables gleaned from backyards to farmer's markets. I usually use dried or fresh Chinese egg noodles, but spaghetti or fettuccine also works great!

Serves 6–8
Prep Time: 10 minutes
Cook Time: 11–13 minutes

8 oz (250 g) dried Chinese egg noodles or dried spaghetti
1 teaspoon plus 2 tablespoons dark sesame oil, divided
$3^1/_2$ tablespoons soy sauce
2 tablespoons rice vinegar
2 tablespoons sesame paste or 4 tablespoons tahini
1 tablespoon smooth peanut butter
1 tablespoon sugar
1 tablespoon peeled and grated fresh ginger
2 teaspoons minced garlic
2 teaspoons sriracha sauce
Half a cucumber, peeled, deseeded and cut into $^1/_8$-in (3-mm) x $^1/_8$-in (3-mm) x 2-in (5-cm) sticks, for garnish
4 tablespoons chopped roasted peanuts, for garnish
Toasted sesame seeds, for garnish
Finely chopped green onions, for garnish

Cook the noodles according to the package directions. Rinse with cold water and drain. Toss with 1 teaspoon of the dark sesame oil and set aside.

In a medium bowl, whisk together the remaining 2 tablespoons sesame oil, the soy sauce, rice vinegar, sesame paste, peanut butter, sugar, ginger, garlic and sriracha sauce.

Pour the sauce over the noodles and toss. Transfer to a serving bowl, and garnish with cucumber, peanuts, sesame seeds and green onions.

COOK'S NOTE
Want to go gluten-free with this recipe? Swap out the egg noodles with rice noodles and used Bragg's Liquid Aminos or San-J tamari instead of soy sauce.

Quick & Easy Penne Bolognese

Let's face it. We all rely on the handy, time-saving jars of store-bought pasta sauce in our pantries—especially on busy weeknights. When you have a bit of extra time, though, it's nice to treat yourself and your family to homemade Bolognese sauce. This is a quick Bolognese recipe you can get from your stovetop to your table in under an hour, yet it tastes like you've been simmering the sauce all day (even my sister Jeanie who studied cooking in Tuscany said so)! Nothing beats coming home to a house filled with the aroma of a flavorful tomato meat sauce brimming with fresh herbs. Now, that's amore!

Serves 4–6
Prep Time: 15 minutes
Cook Time: 35 minutes

One 16-oz (453-g) package penne pasta
2 teaspoons plus 3 tablespoons extra virgin olive oil, divided
4 cloves garlic, minced
1 small sweet onion, finely chopped
1 medium carrot, finely chopped
1 medium stalk celery, finely chopped
1 lb (500 g) lean ground beef
1/2 teaspoon salt
1/2 teaspoon freshly ground black pepper
2 tablespoons tomato paste
1/2 cup (125 ml) red wine
One 28-oz (794-g) can crushed tomatoes
10 leaves fresh basil, roughly chopped
2 sprigs fresh thyme
1 bay leaf
Grated fresh Parmesan cheese, for serving

Prepare the pasta according to the package directions. Drain while reserving 1/2 cup (125 ml) pasta cooking water. Toss with 2 teaspoons of the extra virgin olive oil to prevent them from sticking together.

Heat the remaining 3 tablespoons of extra virgin olive oil in a non-stick skillet over medium-high heat. Add the garlic, onion, carrot and celery and sauté for about 8–10 minutes or until the vegetables are translucent and tender, stirring occasionally.

Add the ground beef, salt and pepper and sauté for about 10 minutes, breaking the meat up as it cooks. Add the tomato paste and cook for about 2 minutes, or until beef is browned. Add the wine and cook until reduced by half, about 3 minutes. Add the crushed tomatoes, basil, thyme and bay leaf. Reduce the heat and simmer for 8–10 minutes, stirring occasionally until the sauce is thickened. Discard the bay leaf and toss the pasta with the sauce and the reserved water. Serve immediately with grated Parmesan cheese.

Butternut Squash Ravioli in Butter Sage Sauce

My friend Amy tested this recipe and loved it so much she wanted to change the title to "Butternut Squash Ravioli with Lick-the-Pan-Clean Crack Sauce." LOL. This brown butter sauce is one of the easiest things to make yet it turns almost any dish into nothing short of pure luxuriousness. I also cheat here by using store-bought dumpling wrappers instead of making ravioli dough for ease and convenience—one of my favorite go-to kitchen hacks. Besides, Marco Polo brought noodles from China to Italy and so this dish is all about Eurasian persuasion!

Serves 4
Prep Time: 25–30 minutes
Cook Time: 30 minutes

Raviolis

1 cup (450 g) mashed cooked butternut squash
1/2 teaspoon salt
1/4 teaspoon freshly ground black pepper
1 pinch ground red pepper (cayenne)
1/2 cup (112 g) mascarpone cheese
1 egg yolk
1/3 cup (30 g) grated Parmesan cheese
1 package round dumpling wrappers

Brown Butter Sauce

One 8 oz (225 g) stick unsalted butter
1/2 cup (125 ml) chicken stock or broth
1/2 cup (125 ml) heavy whipping cream
1/2 teaspoon freshly squeezed lemon juice
2 tablespoons fresh sage, minced
4 tablespoons freshly grated Parmesan cheese, plus more, for garnish
Salt and freshly ground black pepper, to taste
3–4 additional fresh sage leaves, for garnish

Make the Raviolis: In a medium bowl, combine the mashed butternut squash, salt, black pepper and cayenne pepper until blended. Stir in the mascarpone cheese, egg yolk and Parmesan cheese. Mix until the filling is smoothly combined.

Place a dumpling wrapper onto a cutting board. Wet the tip of a finger in water, and run it all along the outer edge of the wonton skin to moisten it. Place about 1 teaspoon of filling in the center of the wonton. Fold the wonton in half to make a half-moon shape, and press the edges to seal. Repeat with the remaining dumpling wrappers. Cover with a damp paper towel.

Bring a large pot of water to a boil.

While the water is coming a boil, make the Brown Butter Sauce: Melt the butter in a large skillet over medium heat. Swirl to coat. Cook for 3–4 minutes until butter turns golden brown and brown specks appear at the bottom of the pan, stirring continuously (being careful not to allow the butter to burn). Allow the butter to cool for two minutes. Slowly pour in the chicken stock or broth, whisking frequently until combined. Whisk in the cream. Add the lemon juice, sage and Parmesan cheese, whisking until completely combined. Add salt and pepper to taste.

Drop the reserved raviolis into the boiling water, a few at a time, and cook until they float to the top, about 2–3 minutes. Drain the raviolis. Transfer them to the skillet and toss until they are evenly coated with sauce.

Garnish with sage leaves and Parmesan cheese, and serve.

COOK'S NOTE
In a rush? Buy store-bought butternut squash raviolis and toss with the sauce you make at home.

Indonesian Fried Rice Nasi Goreng

Nasi Goreng is considered to be the national dish of Indonesia and was praised by former U.S. President Barack Obama during his 2010 visit to the country. It's customary to serve food on banana leaves on special occasions in Indonesia. Serving this sweet and savory fried rice on banana leaves adds a special touch and will make any guest feel like a VIP.

Serves 4
Prep Time: 20 minutes
Cook Time: 27 minutes

3 eggs, beaten
3 tablespoons oil, divided
1 medium white onion, finely chopped
2 cloves garlic, minced
8 oz (250 g) boneless, skinless chicken breast or thigh, cut into strips
8 oz (226 g) shelled and deveined shrimp
1 teaspoon ground coriander
1 teaspoon cumin
3 cups (450 g) cooked and chilled white rice
3 tablespoons sweet soy sauce (*kecap manis*)
1–2 teaspoons chili garlic sauce (*sambal oelek*)
Salt and freshly ground black pepper, to taste
Banana leaves, for plating (optional)
Finely chopped green onions, scallions, green and white parts, for garnish

Heat a large non-stick skillet over medium heat. Spray with non-stick cooking spray. Pour the eggs into hot skillet. Cook until the eggs begin to set, lifting up the edges of the set eggs to allow the uncooked egg to contact the hot pan, about 1 minute. Flip the omelet in one piece and cook until fully set, about 30 seconds. Remove the omelet from skillet and slice it into 1/2-inch (1.2-cm) strips.

Heat the oil in a wok or large non-stick skillet over medium-high heat. Add the onion and garlic and stir-fry until the onion is softened, about 3–4 minutes. Add the chicken, shrimp, coriander and cumin and stir-fry for about 5 minutes. Add the chilled rice, sweet soy sauce, chili garlic sauce and omelet strips and stir-fry for 3–4 more minutes. Season to taste with salt and pepper. Garnish with green onions. Serve immediately on banana leaves, if using.

COOK'S NOTE
Optionally, place a fried egg on top of the rice before serving (called *nasi goreng istimewa* in Indonesian) which means "special fried rice." Indonesian sweet soy sauce (*kecap manis*) can be found at Asian markets. You can substitute with 1 part molasses and 2 parts soy sauce.

Persian Rice with Crunchy Crust Tadig

Persian stews are always eaten on a bed of fluffy basmati rice. Tadig refers to Persian rice cooked with a crispy bottom layer, and literally translates to "bottom of the pot." Tadig is a staple in Persian cooking. This crispy layer of rice is created through a delicate process. According to my Persian friend Mary, its aroma and flavor coupled with the satisfying crunch is what makes it the most fought over part of any Persian meal. This dish is the perfect accompaniment to the classic Persian Herb Stew *ghormeh sabzi* (see page 126 for the recipe).

Serves 4–6
Prep Time: 10 minutes + soaking time
Cook Time: 45 minutes

2 cups (400 g) uncooked basmati rice
4 tablespoons salt
8 cups (1.75 liters) water
4 tablespoons butter
3 teaspoons saffron, ground and soaked in 1/2 cup
   hot water in a covered dish for about 5 minutes

Rinse the rice in a pot with cold water 2 or 3 times until the water clears. Agitate gently so you don't break the grains. Carefully pour the water out of the pot.

Cover the rice with cool water so that the water level is 1-inch (2.5-cm) higher than the rice. Add the salt. Stir to combine and let the mixture soak for 1 hour. Carefully pour the water out of the pot.

Add the washed and soaked rice to a large pot and cover with water that reaches to a level roughly 1/4 inch above the level of the rice. Bring the contents to a boil, and then reduce the heat to low. Cook until the rice is tender, but still slightly firm (al dente), approximately 5 minutes. Remove from the heat.

Transfer 2 cups (300 g) of the cooked rice to a medium bowl and mix it with the saffron water until combined.

Melt the butter in a large non-stick pot over medium-high heat. Add the saffron rice to the pot, spreading it evenly. Add the remaining rice on top of the saffron rice. Using a wooden spoon, gently form the top layer of rice into a mound or pyramid shape, being careful not to overwork the rice into paste. Using the handle of the wooden spoon, poke 4–6 holes in the mound. insert a sliver of butter into each hole.

Wrap the pot lid in a clean kitchen towel and place on top of the pot. Reduce heat and simmer for 40–45 minutes. The rice will be fluffy and the bottom should be crispy, but not burnt. Flip the pot directly onto a serving dish, creating a rice cake with a crunchy crust on the bottom and sides. Serve with your favorite Persian stew.

COOK'S NOTE

The sign of properly prepared Persian rice is when you can see each individual grain in the finished dish, which is accomplished through gentle washing, and steaming with a cloth-wrapped lid.

Kimchi Fried Rice

I was shopping around Korea Town one day and stumbled upon a café that served Kimchi Fried Rice and was surprised to find melted mozzarella cheese intertwined with the rice and yummy sauce. I was immediately hooked, and ran home to create my own version. The cheese is a surprisingly delicious addition and it adds a gooey texture to this striking fusion dish with its pungent aromas of kimchi and soy sauce. It's all topped with a bright fried egg that is barely set, so that it oozes into the rice. Try it and I guarantee you'll be hooked too!

Serves 2
Prep Time: 15 minutes
Cook Time: 8–10 minutes

2 tablespoons oil, divided
1 large shallot, thinly sliced
2 cloves garlic, minced
1 cup (160 g) finely chopped kimchi
2 teaspoons soy sauce
2 teaspoons store-bought kimchi juice
1/2 cup (50 g) shredded mozzarella cheese
2 cups (300 g) cooked white rice (chilled overnight)
1 green onion (scallion), white and light green parts only, finely chopped
Salt and freshly ground black pepper, to taste
2 eggs
Sriracha sauce, for dotting

Heat 1 tablespoon of the oil in a wok or large non-stick skillet over medium-high heat. Add the shallot and garlic, and sauté until fragrant, about 1 minute. Turn the heat to high and mix in the kimchi and cook for 2 or 3 minutes, until the mixture begins to crisp on the edges. Add the remaining 1 tablespoon of oil and the soy sauce, kimchi juice, shredded cheese and rice and stir-fry, breaking up and incorporating the rice as you stir. Cook until the rice is warmed through and cheese is melted, about 2 minutes. Add the green onions and cook for 1 more minute. Season to taste with salt and pepper.

Just before serving, heat a lightly oiled skillet over medium heat. Cook the eggs sunny side up until beginning to set but still runny.

Transfer the rice to two bowls. Place a fried egg on top of each bowl. Dot the eggs with sriracha sauce. Pierce the egg yolk before serving if you wish so the yolk becomes a sauce for the rice. Serve immediately.

Leeann's Chicken Fried Rice

This is my late mother Leeann Chin's famous fried rice recipe that's been enjoyed by millions at her eponymous restaurant chain in Minnesota. It couldn't be simpler to make, but man, kids of all ages just can't get enough. This is a great one-pot dish on a busy weeknight, especially when you have rice leftover from take-out and a store-bought roast chicken in your fridge. The key to great fried rice is using rice that's been chilled overnight so the grains separate while they're being cooked. Add whatever meat, seafood or veggies you have on hand and make "everything-but-the-kitchen-sink" fried rice with this easy and delicious recipe.

Serves 4–6
Prep Time: 15 minutes
Cook Time: 4–5 minutes

2 eggs, slightly beaten
Salt and white pepper, to taste
3 tablespoons oil, divided
½ cup (40 g) sliced white button mushrooms
½ teaspoon salt
Dash of white pepper
3 cups (450 g) cooked white rice (chilled overnight)
1–2 tablespoons soy sauce, to taste
1 cup (100 g) bean sprouts, trimmed
½ cup (65 g) fresh or thawed frozen peas
2 cups (300 g) diced cooked chicken
2 green onions (scallions), finely chopped, plus more, for garnish

Season the eggs with salt and white pepper. Heat 1 tablespoon of the oil in a wok or large non-stick skillet over medium-high heat. Add the eggs and cook until scrambled but still moist. Remove the eggs from the pan and set aside.

Add the 1 tablespoon of the oil to the wok or skillet. Add the mushrooms, salt and pepper. Stir-fry for 1 minute. Add the remaining oil. Add the rice and stir-fry for 1 minute. Add the soy sauce and stir-fry until combined. Add the bean sprouts and peas and stir-fry for 1 minute. Add the reserved eggs, chicken and green onions and stir-fry for 30 seconds.

Garnish with more green onions (scallions) and serve immediately.

COOK'S NOTE
My mom always taught me to use white pepper in Chinese cuisine for its mellow flavor, but feel free to use freshly ground black pepper for this recipe.

Bowled Over—Grain & Noodle Bowls

Gochujang Noodle Bowl

This Gochujang Noodle Bowl recipe is included in my Asian Noodle Essentials course on Craftsy.com. Made with smoky-sweet-hot Gochujang Sauce (recipe on 33), it's earthy, fiery and delish! Tossed with stir-fried pork and placed on top of noodles, it's a fast and easy lunch or dinner that'll make you feel like you took a pit stop to Korea Town—but without any traffic and without getting out of your sweats (or jammies, often in my case)!

Serves 6
Prep Time: 20 minutes
Cook Time: 8 minutes

Gochujang Sauce (page 33)

12 oz (350 g) fresh egg noodles or 8 oz (250 g) dried spaghetti or linguini
1 tablespoon canola oil
1 clove garlic, minced
1 small shallot, thinly sliced
1 lb (500 g) ground pork or turkey
Finely chopped green onions (scallions), for garnish
Toasted sesame seeds, for garnish

Cook the noodles according to the package directions. Rinse and drain. Set aside.

While the noodles are cooking, make the Gochujang Sauce (see recipe on page 33).

Heat the oil in a wok or large non-stick skillet over medium-high heat. Add the garlic and shallot and sauté until fragrant, about 30 seconds. Add the ground pork or ground turkey and sauté for about 4–5 minutes, breaking it up as it cooks. Add the Gochujang Sauce and stir until meat is well coated, about 30 seconds. Divide the reserved noodles among six bowls. Pour the meat-sauce mixture evenly over each bowl. Garnish with green onions and sesame seeds and serve.

Whole Grain Veggie Burrito Bowl

I'm always looking for ways to get my family to eat more whole grains without a lot of groaning at the dinner table. This simple and delicious whole grain veggie bowl is reminiscent of my kids' favorite Mexican chain where you customize your order. I always get a bowl, my hubby a salad and my kids get burritos. Here, I combine the best of all worlds plus the addition of a knock-your-socks-off cool and spicy sauce. Fresh, flavorful and healthy, you'll want to skip the ordering line and make these bowls all the time.

Serves 4
Prep Time: 20 minutes
Cook Time: 1 hour

Chipotle Cream Sauce
8 oz (226 g) sour cream, brought to room
   temperature
1 clove garlic, minced
2 tablespoons finely chopped red onion
1 whole chipotle pepper in adobo sauce
   (canned), deseeded and chopped
1 teaspoon adobo sauce (from the
   chipotle-pepper-in-adobo-sauce can)
$1/2$ teaspoon ground cumin
$1/8$ teaspoon salt
1 tablespoon finely chopped fresh
   coriander (cilantro) leaves

1 cup (200 g) uncooked brown rice
2 cups (500 ml) vegetable broth
Juice of $1/2$ lime
1 tablespoon extra virgin olive oil
4 tablespoons finely chopped coriander
   leaves (cilantro), plus more, for garnish
Salt, to taste
3 cups (225 g) chopped romaine lettuce
1 cup (150 g) thawed frozen corn
One 15 oz (425 g) can black beans,
   drained and rinsed
$1/2$ cup (120 g) pico de gallo salsa
$1/2$ cup (50 g) Mexican blend shredded
   cheese or soy cheese
1 avocado, diced

COOK'S NOTE
Add some diced roast chicken or shrimp for a power punch of protein.

Place the rice in a fine mesh sieve and run cold water over it until the water runs clear. Place the rice in a covered pot with the vegetable broth and bring the mixture to a boil. Reduce to a simmer and keep covered until all of the liquid is absorbed, about 55–65 minutes.

While the rice is steaming, make the Chipotle Cream Sauce: Whisk all of the ingredients together in a small bowl. Set aside.

Transfer the cooked rice to a medium bowl and fluff with a fork. Add the lime juice, olive oil, cilantro and salt (to taste), and stir to combine.

To assemble the bowls, divide the rice mixture into serving 4 bowls. Top with lettuce, corn, black beans, pico de gallo, cheese and avocado.

Drizzled with Chipotle Cream Sauce and garnish with cilantro. Serve immediately.

Quinoa Bibimbap Bowl

Bibimbap is one of the most popular dishes in Korean cuisine. It literally translates as "mixed rice" and is topped with sautéed veggies and Gochujang Sauce. Here, I put a unique spin on this dish by swapping out the rice for quinoa, giving it an extra boost of plant-based protein. This low-carb bowl is brimming with garlicky flavors, crisp Asian slaw, finished with sweet and smoky gochujang sauce and topped with a gooey fried egg. My brother Bill and his friend John Harkness helped test this recipe and they exclaimed in unison, "SO YUM!"

Serves: 4
Prep Time: 30 minutes
Cook Time: 8–10 minutes

Asian Slaw

2 cups (178 g) shredded red cabbage
2 green onions (scallions), white and green parts, finely chopped
4 tablespoons shredded carrots
2 cloves garlic, minced
1 tablespoon soy sauce
1 tablespoon seasoned rice vinegar
2 teaspoons dark sesame oil
1 tablespoon sugar
2 teaspoons toasted sesame seeds
Salt and freshly ground black pepper, to taste

Bibimbap

4 teaspoons oil, divided
4 teaspoons minced garlic, divided
4 cups (120 g) fresh baby spinach
4 oz (113 g) sliced fresh shiitake mushrooms
1 cup (100 g) bean sprouts, trimmed
1$^1/_2$ teaspoons soy sauce
1 teaspoon dark sesame oil
4 eggs
2 cups (370 g) cooked quinoa
2 tablespoons toasted sesame seeds
Finely chopped green onions (scallions), white and green parts, for garnish

Gochujang Sauce (page 33) or store-bought

Make the Asian Slaw: Toss of all the slaw ingredients in a medium bowl until combined. Set aside.

Heat 2 teaspoons of the oil over medium-high heat in a large non-stick skillet. Add 2 teaspoons of the minced garlic and the spinach and sauté until wilted, 2–3 minutes. Remove from the pan and set aside.

Add the remaining 2 teaspoons of the oil to the pan. Add the remaining 2 teaspoon of minced garlic and sauté until fragrant, about 30 seconds. Add the mushrooms and bean sprouts and sauté for about 4 minutes or until mushrooms are tender. Transfer to a bowl and toss with the soy sauce and sesame oil.

Just before serving, heat a lightly oiled skillet over medium heat. Cook the eggs sunny side up and runny (or to desired doneness).

Divide the cooked quinoa among 4 bowls. Top with small mounds of the spinach, mushrooms and bean sprouts. Top with toasted sesame seeds, a fried egg, slaw and the green onions. Drizzle with Gochujang Sauce before serving.

COOK'S NOTE
The Gochujang Sauce will yield approximately 1 cup so halve the recipe for the bibimbap bowl or store the remainder covered in your fridge to drizzle on your favorite meat.

Ahi Tuna Poke Bowl

Your family will be "bowled over" by this fresh and healthy poke bowl recipe. Poke bowl joints have popped up all over LA, and it makes me so happy when my kids ask for poke over burgers or pizza. The expense of all those trips to our local fave poke spot started to add up, so we decided to start making them at home when we have the time. Make sure you ask for sushi grade tuna at your market and place it in your fridge as soon as you get home before using it. I think the poke toppings are the best part, so I include a big list of options. Feel free to mix and match to your liking!

Serves 4
Prep Time: 25 minutes + resting time + marinating time
Cook Time: 20 minutes

Sushi Rice

1 cup (200 g) uncooked sushi rice
1$^1/_2$ cups (375 ml) water
$^1/_4$ teaspoon salt
1$^1/_2$ tablespoons rice vinegar
2 teaspoons sugar

Sriracha Mayo

3 tablespoons mayo
1 tablespoon sriracha sauce

Poke

6 tablespoons soy sauce or tamari
2 tablespoons oil
1 tablespoon dark sesame oil
2 tablespoons honey
1 tablespoon sriracha sauce
1 teaspoon peeled and minced fresh ginger
2 green onions (scallions), white and green parts, finely chopped
Toasted black and/or white sesame seeds
1 lb (500 g) sushi-grade ahi tuna, diced into $^1/_4$-in (6-mm) pieces
1 avocado, diced, for topping

Additional Suggested Toppings

Diced cucumber
Edamame
Chopped green onions (scallions)
Diced mango
Diced pineapple
Seaweed salad
Sliced jalapeño pepper
Crispy garlic or onions
Furikake
Pickled Ginger

> ## COOK'S NOTE
> You can find *furikake* (a classic all-purpose Japanese seasoning made with dried seaweed and sesame seeds) at Japanese markets.

Make the **Sushi Rice:** Rinse the rice in a fine sieve until the water runs clear. Bring the water, rice and salt to a boil in a medium saucepan. Reduce the heat to low, cover and cook until the rice is tender and the water has been absorbed, about 20 minutes. Let sit, covered, 10 minutes.

Combine the vinegar, sugar and 1 teaspoon salt in a small microwave-safe bowl and microwave until the sugar is dissolved, 30 seconds to 1 minute. Stir and allow to cool. Transfer the rice into a large wooden or glass mixing bowl and add the vinegar mixture. Fold thoroughly to combine and coat each grain of rice with the mixture. Allow to cool to room temperature.

Make the **Sriracha Mayo:** Whisk together the mayonnaise and sriracha in a small bowl and set aside.

In a medium bowl, whisk together the soy sauce, oil, sesame oil, honey, sriracha sauce, ginger, green onions and sesame seeds. Add the tuna and toss to coat. Let the mixture sit in the fridge for at least 15 minutes or up to 1 hour.

Divide the sushi rice evenly among 4 bowls. Top with tuna poke, avocado and other desired toppings, if using. Drizzle with Sriracha Mayo and serve.

My mother taught us all about the symbolic foods to eat to usher in wealth, good fortune, prosperity and longevity in the new year.

LUNAR NEW YEAR

Every year, my mother pulled out all the stops for Lunar New Year while we were growing up in Minnesota. She taught us all about the symbolic foods to eat to usher in wealth, good fortune, prosperity and longevity in the new year. TV personality Jeannie Mai and her mom, Mama Mai join me for a special Lunar New Year celebration in highlighting auspicious recipes and centuries-old traditions.

Potstickers

Potstickers are customarily served during Lunar New Year to symbolize wealth and prosperity, as their shape resembles that of a gold ingot (an ancient form of Chinese currency). Serve these all year round and you're sure to feel prosperous—or at least your belly will!

  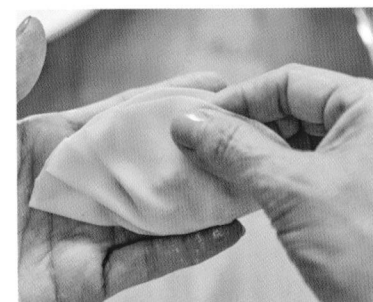

Serves 6–8
Prep Time: 20 minutes
Cook Time: 10 minutes

4 oz (100 g) napa cabbage, cut into thin strips
1½ teaspoons salt, divided
8 oz (250 g) ground pork or chicken
2 tablespoons finely chopped green onion (scallion), white and green parts
2 teaspoons dry white wine
½ teaspoon cornstarch
Dash of white pepper
20–30 store-bought potsticker wrappers
2–4 tablespoons oil, divided

Dipping Sauce
4 tablespoons soy sauce
1 teaspoon dark sesame oil
½ teaspoon sugar

Toss the cabbage with 1 teaspoon of the salt and set aside for 5 minutes. Roll the cabbage up in a clean dry dish towel. Twist the dish towel to squeeze out the excess moisture.

In a large bowl, mix the cabbage, pork or chicken, green onion, wine, cornstarch, the remaining ½ teaspoon of the salt and the pepper.

Place 1 tablespoon of the meat mixture in the center of the wrapper. Moisten the top edge of the wrapper with a bit of water. Lift up the edges of the circle and pinch several pleats to create a pouch to encase the mixture. Pinch the top together. Repeat with the remaining wrappers and filling.

Heat 1 tablespoon of the oil in a wok or skillet over medium high heat. Place 12 dumplings in a single layer in the wok or skillet and fry them for 2 minutes, or until the bottoms are golden brown. Add ½ cup (125 ml) of water and cover and cook for 6–7 minutes or until the water is absorbed. Repeat with the remaining dumplings.

Make the **Dipping Sauce**: Combine the soy sauce, sesame oil and sugar. Serve with dumplings.

> **COOK'S NOTE**
> If you can't find round dumpling wrappers, you can substitute square wonton wrappers. Just use a cookie cutter to create the round shape.

Long Life Noodles with Chicken

Noodles symbolize longevity, so they're always served during Lunar New Year and birthday celebrations. My mother always told me, "The longer the noodle, the longer the life!" You should also serve your noodles uncut for maximum longevity. This easy and delicious recipe filled with tender chicken and tender-crisp veggies is sure to be a hit in your family for years to come!

Serves 4
Prep Time: 20 minutes + marinating time
Cook Time: 5 minutes

8 oz (250 g) dried spaghetti, linguine or Chinese noodles
12 oz (350 g) boneless, skinless chicken breast, cut into bite-size pieces
1 teaspoon cornstarch
$1/_2$ teaspoon salt
$1/_8$ teaspoon white pepper
$3/_4$ cup (75 g) snow peas, tips and strings removed, julienned
3 tablespoons oil, divided
1 clove garlic, minced
1 red bell pepper, thinly sliced
$1/_2$ cup (50 g) bean sprouts
$1/_2$ cup (25 g) carrots, julienned
4 tablespoons soy sauce
1 teaspoon oyster sauce
1 teaspoon sesame oil
$1/_4$ teaspoon white pepper
$1/_8$ teaspoon sugar

Prepare the noodles according to the package directions. Rinse, drain and set aside.

Toss the chicken pieces with the cornstarch, salt and white pepper. Cover and refrigerate for 10 minutes.

Blanch the snow peas in boiling water, about 1 minute. Using a slotted spoon, transfer the pea pods to an ice bath for 1 minute. Drain and set aside.

Heat 1 tablespoon of the oil in a wok or large non-stick skillet over medium-high heat. Add the garlic and stir-fry until fragrant, about 30 seconds. Add the chicken and stir-fry until it turns white, about 2 minutes. Remove the chicken from the pan and set aside.

Add the remaining 2 tablespoons of oil. Add the red pepper and stir-fry for 1 minute. Add the bean sprouts, snow peas and carrots and stir-fry for 1 minute. Add the soy sauce, oyster sauce, sesame oil, white pepper and sugar, and stir-fry until blended, about 1 minute. Add the reserved chicken and stir-fry for 1 minute. Add the reserved noodles and toss until coated. Transfer to a platter and serve immediately.

Crispy Whole Fish with Ginger & Green Onion Sauce

The Chinese word for fish, *yu*, is the same word as that for "abundance," so we eat this for good luck and prosperity on Lunar New Year. The fish is marinated, battered and then flash fried, resulting in the most tender, flaky fish. Topped with a sizzling sauce, there's nothing quite like it.

Serves 4 as part of a multicourse meal
Prep Time: 30 minutes + marinating time
Cook Time: 15 minutes

Ginger-Green Onion Sauce
2 tablespoons oil
2 teaspoons peeled and minced fresh ginger
2 cloves garlic, minced
1/2 cup (125 ml) chicken stock or broth
4 tablespoons white vinegar
4 tablespoons soy sauce
1 tablespoon sugar
1 finely chopped green onion (scallion)

Crispy Whole Fish
1 1/2 lbs (750 g) whole tilapia, catfish or red snapper, well cleaned
2 1/8 teaspoons salt, divided
2 teaspoons peeled and minced fresh ginger
1/8 teaspoon sugar
2 teaspoons dark sesame oil
2 green onions (scallions), cut into 2-in (5-cm) lengths
4 tablespoons all-purpose flour
2 tablespoons cornstarch
1/4 teaspoon baking soda
4 tablespoons water
1/2 tablespoon oil
Oil, for frying

Make the **Ginger-Green Onion Sauce**: Heat the oil in a small saucepan over medium-high heat. Add the ginger and garlic and stir-fry for 1 minute. Add the chicken stock or broth, vinegar, soy sauce and sugar and bring to a boil. Remove from the heat and allow to cool. Add the chopped green onions when ready to serve.

Make the **Crispy Whole Fish**: Make 3 cuts across the fish, almost down to the bone. In a small bowl, combine 2 teaspoons of the salt, the ginger, sugar and the sesame oil and rub the inside and outside of the fish. Marinate for at least 20 minutes (if marinating for longer, cover and refrigerate). Stuff the fish cavity with the sliced green onions and place on a platter.

In a small bowl, combine the all-purpose flour, cornstarch, baking soda, water, oil and the remaining 1/8 teaspoon of the salt. Mix into a smooth batter and brush it over the fish.

Heat 2–3 inches (5–7.5 cm) of the oil in a wok or pot to 350°F (175°C). Deep-fry the fish for 6–7 minutes. Turn the fish over and fry for another 6–7 minutes until golden brown. Drain well on a paper towel-lined sheet pan. Place on a platter. Serve with the Ginger-Green Onion Sauce on the side.

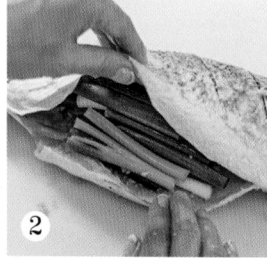
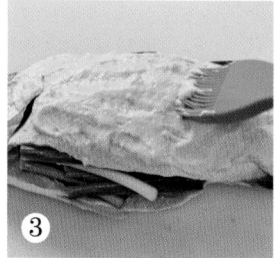
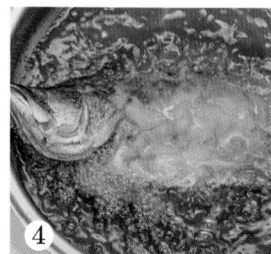

Mama Mai's Good Fortune Pork with Eggs

I was fortunate enough to have Jeannie Mai's mom, Mama Mai, contribute her famous Lunar New Year recipe that they made together on Jeannie's TV show *The Real*. Mama Mai told me her mom used to make it for her and now she makes it for her own kids to usher in good fortune in the New Year.

Serves 4
Prep Time: 20 minutes
Cook Time: About 70–80 minutes

14 oz (370 g) pork belly with skin
3 tablespoons caramel sauce (*nuoc mau*)
1 onion
3 cloves garlic
1 teaspoon salt
1 teaspoon pepper
2 tablespoons fish sauce (*nuoc mam*)
1 cup (250 ml) coconut water
4 eggs, hard boiled and peeled
Pinch of salt and freshly ground black pepper

Brown the pork belly in a large dutch oven or pot over medium-high heat. Add the caramel sauce, onion, garlic, salt and pepper and fish sauce for seasoning. Add coconut water and bring to a boil.

Reduce heat and simmer for about 1 hour.

While simmering, prepare the hard boiled eggs. Place the eggs in a single layer in a large saucepan. Add enough cold water to cover them by 1 inch (2.5 cm). Cover and quickly bring to a boil. Remove from the heat. Let stand for 15 minutes. Rinse eggs in cold water and place in ice water until completely cooled. Drain and peel.

During the last 15 minutes of cooking the pork, add the hard boiled eggs.

Place the pork belly mixture and the eggs on a bed of steaming hot white rice and serve immediately with pickled vegetables.

> **COOK'S NOTE**
> *Nuoc mau* (Vietnamese caramel sauce) can be purchased at Vietnamese markets or online.

Green Beans with Cashews

Vibrant, tender-crisp green beans are a wonderful addition to any Lunar New Year feast, especially when they're stir-fried with garlic, hoisin sauce and oyster sauce, and topped with crunchy cashews. Blanching the beans before stir-frying ensures that they come out bright green and juicy but not overcooked. If you can find Chinese long beans, substitute those, as they're more authentic and their length is another symbol of long life to usher in longevity at your Lunar New Year celebration.

Serves 4
Prep Time: 5 minutes
Cook Time: 3 minutes

1 lb (453 g) green beans, trimmed and cut into 2-in (5-cm) pieces
2 tablespoons oil
2 cloves garlic, minced
2 tablespoons hoisin sauce
2 tablespoons oyster sauce
2 oz (50 g) roasted cashews

Cook the green beans in boiling water until tender-crisp, about 5 minutes. Transfer the beans with a slotted spoon to an ice bath until cool. Drain. Set aside.

Heat the oil wok or skillet over medium-high heat. Add the green beans and stir-fry for 2 minutes. Add the garlic, hoisin sauce and oyster sauce and stir-fry for 30 seconds.

Garnish with roasted cashews. Dish out and serve immediately with steaming hot rice.

COOK'S NOTE
You may substitute green beans with Chinese long beans, but blanch them for just 2 minutes instead of 5 minutes.

Caramel-glazed Brandied Oranges

I taught a group of influencers how to make this at a blogger event celebrating Lunar New Year in Boston. They were blown away at how easy yet sophisticated this recipe is. It's light and refreshing but also decadent from the brandy and caramelized sugar. It's so simple that you can throw it together in just a few minutes. Chill the slices while you're enjoying dinner and then emerge from the kitchen with these beauties as the entertaining goddess that you are.

Serves 3–4
Prep Time: 15 minutes + chilling time
Cook Time: 5 minutes

3 large navel oranges
2 tablespoons brandy
1/2 cup (104 g) sugar

With a vegetable peeler, remove three 3-inch (7.6-cm) long strips of peel, about 3/4-inch (1.9-cm) wide each, from the oranges. Cut the strips lengthwise into very thin slivers.

Remove the remaining peel and white pith from oranges with a sharp paring knife. Slice the oranges into about 6 thin rounds and place them into a deep platter, overlapping slices. Sprinkle the orange slices with brandy and orange peel slivers.

In a small saucepan, cook the sugar over medium heat until it melts and becomes a deep amber color, stirring to dissolve any lumps. Drizzle the caramelized sugar over oranges. Place the platter in the refrigerator and chill the orange slices for 15–20 minutes and up to 2 hours before serving.

Join my family and friends—including Nate Berkus and Jeremiah Brent—as we kick off this 8-day Festival of Lights with traditional dishes.

HANUKKAH

Ours being a multicultural family, my kids always
look forward to the holiday season as they get to
celebrate both Hanukkah *and* Christmas. (I know,
what lucky kids!) Join my family and friends
as we kick off this 8-day Festival of Lights with
traditional dishes—including Hanukkah *sufganiyot*
(doughnuts), provided by renowned food writer,
Faye Levy.

Matzo Ball Soup

This recipe appeared in *Faye Levy's International Jewish Cookbook*. Matzo ball soup is prepared year-round in many Jewish households, and is perfect for Shabbat during Hanukkah week, when the weather is cold. Matzo balls are the subject of an ongoing controversy in many families—some people like them light and airy, while others prefer them more substantial. Faye Levy prefers light matzo balls, which require a very soft batter and gentle shaping. If the batter is firm enough so the balls can be formed in a neat, perfectly round shape, they will not be fluffy.

Serves 8
Prep Time: 1 hour and 15 minutes
Cook Time: 2 hours

Broth
2 lbs (1 kg) chicken wings or drumsticks
2 quarts (2 liters) cold water
1 whole onion, peeled
1 whole carrot, peeled
1 small parsnip, peeled (optional)
2 stalks celery, including leafy tops
5 sprigs parsley
3 sprigs fresh dill
Pinch of salt
Freshly ground black pepper, to taste
1 tablespoon chopped fresh dill

Matzo Balls
2 eggs
2 tablespoons vegetable oil
$\frac{1}{2}$ cup (58 g) matzo meal
$\frac{1}{2}$ teaspoon salt
$\frac{1}{2}$ teaspoon baking powder
1–2 tablespoons water or broth
2 quarts (2 liters) water salted with 1
  teaspoon kosher salt, for simmering

Make the **Broth**: Combine the chicken wings, water, onion, carrot, parsnip (if using), celery, parsley, dill sprigs and salt in a large saucepan and bring to a boil. Partially cover and simmer for 2 hours, skimming occasionally. If possible, make ahead and refrigerate, skimming off the excess fat once it's chilled.

Make the **Matzo Balls**: In a medium-sized bowl, lightly beat the eggs with the oil. Add the matzo meal, salt and baking powder and stir until smooth. Stir in the water or broth. Let the mixture stand for 20 minutes while the matzo meal absorbs the liquid.

Bring the salted water to a boil. While the water is heating, with wet hands, take about 1 teaspoon of matzo ball mixture and roll it into a ball between your palms; the mixture will be very soft. Set the balls on a plate. With a rubber spatula, carefully slide the balls into the boiling water. Cover and simmer the matzo balls over low heat for 30 minutes or until firm. Keep covered to keep them warm until ready to serve.

To serve the soup, remove the chicken wings, onion, celery, parsnip, parsley and dill sprigs. Reheat the broth to a simmer. Add pepper, stir in the chopped dill and taste the broth for seasoning. Add a few carrot slices to each bowl. Add a few matzo balls to each bowl with a slotted spoon. Serve hot.

Potato Latkes

Faye Levy contributed this recipe, which appeared in her book, *Jewish Cooking for Dummies*. She notes that these lacy, crisp potato pancakes are always a hit at Hanukkah parties, dinners or as a savory snack. Some grate the potatoes by hand but Faye uses a food processor to save time. Serve them with their traditional partners—applesauce and sour cream. Yogurt is a good accompaniment too.

Serves 4
Prep Time: 30 minutes
Cook Time: 30 minutes

1¼ lbs (600 g) large potatoes (preferably baking potatoes), peeled
1 medium onion
1 egg
1 teaspoon salt
¼–½ teaspoon ground white pepper, to taste
2 tablespoons all-purpose flour
½ teaspoon baking powder
½ cup (125 ml) vegetable oil, plus more if needed

Suggested Toppings
Applesauce
Sour cream
Chopped chives
Yogurt

Using the coarse grating disc of a food processor or large holes of a hand grater, grate the potatoes and onion, alternating them to mix. Transfer them to a colander. Squeeze the mixture by handfuls to press out as much liquid as possible; discard the liquid.

Put the potato-onion mixture in a bowl. Add the egg, salt, pepper, flour and baking powder.

Heat the oil in a deep, heavy 10 to 12-inch (25 to 30-cm) skillet over medium heat. For each pancake, add about 2 tablespoons of potato mixture to the pan. Flatten the pancake with the back of a spoon to make a 2½-inch (6.3-cm) disc. Fry for 4–5 minutes. Using 2 pancake turners, turn the latkes carefully. Fry the second side for about 4 minutes, or until the pancake is golden brown and crisp. Drain on a paper towel-lined plate.

Stir the potato mixture before frying each new batch. If all the oil is absorbed during frying, add 2 or 3 tablespoons more oil to the pan. Serve hot with your preferred toppings.

COOK'S NOTE

Here are Faye's tips for making potato latkes ahead: fry them and put them on a cookie sheet, then refrigerate or freeze them. Once they are frozen, you can transfer them to a freezer bag. Before serving, preheat the oven to 450°F (232°C) and, if your latkes are frozen, remove them from the freezer so they partially thaw. Bake the refrigerated or frozen latkes on an ungreased cookie sheet for about 5 minutes or until they are hot. Frying potato latkes in advance is better than making the batter ahead, as the raw potatoes in the batter tend to discolor.

Apple-cinnamon Noodle Kugel with Sour Cream

Faye Levy contributed this recipe, which appeared in her book, *1,000 Jewish Recipes*. This kugel makes a delightful dairy entrée for Hanukkah or Shavuot. Delicately sweet and rich in flavor, it's also great for Sunday brunch. An added benefit is that it's an easy kugel to make. Serve it with sour cream, its traditional accompaniment.

Serves 8
Prep Time: About 45 minutes
Cook Time: About 1 hour

14 oz (396 g) medium egg noodles
Pinch of salt
4 tablespoons melted butter, divided
Pinch of salt
1 cup (240 g) sour cream
4 large eggs
6 tablespoons sugar, divided
1 teaspoon vanilla extract
$1^1/_2$ teaspoons ground cinnamon, divided
3 Golden Delicious apples (about $1^1/_2$ lbs / 750 g)
Sour cream, for serving

Preheat the oven to 350°F (175°C). Grease a 13 x 9 x 2-inch (33 x 23 x 5-cm) baking dish. Cook the noodles in a large pot of boiling salted water until barely tender, about 5 minutes. Drain, rinse with cold water, and drain well.

Transfer the noodles to a large bowl. Separate them with your fingers. Add 3 tablespoons of the melted butter and a pinch of salt and mix well. Stir in the sour cream, eggs, 2 tablespoons of the sugar and the vanilla. Mix the remaining 4 tablespoons of the sugar with 1 teaspoon of cinnamon in a bowl and set aside.

Peel the apples, halve and core them, and cut them in thin slices. Mix half the apples with the noodle mixture.

Add half of the noodle mixture to the greased baking dish. Top with the remaining apples in an even layer and sprinkle them with the cinnamon mixture. Top with the remaining noodle mixture. and spread it gently to cover the apples. Sprinkle with the remaining $1/_2$ teaspoon of the cinnamon, and then with the remaining 1 tablespoon of melted butter. Cover the dish with foil and bake for 30 minutes. Uncover and continue baking for another 15–20 minutes or until set. Serve hot or warm.

Brisket, American-Jewish Style

This recipe is from Faye Levy. It first appeared in *Faye Levy's International Jewish Cookbook*. In the US, brisket has been associated with Jewish cooking, perhaps because Jewish cooks have developed cooking methods and tasty recipes for using this cut of meat. Brisket is sometimes cooked in stew, but the image that comes to mind most often is of brisket that is roasted slowly as one succulent piece, either pot-roasted on top of the stove or cooked in a covered pan in the oven, as below.

Serves 5 or 6
Prep Time: About 1 hour + marinating time
Cook Time: About 2¾ hours

4 large cloves garlic, minced
¾ teaspoon freshly ground black pepper
1 teaspoon paprika
1 teaspoon salt, plus more, to taste (if using potatoes)
1 teaspoon vegetable oil
One 3-lb (1.5-kg) brisket, excess fat trimmed
2 onions, sliced
1 cup (235 g) ketchup
½ cup (125 ml) water, plus more, if needed
2 lbs (1 kg) large baking potatoes (optional)

Mix the garlic, pepper, paprika, salt and oil into a paste and rub it into the meat. Let stand about ½ hour. Preheat the oven to 400°F (200°C).

Put the onions in a small roasting pan and top with the brisket, fat side up. Cover with foil and roast for 15 minutes. Reduce the oven temperature to 325°F (160°C). Pour the ketchup over the brisket and spread lightly. Add the water to the pan, pouring it around, not over, meat. Cover and cook for 1½ hours, occasionally adding a few tablespoons water to the pan if it becomes dry.

Peel and quarter the potatoes, if using. Add them to the pan around the meat. Baste the meat and potatoes with the pan juices and sprinkle the potatoes lightly with salt. Cover and roast for 45 minutes; turn the potatoes over and roast 45 minutes longer or until the brisket and potatoes are very tender when pierced with a fork.

If you are not adding potatoes: Baste the meat after cooking it for 1½ hours. Continue cooking for 1½ hours longer or until the meat is very tender when pierced with a fork.

Remove the meat to a cutting board, ketchup side up. Remove the onions with slotted spoon. Put ½ cup (75 g) of the onions in a medium saucepan and add the roasting juices from meat. Boil the mixture for about 5 minutes or until the sauce is well flavored and slightly thickened. Taste the sauce and adjust seasoning. If desired, heat the remaining onions in a separate small saucepan to serve on the side.

With a thin-bladed sharp knife, carve the meat crosswise into thin slices. Serve the sauce and onions separately.

COOK'S NOTES
Flavoring brisket with ketchup adds a tangy note. Faye Levy learned this method from her aunt, Sylvia Saks.

You can roast potatoes around the brisket. Or, if you are preparing brisket for Hanukkah, accompany it with potato pancakes.

Israeli Hanukkah "Doughnuts" Sufganiyot

Faye Levy contributed this recipe, which appeared in *Faye Levy's International Jewish Cookbook*. In Israel *sufganiyot* are the most popular Hanukkah food. Fluffy doughnuts without holes similar to these are known by many names—Faye Levy has come across them as Bismarck jelly doughnuts, *krapfen*, and in France as *boules de Berlin* (Berlin balls). Probably Austrian bakers brought them to Israel. Other common flavorings for these doughnuts, besides the brandy used in this recipe, are vanilla, grated lemon rind, cinnamon and nutmeg.

Makes 14 (more if you use the scraps too)
Prep Time: About 2 hours + rising time
Cook Time: 30 minutes

3/4 cup (185 ml) lukewarm water, divided
2 envelopes active dry yeast (1/4 oz/ 7 g each)
4 tablespoons sugar, divided
4 cups (480 g) all-purpose flour, plus 2 tablespoons more, if necessary
2 large eggs
2 large egg yolks
7 tablespoons unsalted butter or margarine, room temperature
2 tablespoons brandy
2 teaspoons salt
4 tablespoons apricot or strawberry preserves
At least 5 cups (1.25 liters) vegetable oil (for deep frying)
Sifted confectioners' sugar, for sprinkling

> **COOK'S NOTE**
> Don't serve the doughnuts immediately after frying—the filling will be boiling hot!

Pour 1/2 cup (125 ml) of the lukewarm water into a small bowl. Sprinkle the yeast on top and add 1 teaspoon of the sugar. Let stand 10 minutes.

Meanwhile, add the flour to a mixer bowl or another large bowl. Make a well in the center. Add the remaining sugar and the eggs, egg yolks, butter, brandy, the remaining lukewarm water and the salt. Mix with a mixer dough hook or a wooden spoon until the ingredients are combined. Add the yeast mixture. Mix with the dough hook at low speed or with the spoon until the ingredients come together into a dough. Beat at medium speed, scraping the dough down occasionally, for 5 minutes; or knead it by hand for 5 minutes. If the dough is very sticky, add 2 tablespoons of flour. Knead 5–10 minutes more until very smooth.

Put the dough in a clean oiled bowl, and turn the dough to coat it with oil. Cover the bowl with a damp cloth and let the dough rise in a warm place for 1–1 1/2 hours, or until doubled in volume.

On a floured surface, roll out half of the dough until it is 1/4-inch (6-mm) thick, flouring it occasionally. Using a 2 1/2 to 3-inch (6.5 to 7.5-cm) cutter, cut the dough into rounds. Put 1/2 teaspoon apricot or strawberry preserves on the center of half of them. Brush the rim of a round holding preserves lightly with water. Set a plain round on top. With floured fingers, press the dough firmly all around to seal it. Transfer this "sandwich" immediately to a floured tray. If it has stretched out into an oval, plump it gently back into a round shape. Continue with the remaining dough. Cover the pastries with a slightly damp cloth and let them rise in a warm place for 1/2 hour.

If you want to use the scraps of dough, knead them, put them in an oiled bowl, cover with a damp cloth and let stand for about 1/2 hour.

Add several inches of oil for deep frying to a large heavy saucepan or dutch oven. Do not fill the pan more than half full with oil. Heat the oil over medium heat until it reaches 350°F (175°C). If a deep-fry thermometer is not available, heat the oil until it bubbles gently around a small piece of dough added to it. Add 4 doughnuts at a time, or enough to fill the pan without crowding. Adjust the heat as you fry to maintain the temperature. Fry the doughnuts for about 3 minutes on each side, or until golden brown. Drain on paper towels. Pat the tops gently with paper towels to absorb the excess oil.

Make more doughnuts with the scraps if you like; they won't be as light, but will still be good.

Serve the doughnuts warm or at room temperature, sprinkled with confectioners' sugar.

Join me and my Greek besties, Christos Garkinos and Debbie Matenopoulos at our Greek Easter feast.

GREEK EASTER

Greek Easter is considered to be the most significant time in the Greek Orthodox Church calendar. It's celebrated with a large family feast filled with avgolemono soup, roast lamb and spanakopita, among other delicious dishes. Join me and my Greek besties, Christos Garkinos and Debbie Matenopoulos at our Greek Easter feast featuring recipes from Debbie's cookbook, *It's All Greek to Me*.

Classic Roast Leg of Lamb with Potatoes

Arni kai Patates

This recipe is contributed by TV personality Debbie Matenopoulos from her cookbook, *It's All Greek to Me*. Although Debbie was a vegetarian for 12 years, she still craved lamb. She has such fond memories of her father roasting a whole lamb on a spit in their backyard, which is a traditional selection for Greek Easter. Chances are you don't have enough space or time to roast an entire lamb, so try this recipe for roasted leg of lamb, which is just as juicy and delectable.

Serves 6 to 8
Prep Time: 20 minutes + resting time
Cook Time: 2–2½ hours

½ cup (125 ml) freshly squeezed lemon juice
  (3–4 lemons)
6 tablespoons extra virgin olive oil
1 tablespoon finely chopped fresh rosemary,
  plus 16 individual leaves, divided
1 tablespoon dried oregano
1 tablespoon plus ½ teaspoon sea salt,
  divided
1¼ teaspoons freshly ground black pepper,
  divided
15–20 small new potatoes, scrubbed clean
  and dried
1 bone-in leg of lamb, 7–8 lbs (3.1–3.6 kg),
  aitchbone removed by butcher, rinsed,
  patted dry, fat trimmed to ¼-in (6-mm)
  thick
4 cloves garlic, peeled and sliced into
  quarters

Whisk together the lemon juice, 4 tablespoons of the extra virgin olive oil, the chopped rosemary, oregano, 1 tablespoon of the salt, and 1 teaspoon of the pepper. Set aside.

Lightly oil a large roasting pan. Add the potatoes to the pan, and toss them with the remaining 2 tablespoons of the olive oil and the remaining ½ teaspoon of salt and the remaining ¼ teaspoon of the pepper.

Make 16 evenly distributed ¾-inch (1.9-cm) deep slits in the lamb (covering both sides) with a sharp paring knife. Insert a slice of garlic and 1 leaf of the rosemary into each slit. Place the leg of lamb, fat side up, on top of the potatoes. Spread the herb mixture all over the lamb, allowing any excess to drip down and coat the potatoes. Set aside to rest at room temperature for 30 minutes.

Preheat the oven to 425°F (220°C).

Roast the lamb and potatoes for 20 minutes. Reduce the temperature to 350°F (175°C) and continue to cook until a meat thermometer inserted 2 inches into the thickest part of the roast (do not touch the bone) reads between 135°F (57°C) and 140°F (60°C) (medium rare), 1½ to 2 hours. Baste every 20 minutes with the pan juices.

When the lamb is done, remove the pan from the oven, and transfer the meat to a large cutting board or platter. Cover with aluminum foil, and set aside to rest for 20 minutes before carving. Meanwhile, transfer the potatoes to a serving bowl with slotted spoon, and cover them with foil. Pour the pan juices into a glass measuring cup. Skim and discard any fat that floats to the surface. Keep the juices warm while the lamb rests, adding any juices that drip from the resting meat to the measuring cup.

Carve the lamb, slicing against the grain. Serve with the potatoes, drizzled with the reserved pan juices (reheated if necessary).

Baklava

This recipe is contributed by TV personality Debbie Matenopoulos from her cookbook, *It's All Greek to Me*. Here is her family's "secret recipe" for the best Baklava ever. Rolling it—as described below, instead of baking it in a flat pan—imparts a light flakiness and just the right amount of the honey syrup running throughout. Around the holiday season, when she was growing up, her mom would make big batches of this so that her sister, brother, and she could give platters of it to their teachers. Needless to say, every new school year, teachers were very excited to see one of the Matenopoulos kids on their class rosters!

Makes approximately 39 pieces
Prep Time: 40 minutes + resting time
Cook Time: 66–68 minutes

Baklava
5 cups (600 g) finely chopped walnuts
2 tablespoons granulated sugar
2 teaspoons ground cinnamon
One 1-lb (453-g) 18-sheet package phyllo dough
   (13 x 18-in / 33 x 45-cm), thawed
1 cup (113 g) (2 sticks) unsalted butter, melted

Syrup
2 cups (400 g) sugar
2 cups (500 ml) water
1 cup (340 g) honey
2 tablespoons freshly squeezed lemon juice
   (1 lemon)
One 2-in (5-cm) wide piece fresh lemon peel

Preheat the oven to 325°F (160°C).

Make the **Baklava**: In a medium mixing bowl, stir together the walnuts, sugar and cinnamon, and set aside.

Working quickly, and keeping the unused phyllo sheets covered, lay out 1 sheet of phyllo on a clean flat surface. Lightly brush the phyllo sheet with the melted butter. Cover with a second phyllo sheet, and butter. Sprinkle about ½ cup (65 g) of the walnut mixture over the top sheet. Repeat the process with 2 more sheets of phyllo, then again with a final 2 phyllo sheets. You will have used 6 sheets of phyllo (three 2-sheet layers). Starting at the long end (the 18-in /45-cm side), roll the layered phyllo sheets up into a fat roll. Brush the seam with butter to seal. Repeat the entire process twice more. One phyllo dough package will make 3 rolls.

Using a large, very sharp knife, cut the rolls into 1-inch (2.5-cm) pieces. Lay the pieces cut side down on two large ungreased rimmed baking sheets. Bake for 20 minutes. Remove the baking sheets from the oven.

Using a large spatula or tongs, quickly flip the baklava pieces over. Return the baking sheets to the oven, and bake 20 minutes more, or until cooked through, golden and flaky.

While the baklava is baking, make the **Syrup**: Combine all of the syrup ingredients except the lemon juice in a medium, nonreactive saucepan over medium-high heat. Bring the mixture to a boil, reduce the heat, and simmer for 12 minutes, stirring occasionally. After 12 minutes, stir in the lemon juice, and cook 3 more minutes. Remove from the heat, and carefully remove and discard the lemon peel. Let the syrup cool slightly.

Remove the baklava from the oven, and slowly pour the warm syrup over the pieces on the cookie sheets. Let stand 1 hour to soak up the syrup.

Transfer to individual cupcake wrappers, if desired, and serve. The baklava will keep, covered loosely, at room temperature for up to 1 week.

> ## COOK'S NOTES
> To make a vegan baklava, substitute a vegan butter (like Earth Balance Vegan Buttery Sticks) for the dairy butter. Use maple sugar or organic (vegan) sugar in place of the honey, if desired.

Greek Easter Bread Tsoureki

This recipe is contributed by TV personality Debbie Matenopoulos from her cookbook, *It's All Greek to Me*. Every Easter, Debbie's mom makes a huge batch of *tsoureki* for us to enjoy and to give away to friends and family. Easter is one of her mom's favorite days, because she can share this bread, which she makes with so much love, with those she cares for. With her mom's heart and spirit in mind, this recipe yields 7–8 loaves so that you, too, can give them away to those you love.

Makes 7 to 8 loaves
Prep Time: 45–60 minutes + resting and rising time
Cook Time: About 40 minutes

9¹/₂ cups (1.15 kg) all-purpose flour
3 envelopes active dry yeast (¹/₄ oz / 7 g each)
¹/₂ cup (125 ml) warm water (110°F / 43°C)
2 cups (500 ml) milk
1 cup (113 g) (2 sticks) unsalted butter at room temperature
1¹/₂ cups (300 g) sugar
¹/₄ teaspoon sea salt
5 large eggs, divided
¹/₄ teaspoon room-temperature water
1 tablespoon sesame seeds or 4–6 tablespoons sliced almonds (optional)

Sift the flour into a very large wooden or plastic salad bowl. Make a small well in the center of the flour. Dissolve the yeast in the warm water, and slowly pour the yeast mixture into the well in the flour. With a small spoon, mix a little bit of the flour into the yeast and water mixture, but keep the yeast mixture liquid and not too thick. Cover the bowl with a kitchen towel, and set it in a warm place for 20 minutes.

Heat the milk in a medium saucepan set over medium heat until it just begins to boil. Remove from the heat, and add the butter, sugar and salt. Allow the butter to melt, and stir the contents of the saucepan together to combine the mixture. Set aside to cool slightly.

After the flour and yeast mixture has remained covered for 20 minutes, beat together 4 of the eggs. Remove the towel from the bowl. Very slowly pour half of the warm milk mixture around the edges of the bowl, stirring the flour into the milk mixture with a wooden spoon. Begin to incorporate the yeast as you stir. Then, stir half of the beaten eggs into the flour mixture in the same manner. Follow with the remaining milk, then with the remaining beaten eggs. Once everything has just come together, begin to knead the dough in the bowl. It will be very sticky at first, but as you work the dough, it will come together and stop sticking to your hands. Knead the dough for 13–15 minutes, until it becomes smooth and soft and no longer sticks to your fingers or the sides of the bowl.

Put the entire bowl into a large plastic bag. Cover the bowl with a large towel or a small blanket, and set it in a warm place, away from any air conditioning or drafts. Debbie's mom actually set it on the sofa in the living room—where, by the way, she and her siblings were never allowed as children! Let the dough rise for 1 hour.

After 1 hour, remove the dough from the bag. Set out a large wooden cutting board to assemble the loaves. Warm up 2 large baking sheets by running them under very warm water. Dry them well, and line them with unbleached parchment paper.

Pull a softball-size piece of dough from the bowl,

cut it, and put it on the cutting board. Cut the small piece of dough into 3 equal pieces. Using your hands, roll the 3 pieces of dough into 3 even logs, each 1 foot (30 cm) in length. If the dough gets too sticky, coat your hands with a little olive oil. Braid the 3 logs together, all the way to the end, and gently pinch the ends together to form loaves. Repeat this braiding process with the remaining dough. Transfer the braided dough to the prepared cookie sheets. Put each baking sheet into its own plastic bag, cover with a towel or blanket, and set aside in a warm place for the dough to rise again for 1 hour.

Preheat the oven to 350°F (175°C).

After the loaves have risen, remove the cookie sheets from the bags. Beat the remaining egg with the 1/4 teaspoon of water to create an egg wash. Using a large pastry brush, brush each loaf evenly with the egg wash, and then sprinkle each loaf evenly with the sesame seeds or sliced almonds. Put the cookie sheets in the preheated oven. Bake until the tops are richly golden and the loaves sound hollow when tapped, 35–40 minutes. Watch closely for the last couple of minutes.

Remove the loaves from the oven, and immediately transfer them to kitchen or paper towels on the counter to cool. When the loaves are cool, you can serve the bread right away or put them into decorative plastic bags to give as gifts.

Spinach Feta Pie Spanakopita

This recipe is contributed by TV personality Debbie Matenopoulos from her cookbook, *It's All Greek to Me*. She loves sharing this Greek favorite with her friends. Over the years she has mastered making an excellent spanakopita, and you'd be hard pressed to find someone working in entertainment news in Hollywood who wouldn't agree that it's pretty darn delicious. Still, she admits that hers will never be quite as good as her mother's. Her mom has the magic touch. Practice makes perfect, and while her mom's is still the best, yours will be pretty fantastic too!

Serves 8 to 10
Prep Time: 40 minutes
Cook Time: 55–65 minutes

¹/₂ cup (125 ml) extra virgin olive oil, divided, plus more for baking pan
1 bunch green onions (scallions), white and green parts, thinly sliced
¹/₂ large sweet onion, finely chopped
2 lbs (1 kg) fresh spinach, coarse stems removed, washed in several changes of cold water, drained and chopped
1 lb (500 g) brine-packed Greek feta
1 cup (10 g) finely chopped fresh dill
4 large eggs, beaten
¹/₄ teaspoon freshly ground black pepper
One 1-lb (453-g) 18-sheet package phyllo dough (13 x 18-in/33 x 45-cm), thawed

Preheat the oven to 350°F (175°C). Oil a 9 x 13-inch (23 x 33-cm) baking pan.

Heat 2 tablespoons of the extra virgin olive oil in a large pot over medium heat. Add the green onions and the sweet onion, and sauté until translucent, about 5–6 minutes. Add the spinach, and sauté until just wilted. Remove from heat, let cool slightly, and transfer to a fine-mesh strainer. Cool further, and then squeeze as much excess water as possible from the spinach, and transfer it to a large mixing bowl.

COOK'S NOTE

As with most phyllo pies, spanakopita can be made with either melted butter or extra virgin olive oil. Debbie finds the olive oil version to be a lighter, more healthful dish, but she also loves to indulge in her mom's decadent, traditional version once in a while. To make it her mom's way, replace the extra virgin olive oil used to brush the phyllo with 6 tablespoons of melted butter, add an extra egg and use 1¹/₂ lbs (750 g) of feta instead of 1 lb (500 g). It's over-the-top delicious!

Crumble the feta into small pieces, and add it to the spinach mixture. Add the dill, and mix gently to combine. Add the eggs and pepper. Mix well to combine with clean hands or a silicone spatula.

Roll the phyllo dough out on a flat surface, working quickly and keeping it covered to prevent it from drying out. Place 2 phyllo sheets into the baking pan at a time, centering them and letting the edges hang over the sides. Brush the top sheet of each 2-sheet layer with a little of the remaining olive oil, but do not brush the overhanging edges. Continue in this manner until you have used 10 of the phyllo dough sheets. Spread the spinach-feta mixture evenly over the phyllo dough layers in the prepared dish. Fold the overhanging phyllo dough over the filling, and then continue to layer the phyllo dough, brushing each 2-sheet layer with olive oil, until you have used all of the dough. Trim the top layers of phyllo to fit the pan. Slowly pour the remaining olive oil on top, and spread evenly.

Before baking, using a large knife, very carefully score the pie into 8–10 pieces, cutting through the top layers just until you reach the filling. Precutting makes it much easier to serve, as the phyllo dough becomes crisp and very fragile after baking.

Bake 50–60 minutes, or until the top is golden brown and flaky. Watch closely for the last couple of minutes.

Cool for 10 minutes, and then slice the precut pieces all the way through, and serve.

Greek Chicken Soup   Kotosoupa Avgolemono

This recipe is contributed by TV personality Debbie Matenopoulos from her cookbook, *It's All Greek to Me*. Not only is this chicken soup super delicious, it is believed to have magical curative powers. Debbie's mom, along with every other Greek mother she knows, refers to this delicious soup as "Greek penicillin." We have to be honest with you—it really does the trick! Give it a try, especially if you're not feeling well.

Serves 6
Prep Time: 30 minutes
Cook Time: About 1 hour + 45 minutes

Soup
1 whole chicken, about 4 lbs (2 kg), skin removed
12 cups (2.75 liters) water
1 onion, peeled and cut into quarters
2 teaspoons sea salt
3/4 teaspoon freshly ground black pepper
2 bay leaves
1/2 cup (100 g) uncooked long-grain white rice or orzo

Egg Lemon Sauce
2 large eggs
1/4 cup (175 ml) plus 2 tablespoons freshly squeezed lemon juice (2–3 lemons)
1 cup (250 ml) hot chicken stock (not boiling, taken from the soup)

Rinse the chicken very well, inside and out, under cold water. Add the water, chicken, onion, salt, pepper and bay leaves to a large stockpot. Bring to a boil over medium-high heat. Skim any scum or foam that rises to the top. When foam stops rising to the top, reduce the heat to low and simmer, partially covered, until the chicken is falling off the bone, about 1 1/2 hours.

Remove the chicken from the pot, and set aside to cool.

Strain the broth through a fine-mesh sieve into a large bowl. Remove 1 cup (250 ml) of the stock and set aside. Return the strained stock to the pot, and return it to a boil over medium-high heat. Stir in the rice or orzo, reduce heat to medium, and simmer, uncovered, until it is tender, about 15 minutes.

Meanwhile, remove the chicken meat from the bones, and shred it into small pieces. Return the shredded chicken to the pot, and reduce the heat to medium. Simmer the soup until the chicken is warmed through. Remove from the heat.

Make the **Egg Lemon Sauce**: In a medium saucepan, beat the eggs with a whisk until they are frothy. Gradually whisk in the lemon juice until combined. Slowly add the reserve 1 cup (250 ml) hot stock (from the soup you just made), a little at a time, being careful not to add it too quickly (see Cook's Note) and stirring constantly.

Slowly stir the sauce back into the remaining chicken broth, mixing well so as not to scramble the eggs. Do not boil again after the sauce has been added.

Taste and adjust seasonings, if necessary. Serve immediately.

COOK'S NOTE
Slowly incorporating the hot broth into the egg mixture while whisking vigorously is a technique called tempering. For best results, have your eggs at room temperature and the broth hot but not boiling. Adding the broth too quickly will result in a wet mess of scrambled eggs. Don't be intimidated! Do it once, and you will forever have a knack for tempering.

Cinco de Mayo is celebrated all over the world, and here in Los Angeles, the tequila is always plentiful.

CINCO DE MAYO

In case you didn't know, Cinco de Mayo celebrates Mexico's victory over France in the 1800s during the Franco-Mexican War. Cinco de Mayo is celebrated all over the world, and here in Los Angeles, the tequila is always plentiful. Come celebrate with me and my dear friend and cookbook author Jeffrey Saad at our Mexican fiesta, and savor authentic Mexican recipes with your family and friends!

Cumin-spiced Tortilla Soup with Pork

"Mexican comfort food" is what jumped to mind when Jeffrey shared this recipe and I made it for my family. We loved the creamy texture and flavor that comes from puréeing the tortilla right into the broth! Our house was filled with intoxicating aromas from the cumin, chili peppers and splash of lime juice, and every taste was the ultimate spoonful of Mexican tortilla chicken soup for the soul!

Serves 3
Prep Time: 15 minutes
Cook Time: 26–46 minutes

$1/2$ teaspoon cumin seed
4 oz (100 g) pork shoulder or tenderloin
$1^3/4$ teaspoons salt, divided
Freshly ground black pepper, to taste
1 tablespoon oil
$3/4$ cup (86 g) thinly sliced white onions
1 clove garlic, roughly chopped
$1/2$ teaspoon dried Mexican oregano
3 cups (750 ml) chicken stock or broth
One 6-in (15-cm) corn tortilla
1 guajillo chili pepper, stemmed and deseeded or $1/4$ oz (10 g) ground guajillo chili pepper
$1/2$ ancho chili, stemmed and deseeded or $1/2$ oz (15 g) ground ancho chili pepper
4 tablespoons freshly squeezed lime juice
$1/2$ cup (85 g) pinto beans, rinsed and drained

Garnishes
6 tortilla chips, crushed
$1^1/2$ tablespoons grated cotija cheese or grated Parmesan cheese
4 tablespoons roughly chopped fresh coriander leaves (cilantro)
$1/2$ avocado, cut into 8 slices

COOK'S NOTE
Substitute whole cumin seeds with ground cumin and skip the grinding step if whole cumin seeds aren't available.

Grind the cumin seed to a rough, sandy texture using a mortar and pestle or a coffee grinder. Rub the cumin all over the pork, coating it evenly. Season with $3/4$ teaspoon of the salt and pepper to taste.

Sauté the pork and onions together: Heat the oil over medium-high heat in a large dutch oven or large pot (large enough to brown the pork and onions at the same time), Place the pork on one side of the dutch oven or pot. Sauté, flipping frequently, until golden brown on both sides, about 6 minutes.

Meanwhile, add the onions to the other side of the dutch oven or pot (being careful not to overcrowd, as the pork will then braise instead of sauté). Once the pork and onions are browned, add the garlic and oregano, and stir to combine until fragrant. Add the chicken stock or broth and $1/4$ teaspoon of the salt, and bring to a boil. Reduce the heat and simmer.

Add the whole corn tortilla. Cover and continue simmering on low. Add the guajillo and ancho chili peppers. Simmer for about 20 more minutes if using pork tenderloin, 40 minutes if using pork shoulder.

Remove the pork and transfer to a plate.

In a blender, purée the broth and ingredients from the dutch oven or pot. Pour it back into the pot. Add the remaining $3/4$ teaspoon of the salt and stir to combine and continue simmering.

Shred the pork with two forks. Add the shredded pork to the dutch oven or pot. Add the lime juice and the beans. Stir to combine while the soup returns to a simmer.

Ladle the soup into bowls and garnish with crushed tortilla chips, cotija cheese, cilantro and sliced avocado.

Grilled Corn with Mexican Pesto

This Mexican pesto has bold flavor that's delicious on corn, but is so versatile that you can also use it on grilled chicken or fish. The roasted pumpkin seeds add an appealing chunky texture to this dish. Jeffrey removed the kernels from the cob for my braces-wearing daughter Becca and tossed them with some of the pesto and he gained yet another fan!

Serves 4
Prep Time: 20 minutes
Cook Time: 20–25 minutes

Seasoned Pumpkin Seeds
2 tablespoons green-shelled pumpkin seeds
1/2 tablespoon oil
1 teaspoon chili powder
1/4 teaspoon salt, plus more, to taste

Pesto
1 clove garlic, minced
2 cups (120 g) fresh coriander leaves (cilantro)
4 tablespoons grated cotija cheese, plus more, for topping
6 1/2 tablespoons oil, divided
Salt, to taste

4 ears fresh corn

Preheat the oven to 450°F (230°C).

Prepare the Seasoned Pumpkin Seeds: Combine the pumpkin seeds, 1/2 tablespoon oil, chili powder and salt in a small bowl. Spread the pumpkin seeds out evenly on a baking sheet and place on the middle rack of the oven. Toss the seeds every few minutes until they are golden brown and crackling, about 10 minutes. When the seeds are done, transfer to another flat pan to cool. Set aside.

Make the Pesto: In a food processor, purée the garlic, cilantro, roasted pumpkin seeds and cotija cheese. With the motor running, pour in the 6 tablespoons of oil in a stream and process until slightly chunky. Season with salt, to taste.

Prepare the corn: heat a grill to high. Husk the corn and place it on the grill. Leave the grill open and turn the corn every 2 minutes to evenly roast it all around. Grill until char marks appear, about 10 minutes. Transfer the corn to a platter.

Using a pastry brush, slather the pesto over each ear of corn. Roll the corn around in the pesto that drips onto the platter to completely cover it with pesto. Sprinkle with more cotija cheese if desired. Serve immediately.

COOK'S NOTE
Feel free to substitute cotija cheese with grated Parmesan cheese.

Scallop Tacos with Chipotle Chili Chutney

I was celebrating my birthday one night at Jeffrey's restaurant Sweet Heat with my friends Patrick, Rita, Kristin. We were fortunate enough for Jeffrey to have a rare moment to pull up a chair and chat. He regaled us with stories about his culinary adventures in Mexico and how he found inspiration for the amazing seared scallop tacos we were enjoying that night. He recreated the smoky heat and crunchy textures he experienced during one of his many trips. He decided to put his own signature spin on the creation with the addition of Chipotle chutney. Enjoy this incredible recipe from his table to yours.

Serves 6–8
Prep Time: 20 minutes + cooling time
Cook Time: 10 minutes

12 green Anaheim chili peppers
2 small jalapeño peppers
16 large sea scallops
Salt and freshly ground black pepper, to taste
2 tablespoons oil
1 teaspoon dried cumin
4 teaspoons dried Mexican oregano
1/2 cup (125 ml) apple cider vinegar or lemon juice
1/4 cup (50 g) sugar
1 1/2 teaspoons salt, divided
2 teaspoons smashed chipotle peppers in adobo sauce
1 cup (240 g) sour cream or plain Greek yogurt
Juice of 4 limes
12–16 corn or flour tortillas
1 cup (70 g) shredded red cabbage
1 cup 70 g) shredded green cabbage

Preheat the oven to broil.

On the highest rack in the oven, place the Anaheim chili peppers on a baking sheet. Turn the chilis every minute with tongs until they are completely black on all sides. Place the chilis in a bowl, cover tightly with aluminum foil and let sit for 10 minutes to cool and allow the steam to loosen the skin. Once the chilis are cool, wipe off the skins gently with your fingers. Don't use water to remove the skin as their flavorful oils will get washed away. Remove the seeds and finely chop the chilis. Set aside.

Deseed the jalapeño peppers and chop fine. Add the jalapeños to the Anaheims and set aside.

Rinse the scallops well and pat dry with a paper towel. Remove the side muscle if necessary from the side of each scallop. Season the scallops with salt and pepper.

Heat the oil in a large non-stick skillet over medium-high heat. Add the scallops and sear on the first side until a golden crust forms. Flip over the scallops and continue cooking until the sides of the scallops turn from translucent to opaque, about 1 minute. Be careful not to overcook. Remove from the heat.

Heat a separate medium non-stick skillet over medium heat. Add the cumin and oregano and toast for 1 minute, until fragrant. Add the vinegar, sugar and 1 teaspoon of the salt and bring to a boil. Add the chopped Anaheim and jalapeño chilis and simmer until the mixture thickens (but still easily flows from side to side as you tilt the pan). Remove the chutney to a bowl using a rubber spatula and let cool.

In a medium bowl, combine the smashed chipotle chili peppers, sour cream and the remaining 1/2 teaspoon of the salt with a fork. Pour in the lime juice and mix well. Set aside at room temperature.

Toast the tortillas on a grill, or in a non-stick pan or under a broiler until warm, soft and slightly golden. Lay them on six or eight plates. (Place the tortillas in a bowl and cover with a dry towel if not serving right away.)

Divide the shredded cabbage evenly among the tortillas. Slice the scallops and lay them on the cabbage. Top with chutney, and then seasoned sour cream.

COOK'S NOTE
Leave the seeds intact before chopping the peppers if you prefer maximum heat!

Fiery Pineapple Salsa

Jeffrey tells me this spicy pineapple salsa was all the rage at his Sweet Heat restaurant and they could barely keep up with the demand. Great on fish tacos or any grilled meat or seafood you like. I love to double the recipe when I'm entertaining and serve with tortilla chips and a big batch of his Spicy Habanero Margaritas (see below).

Serves 4 to 6
Prep Time: 15 minutes

3/4 cup (130 g) chopped
    fresh pineapple
4 tablespoons fresh
    coriander leaves
    (cilantro)
1/2 orange habanero chili,
    stemmed and chopped
4 tablespoons chopped
    white onion
Juice from 1 lime
1/4 teaspoon kosher salt
4 tablespoons water

In a blender or food processor, purée the pineapple, cilantro, habanero, onion, lime juice, salt and water until smooth. Serve with tortilla chips or drizzle over fish, chicken, beef or tacos.

COOK'S NOTE
You may use canned or frozen pineapple instead of fresh but it won't be as tangy fresh.

Spicy Habanero Margarita

This is Jeffrey's signature Spicy Margarita loved by his legions of friends and customers. The secret is infusing tequila with habanero chili. The chili may remain in the bottle indefinitely so you can enjoy spicy margaritas anytime!

Serves 4
Prep Time: 10 minutes
    + resting time

1 orange habanero chili,
    cut in half
1 bottle tequila, preferably
    Herradura Silver
2 handfuls of ice
2 oz (60 ml) Cointreau
    (orange liqueur) or Triple
    Sec
Juice of 3 limes
4 teaspoons honey or agave
    syrup

Wearing a latex glove, push the habanero halves into the bottle of tequila. Close the bottle and let it sit for at least 24 hours.

In a pitcher, add handfuls of ice, 6 oz (185 ml) of the spiced tequila, the Cointreau, lime juice and honey or agave syrup. Stir vigorously and strain through a fine mesh sieve into martini glasses.

COOK'S NOTE
Avoid aged tequila as the woody notes inhibit the full flavor of the habanero from coming out.

QUENCHING & SWEET

All cultures have signature drinks that hold a cherished place in their cuisine. All the beverages in this chapter can be served with a variety of world flavors and are not limited to the ethnicity they're associated with. For example, **Ginger Beer Sangria** is of course fantastic with Spanish Tapas-style Meatballs (page 71) but it goes just as well with a Cherry Tomato & Basil Pizza on Cauliflower Crust (page 46). The **Mexican Frozen Hot Chocolate** is an anytime treat for kids of all ages. Anyone enjoying a spicy dish will benefit from the cooling **Bombay Mango Shake**. We wouldn't be having any fun if I didn't include some grown-up libations so please treat your friends to the **Tipsy Thai Basil Lemon Soda**. They'll be glad you did.

Sweets for my sweet. My sweet friends, that is! Every cuisine has delectable desserts they claim to be the best in the world. I've taken inspiration from many traditional dessert ingredients and infused them into everyday classics like **Dulce de Leche Poke Cake** or **Thai Basil Coconut Ice Cream.** In China, most desserts are of the red bean paste variety and not necessarily kid-friendly, so I married traditional wonton wrappers with banana walnut filling for **Banana Walnut Wontons** (served over French vanilla ice cream... so yum!). Other offerings include **Peanut Butter Cup Biscotti** and **Raspberry Chocolate Crepes.** Is your mouth watering yet?

Tipsy Thai Basil Lemon Soda

This is a recipe I included in my Thai cookbook—except that one didn't include vodka. My friend Jenna was over one day and she said, "You know what? This would be so delicious if we added some vodka." And the rest is history (I'm not gonna lie, we definitely enjoyed testing this one a few times). Thai basil is peppery with a slight note of anise, which makes for an amazing cocktail. If you don't have Thai basil, you can use Italian basil—but I highly recommend seeking Thai basil out at an Asian market, as it adds an exotic and unique flavor to this drink.

Makes 4 Servings
Prep Time: 10 minutes

4 tablespoons freshly squeezed lemon
   juice
2 tablespoons sugar
10 fresh Thai basil leaves
Pinch of salt
3 cups (750 ml) sparkling water
6 oz (185 ml) vodka
Ice
Lemon slices, for garnish

In a pitcher, add the lemon juice, sugar, basil leaves and salt. Muddle the ingredients with a muddler or the handle of a wooden spoon until the sugar dissolves. Add the sparkling water and vodka. Strain and pour into four 8 oz (240 ml) highball glasses with ice. Garnish with lemon slices and serve.

COOK'S NOTE

Throw all of the ingredients less ½ cup (125 ml) sparkling water with a couple of handfuls of ice in the blender for a frosty Tipsy Thai Basil Lemon Slushie version of this drink. So divine on a hot summer day!

Ginger Hibiscus Iced Tea

Sweet, tangy and tart, hibiscus tea is known for its signature crimson color. So refreshing, it perks you up without caffeine. Paired with ginger, it's a gorgeous and fresh take on iced tea. Hibiscus is also the state flower of Hawaii. So pin one behind your ear while sipping on a tall glass of this and you'll feel like you're on a mini holiday. Aloha!

Serves 6
Prep Time: 5 minutes + steeping time + chilling time
Cook Time: 5 minutes

$4^{1}/_{2}$ cups (1 liter + 125 ml) water, divided
12 hibiscus tea bags
2 tablespoons honey
2 tablespoons minced fresh ginger
Mint leaves, for garnish

Bring 1 cup (250 ml) water to a boil and place the rest in a large pitcher in the fridge. Remove the boiling water from the heat and add the hibiscus tea bags, honey and ginger. Steep for 20 minutes. Strain the tea into the pitcher, discarding the solids. Refrigerate until cold. Serve in tall glasses over ice and garnish with mint leaves.

COOK'S NOTE

You can find hibiscus tea bags at health food stores, online and in many grocery stores. You may also use the widely available Celestial Seasonings Red Zinger Herbal Tea, which contains hibiscus.

Ginger Beer Sangria

I wanted to add a fresh, gingery twist to this classic Spanish libation and "OMG yum, hand me another!" was the reaction from my friends Ann and Jenna, who were over on a scorching afternoon the other day. The fresh citrus juices lend a sweet-tart finish along with a POW inducing punch from the ginger syrup. Serve with Easy Seafood Paella (page 139) and Spanish Tapas-style Meatballs (page 71) to complete your Spanish Soirée.

Serves: 6–8
Prep Time: 10 minutes + chilling time
Cook Time: 4 minutes

Ginger Simple Syrup
$^{1}/_{2}$ cup (250 ml) water
4 tablespoons sugar
One 3-in (7.5-cm) piece fresh ginger, peeled and sliced

1 bottle dry white wine i.e. sauvignon blanc or chardonnay
1 cup (250 ml) freshly squeezed orange juice
4 tablespoons freshly squeezed lime juice
4 tablespoons freshly squeezed lemon juice
12 oz (355 ml) ginger beer
Orange, lime and lemon slices, for garnish
Mint sprigs, for garnish

Make the **Ginger Simple Syrup:** Place the water, sugar and ginger root in a small saucepan and bring to a simmer. Stir for 60 seconds or until the sugar dissolves. Remove from the heat and let cool to room temperature.

Place the white wine in a large pitcher and add the orange, lime and lemon juices.

Once the Ginger Simple Syrup has cooled, discard the ginger slices and add the syrup to the pitcher of wine. Stir well and let the mixture chill in the refrigerator for 4 hours or up to overnight.

Pour the sangria over ice in glasses until $^{3}/_{4}$ full. Top each glass with ginger beer. Garnish with extra citrus slices and a sprig of mint. Serve immediately.

Mexican Frozen Hot Chocolate

My friend Karen's daughter Kate is already a foodie at age 12 and loves to cook. She was super excited about testing a recipe for me with her mom and jumped (like a Mexican jumping bean) at the chance to make this Mexican Frozen Hot Chocolate. This recipe is inspired by the trip my daughter Becca took to Serendipity in NYC where she tried its famous Frozen Hot Chocolate. We decided to put a Mexican twist on this popular treat with the addition of cayenne pepper and the use of Mexican chocolate (although it's totally fine to use bittersweet chocolate in this recipe).

Serves 3–4
Prep Time: 10 minutes
Cook Time: 6 minutes

One 2.7-oz (76-g) package of Mexican chocolate discs or bittersweet chocolate, chopped fine
2 tablespoons maple syrup
2 tablespoons cocoa powder
1 cup (250 ml) milk, coconut milk, almond milk, oat milk or soy milk
$1/8$ teaspoon ground cinnamon
Ground red pepper (cayenne), to taste
$2^1/2$ cups (340 g) crushed ice
Shaved chocolate, for garnish

Melt the chocolate in a double boiler. Transfer the melted chocolate to a medium bowl and whisk in the maple syrup, cocoa powder, milk, cinnamon and cayenne pepper until smooth.

Place the bowl in the refrigerator until the mixture is cool to the touch. Place the cooled chocolate mixture in a blender along with ice and blend until thick but pourable (adding more milk or ice as needed.) Pour into glasses and top with shaved chocolate. Serve immediately.

COOK'S NOTE
Some grocery stores carry Mexican Chocolate discs, or you can find them online or at Latin markets. I recommend the Taza brand, which is widely available.

Iced Vietnamese Coffee

"Strong and sweet" is the best way to describe this popular Vietnamese coffee concoction (my hubby describes me this way, too—with the addition of "sometimes" before sweet, just kidding. Haha). My friends just love to meet up for some pho and chilled summer rolls at our favorite Vietnamese restaurant and of course, iced Vietnamese coffee. If it's one of your go-tos too, now you can make it at home in a matter of minutes. Allowing your guests to pour the coffee over the ice—accompanied by the subsequent happy clanging sound of eager stirring—is the traditional way to serve this popular drink in Vietnam. If you really want to impress your family and friends and skip the restaurant lines, serve it with my Easy Beef Pho Soup (recipe on page 92).

Serves 4
Prep Time: 10 minutes

4 cups (1 liter) very strong hot dark roast coffee
$^{1}/_{2}$ cup (125 ml) sweetened condensed milk
16 ice cubes

Divide the coffee into 4 cups. Pour 2 tablespoons of condensed milk into each cup. Stir to dissolve the milk.

Divide the ice cubes into 4 tall glasses. Serve each guest a cup of coffee, a glass with ice cubes and a long handled spoon. Instruct your guests to pour the hot coffee over the ice cubes and stir briskly with the spoon.

Bombay Mango Shake

Although I'm terrible at following choreography, I take a super fun dance exercise class with my friend Karen, taught by the eclectic Marise Freitas. The other day she put on a Bollywood number and we belly-folk-modern Indian danced our hearts out (believe me, I danced like I thought no one was watching!) It inspired me to run home and whip up this classic Bombay Mango Shake. It's a healthy vegan and gluten-free shake that is super refreshing, with exotic hints of cardamom and saffron that's sure to make your taste buds dance!

Serves: 4
Prep Time: 5 minutes

1 lb (453 g) frozen mango chunks
4 cups (1 liter) coconut milk, almond milk, oat milk or
  soy milk
$^{1}/_{2}$ teaspoon ground cardamom
1–2 teaspoons sugar (optional)
1 pinch saffron
4–6 ice cubes
Finely chopped pistachio nuts, for garnish

Place the mango chunks in a blender and purée until blended. Add the milk, cardamom, sugar (if using) and saffron, and blend. Add the ice cubes and blend until smooth. Pour into glasses. Garnish with pistachio nuts and serve.

> **COOK'S NOTE**
> If your mango chunks are quite ripe,
> you may not need to add sugar.

Banana Walnut Wontons

If you know me, you know I love to dance and sing on a stage so I naturally had to include this show-stopping dessert in my book. It's amazingly simple to make yet so elegant and festive when served in martini glasses over French vanilla ice cream and drizzled with caramel sauce. It's sure to garner a round of applause with your friends chanting, "encore!"

Makes 20
Prep Time: 10 minutes
Cook Time: 8–10 minutes

2 ripe bananas, chopped fine
2 tablespoons sugar
1 cup (125 g) store-bought candied walnuts, chopped coarsely
20 square wonton wrappers
Oil, for frying
French vanilla ice cream
Store-bought caramel sauce
Mint leaves, for garnish

Gently combine the banana pieces, sugar and walnut pieces in a medium bowl (do not mash the banana pieces).

Place a wonton wrapper in your hand. Place a teaspoon of the banana mixture in the center of the wrapper. Use your finger to moisten the edges of the wrapper with water. When the edges have been moistened, fold the wrapper in half to create a rectangular shape, pressing any air that might be trapped around the filing. Fold the sides inward so that they overlap. Wet the portion where the sides meet. Pinch and close to seal. The wontons should resemble a cute nurse's cap. Repeat with the remaining wrappers.

In a large wok or deep skillet, heat 2–3 inches (5–7.5 cm) of the oil to 350°F (175°C). Fry 8–10 wontons at a time until golden brown, turning 2 or 3 times, about 3 minutes. Drain on a paper towel-lined sheet pan.

Fill martini glasses with a scoop of French vanilla ice cream and place 2–3 wontons on top.

Drizzle with caramel sauce and garnish with mint leaves. Serve immediately.

Thai Basil Coconut Ice Cream

Cool, creamy and infused with exotic Thai basil, this Thai Basil Coconut Ice Cream is a wonderful accompaniment to a rich dish such as Indonesian Short Ribs Braised in Coconut (page 130) or something on the spicier side like Thai Chicken with Mint & Chilis (page 108). Serving the ice cream in a coconut shell is a fun and unexpected treat for your guests, and will have them raving about your dinner party for days to come.

Makes 6 to 8 Servings
**Prep Time: 10 minutes + steeping time +
  freezing time**
Cook Time: 5 minutes

1/2 cup (125 ml) heavy cream
1 cup (250 ml) whole milk
One 13.5-oz (396-ml) can coconut milk
3/4 cup (150 g) sugar
1/4 cup (5 g) fresh Thai or Italian basil leaves,
  lightly packed
6 egg yolks
3–4 whole coconuts
Fresh mint leaves, for garnish

Combine the heavy cream, milk, coconut milk and sugar in a medium saucepan and bring to a simmer over medium-low heat. Remove from the heat and add the basil leaves. Cover with plastic wrap and allow to steep for 1 hour.

Remove the plastic wrap and return the mixture to a simmer. Slowly whisk the mixture into a bowl containing the egg yolks. Strain into another bowl, pressing on the basil leaves with a spatula. Chill until the mixture is very cold, for at least 2 hours or up to overnight. Spin the chilled mixture in an ice cream maker according to manufacturer's instructions. Place the thickened mixture into a covered container freeze until solid.

Cut the coconuts in half. Scoop the ice cream into the coconut shells. Garnish with mint leaves and serve immediately.

COOK'S NOTE
Look for coconuts at your grocery store that are pre-scored, because they're easier to cut in half.

Dulce de Leche Poke Cake

Poke Cake was invented in the '70s and famously calls for using a store-bought cake mix. It's been a popular go-to classic ever since. I know what you're thinking; "Store-bought cake mix?" Well, don't go "poking" holes in it just yet. Wait until you actually poke holes in this cake and discover how unbelievably moist and delicious the results are. Topped with warm dulce de leche (which seeps into the holes), toasted pecans and toffee bits, it's simply a slice of heaven on your plate.

Makes: One 9 x 13-in (23 x 33-cm) cake
Prep Time: 25 minutes + cooling time
Cook Time: Baking time per package instructions

One 15.2-oz (425-g) box yellow cake mix or butter pecan cake mix plus the ingredients called for in package instructions

Dulce de Leche Glaze and Whipped Topping
One 15-oz (425-g) jar dulce de leche (milk caramel)
2 cups (500 ml) heavy cream
2 teaspoons vanilla extract
2 tablespoons confectioner's sugar
1/2 cup (120 g) toffee bits
1/2 cup (63 g) toasted chopped pecans

Prepare the cake according to the package instructions for a 9 x 13-inch (23 x 33-cm) cake. Let the cake cool for 20 minutes.

Microwave the dulce de leche for about 30 seconds so it's pourable. Using a chopstick or wooden spoon handle, poke holes in the cake all over, penetrating all the way to the pan. Pour the dulce de leche over the top to fill the holes.

Whip the heavy cream, vanilla extract and confectioner's sugar with a mixer until stiff peaks form. Spread the whipped cream over the cake. Sprinkle with toffee bits and chopped pecans.

Cover the cake with plastic wrap and refrigerate until it is well chilled and the dulce de leche has been absorbed, at least 1 hour.

COOK'S NOTE
Place your bowl and whisk attachment into the freezer for half an hour before whipping the cream.

Ginger Peach Sorbet

Peaches symbolize romance and love in Chinese culture, so I like to whip up this super easy sorbet with a ginger twist on Valentine's Day. Gone are the days of romantic dinners for two because our twins get upset if we don't celebrate Valentine's Day with them (they're 12 now, but if we're still doing this when they're 30 I may start to worry). We usually have a fun family steak dinner and exchange gifts, and this is the perfect light and refreshing dessert to serve and fall in love with.

Serves 4
Prep Time: 10 minutes + resting time + freezing time
Cook Time: 5 minutes

Ginger Simple Syrup
1 cup (125 ml) water
1/2 cup (100 g) sugar
4 teaspoons peeled and minced fresh ginger

One 20-oz (567-g) package thawed frozen sliced peaches
One 20-oz package (567-g) frozen sliced peaches
2 teaspoons freshly squeezed lemon juice
Fresh mint leaves

Make the **Ginger Simple Syrup**: Combine the water, sugar and ginger in a small saucepan. Bring to a boil over medium-high heat. Reduce the heat and simmer, stirring until the sugar dissolves. Remove from the heat and let stand for 30 minutes. Strain the mixture with a fine mesh strainer and discard the minced ginger solids.

Combine the Ginger Simple Syrup, thawed and frozen peaches and lemon juice in a food processor and blend until smooth. Cover and chill the mixture in the freezer for at least 2 hours before serving. Garnish with mint leaves and serve.

Peanut Butter Cup Biscotti

"You got your peanut butter on my chocolate!" "You got your chocolate in my peanut butter!" If you remember that commercial, then you probably also wore acid wash jeans and had feathered hair in high school (like me!). It's still true today: peanut butter and chocolate are two great tastes that go great together. While this recipe requires more time than the other dessert recipes in this book, it's totally worth the extra effort. I mean, like, totally tubular.

Makes 22–24
Prep Time: 60 minutes
Cook Time: 55 minutes

4 tablespoons whole milk
1½ teaspoons vanilla extract
3 cups (360 g) all-purpose flour
1 tablespoon baking powder
1 cup (240 g) crunchy peanut butter
½ cup (99 g) dark brown sugar
½ cup (99 g) sugar
3 eggs
1½ cups (262 g) peanut butter chips
8 oz (226 g) semisweet chocolate chips
½ cup (65 g) finely chopped roasted peanuts
   (optional)

Preheat the oven to 350°F (175°C).

Line 2 baking sheets with parchment paper.

Mix the milk and vanilla extract together in a small bowl. Set aside. Combine the flour and baking powder in a separate medium bowl.

With an electric mixer, beat the peanut butter, brown sugar and sugar in a large bowl until smooth. Add the eggs one at a time, allowing each egg to blend into the peanut butter mixture before adding the next.

Pour in the flour mixture alternately with the milk mixture, mixing until just incorporated. Fold in the peanut butter chips until combined.

Shape into two 10 x 2-inch (25 x 5-cm) logs and place on a baking sheet lined with parchment paper.

Bake 22–25 minutes. Remove from oven and allow to cool for 30 minutes. Lower the oven temperature to 300°F (150°C).

Once cooled, slice the logs into about ½-inch (1.2-cm) slices and place them back onto the lined baking sheet. Each log will make about 18–20 slices. Bake for 15 minutes. Flip the slices over and bake an additional 15 minutes. Remove to a wire rack to cool.

While the biscotti is cooling, heat the chocolate chips in a microwave-safe glass or ceramic bowl in 30-second intervals, stirring after each interval, until melted and smooth. (Alternatively, use a double boiler).

Once cooled, dip the bottom half of each cooled biscotti into the melted chocolate and sprinkle with chopped peanuts, if using. Set the biscotti onto parchment paper. Repeat with the remaining biscotti. Allow to set for about 20 minutes before serving.

Becca's Tres Leche Cupcakes

My 12 year-old daughter Becca has a YouTube channel called "Becca's Yummytown." She's loved to bake ever since the age of 3. We collaborated on this recipe when a bunch of her besties were over and they were Tres Happy and Tres Grabby over these cupcakes. Light, fluffy and milky sweet, the girls devoured the platter and can't wait for their next to trip to Becca's Yummytown!

Serves: 16–18
Prep Time: 20 minutes + chilling time
Cook Time: 20 minutes

One 4-oz (113-g) stick unsalted butter at room
   temperature
1 cup (200 g) granulated sugar
2 teaspoons vanilla extract
1 large egg
1$^{1}/_{2}$ cups (180 g) all-purpose flour
$^{1}/_{2}$ teaspoon baking powder
$^{1}/_{4}$ teaspoon baking soda
$^{1}/_{4}$ teaspoon salt
1 cup (250 ml) buttermilk

Milk Mixture
4 tablespoons sweetened condensed milk
4 tablespoons evaporated milk
2 tablespoons heavy whipping cream

Topping
1$^{1}/_{2}$ cups (375 ml) heavy whipping cream
4–5 tablespoons confectioners' sugar
Toasted sweetened shredded coconut (optional)
Fresh sliced strawberries

Preheat the oven to 350°F (175°C). Line a muffin tin's cups with paper liners.

Cream the butter and sugar until light and fluffy. Beat in vanilla and egg. In another bowl, whisk together the flour, baking powder, baking soda and salt; add to creamed mixture alternately with the buttermilk, beating after each addition.

Fill the prepared cups about two-thirds full. Bake until a toothpick inserted in center comes out clean, 17–20 minutes. Let cool for 10 minutes on a wire rack. Remove the cupcakes from the muffin tin.

Make the **Milk Mixture**: In a bowl, mix the sweetened condensed milk, evaporated milk and whipping cream. Poke about 6 evenly spaced holes in each cupcake with a skewer. Slowly spoon milk mixture over top (about 1 tablespoon per cupcake), allowing the mixture to be absorbed into the cupcakes. Cover the cupcakes and refrigerate for at least one hour.

Meanwhile, make the **Topping**: beat the cream until it begins to thicken. Add the confectioners' sugar; beat until soft peaks form.

Spread or pipe the topping over the cupcakes. Top with shredded coconut (if desired) and strawberries, and serve.

Raspberry Chocolate Crepes

Oh la la! Impress your friends and family with luscious French crepes filled with the sublime combination of hazelnut spread and raspberries in less time than it takes to make a batch of cookies. They're easier to make than most people think and a great dessert to serve when un-expected guests show up, as you probably have most of the ingredients in your pantry and fridge.

Makes: 8 crepes
Prep Time: 5 minutes + chilling time
Cook Time: 16 minutes

3/4 cup (185 ml) milk
1/2 cup (60 g) all-purpose flour
1 egg
2 tablespoons unsalted melted butter, divided, plus more, as needed
Pinch of salt
1/2 cup (140 g) chocolate-hazelnut spread, such as Nutella
3/4 cup (95 g) fresh raspberries
Confectioners' sugar, for dusting
Cinnamon, for dusting
Mint leaves, for garnish

COOK'S NOTE
Feel free to add sliced bananas or other berries to these delicious crepes.

In blender, combine the milk, flour, egg, 1 tablespoon of the butter and salt. Blend until smooth. Strain to remove lumps if necessary. Let stand at least 20 minutes or put into the refrigerator for up to 12 hours to use later.

Heat a large non-stick skillet over medium heat. Add the remaining 1 tablespoon of the melted butter and swirl to coat. Ladle a small scoop (about 4 tablespoons) of batter into the pan.

Swirl to coat bottom of pan to make a 7½-inch (19-cm) thin crepe. Cook for 1 minute, or until the crepe begins to curl at edges. Flip and cook for 1 minute more.

Transfer the crepe to a plate. Repeat with remaining batter, adding additional butter to pan as needed. Layer the crepes between sheets of waxed paper to prevent them from sticking together.

Spread approximately 1 tablespoon of the chocolate-hazelnut spread on each crepe. Place 6 raspberries on top of the spread and fold the sides over the crepe. Repeat with the remaining crepes. Dust with confectioners' sugar and cinnamon. Garnish with mint leaves and serve immediately.

Index

Photo Credits

123rf.com **24 top left** Diana Taliun. **58** Kia Cheng Boon. **219** Olena Danileiko. *Dreamstime.com* **31 top left** Robyn Mackenzie. **39** Moorereese. **135** Igor Ploskin. *istock.com* **204 bottom left** Juanmonino. **208** Juanmonino. *Shutterstock.com* **Front cover** Joshua Resnick; stockcreations; Kiian Oksana; Elena Eryomenko; Elena Eryomenko. **Back cover top** Piyato; Ostancov Vladislav; nehophoto; Maggiezhu. **Front/back endpapers top middle** smspsy; **top right** Shaiith; **extreme left middle** Tatiana Volgutova; **center** Ostancov Vladislav; Natasha Breen; nehophoto; **extreme right bottom** etorres. **77** farbled. **78** wong yu liang. **4, 72** Maggiezhu. **5 top left, 82** zstock; **5 top right, 109** Liliya Kandrashevich; **5 bottom right, 101 top** Wiktory. **6 top left, 122** Makistock. **7** Julie Mayfeng. **8** Timolina. **10, 142** OlesyaSH. **12** DronG. **14** Luis Echeverri Urrea; B.G. Photography; Dream79; prasit2512; Nattika. **16** KatyaPulina; Yeti studio; snyferok; SMDSS; k_jiena. **16 middle top, 20 left bottom** Keith Homan. **16 middle bottom, 23 middle top, 30 left top & bottom, 31 middle top, 77, 138, 147** Shutterstock.com. **17 left bottom, 33 right** HandmadePictures. **17** Da-ga; Boonchuay1970; baibaz; Piccia Neri; linyoklin. **18, 19 middle top, 155** Robyn Mackenzie. **18** Evgeny Karandaev; Slawomir Zelasko; Nataly Studio; Thanthima Lim; stevemart. **19** Paul_Brighton; Sheila Fitzgerald; Mrklong; akepong srichaichana. **19 middle bottom, 22 right** Olga Popova. **20** Brian Yarvin; Picture Partners; Sakarin Sawasdinaka; nito. **21** mayura benjarattanapakee; Manish Shrivastava; Michael A. Buser; Amallia Eka; carlosdelacalle; Julie Clopper. **22** IngridHS; Photoongraphy. **23** Hortimages; Quang Ho; PIXbank CZ; Mark Brandon; boommaval. **23 right bottom, 24 left bottom** K321. **24** Narsil; perfectlab; Andrii Horulko. **29** Spalnic; Arina P Habich; Fluid Frame. **30** thefoodphotographer; Vitalii Matokha; David Smith; Vadym Zaitsev; CK Bangkok Photography; Atsushi Hirao; Shawn Hempel. **31** Chachamp; bjphotographs; Planner: Lovely Bird. **32, 158** Ildi Papp. **33, 96** Elena Veselova. **34 left, 76** szefei; **34 right** Shebeko. **35 left, 115** Africa Studio; **35 right** nelea33. **38** Magdanatka. **40, 92, 131** Joshua Resnick. **41, 67, 169, 206** Ezume Images. **42** coconutbaby. **43** PI. **44** jreika. **45** Margoe Edwards. **46, 166** Nataliya Arzamasova. **47** Sara Winter. **48** Piyato. **50** Slawomir Fajer. **14 right middle, 51, 53, 54, 70, 94, 120, 123, 179, 209 top** Brent Hofacker. **56** voloshin311. **57** MSPT. **59** NAK Photographer. **60** Bartosz Luczak. **61** juleehophotography. **63** Stepanek Photography. **64** Food Via Lenses. **66** NoirChocolate. **68, 177** Alexander Prokopenko. **69** etorres. **73** isasto. **75** Edalin Photography. **80** Ostancov Vladislav. **86** Elena Eryomenko. **88, 104, 105, 119** from my point of view. **89** Ekaterina Smirnova. **90/91** lunamarina. **93** Ekaterina Markelova. **98** Charlotte Lake. **99** pedphoto36pm. **100** YummyFeast. **71, 102, 221** AS Food studio. **107** Ratov Maxim. **108** kingkanok suwannasi. **111** Kostenko Maxim. **112** Mau Horng. **114** Nina Firsova. **116/117** Larisa Blinova. **124** Tatiana Bralnina. **125** Olexiy Bayev. **127** Shahram Jafari Studio. **128** S and S Imaging. **129** Victority. **130** sungsu han. **132, 133** nehophoto. **136** gkrphoto. **138** Cyril Hou. **139** ilolab. **141** hlphoto. **143** Hassel Sinar. **145** freeskyline. **146** Lili Blankenhship. **147** HHLtDave5. **149** Richy Stocker. **150, 154, 159** vm2002. **152, 210 top left, 218** Tatiana Volgutova. **153** Tatjana Baibakova. **156** Jess Lessard Photography. **160** Selwa Baroody. **161, 198** Zoryanchik. **164, 170** Shaiith. **167** ARENA Creative. **168** Karen Barnaby. **171** petereleven. **172** Fierman Much. **173** bonchan. **174** Nungning20. **175** Take A Pix Media. **187** Barbro Bergfeldt. **192** Dav Rubin. **193** Fanfo. **195** Asya Nurullina. **199** NewFabrika. **207, 220** istetiana. **209 bottom** Dmitry Lobanov. **210 top right, 215 left** Anna_Pustynnikova. **210** Alexander_DG; **210 bottom right, 215 right** Antonina Vlasova. **212, 213 right** 5PH. **213 left** Alp Aksoy. **214** Olyina V.

Acknowledgments

I am so thankful for all the wonderful people that have supported me through the creation of this book. It's been an exciting journey to research, create, test, refine and perfect the 170+ recipes in this book with friends guiding me along at every turn.

I want to thank my awesome hubby Matthew for his support through endless hours of testing, writing and editing as well as taking some amazing photos for this book. My twins Dylan and Becca for inspiring me every day to come up with flavorful, healthy and delicious meals with globally infused flavors. When they came home boasting they were the envy of their friends when leftovers made their way into their lunch boxes at school, I knew I was on to something. They were also true sports when it came to being photographed for the book and came up with ways to make it fun.

Testing is key to a successful cookbook. Thanks go out to my tireless and enthusiastic testers from all over the country: Neil Newman, Amy Schnabel, Ann Koh, Dina Barry, Ryan McShera, Liset Alfieri, Griffin Chin, Candace Ng, Susie Romano, Steven Durbahn, Bill Chin, Laura Chin, David Chin, John Harkness, Jean Chin, Stacy Mearss, Jodi Young and Jenna Carlston (and special thanks to her as well and to my intern Kimberly Pramana for art directing our photoshoots).

Part of the magic of this book comes from those whom contributed recipes from their family vaults: Galina Prosyak, Derakshandeh Sadeghi, Mae Chandran, Monica & Oystein Danielson and Margaret McSweeney.

I was overjoyed to include multi-cultural celebrations in this book and am incredibly honored to feature my rock star friends (along with their recipes) Debbie Matenopoulos, Jeannie Mai & Mama Mai, Faye Levy and Jeffrey Saad.

Special thanks to Hugo Rojas for his stunning photography, Troy Lazaris for his make-up artistry and to Shannon Dellimore and Martina Chaconas & Jennice Tronciale for allowing us to shoot in their stunning homes.

Many thanks to Delfina Garcia for the hours spent washing dishes and keeping my kitchen clean after marathon testing sessions. I also need to thank Jenna Sandez for caring for our munchkins.

Couldn't do it without all the Elite Dance Moms and Dads who carpool and make sure I know where Becca is supposed to be what she's supposed to be wearing (because I usually have no idea!): Alyssa Alison, Nicole Wagg, Amy Rice, Michelle Slobin, Rebecca Aaronson, Maureen McMahon, Brian Skaggs and Shannon Dellimore.

Shout out to celebrity event planner Nicole Hirsty Saine who waved her magic wand over our Greek Easter photoshoot resulting in a magical table-scape.

A round of applause to all the friends who have supported me through the years and fueled my culinary dreams: Christos Garkinos, JJ McKay, Kimlai Yingling, Josh Moreland, Robert Schueller, Linda Grasso, George Leon, Andrea Zito, Chris Vasquez, Jen Prince, Tom Koh, Patrick Martin, Peter Petraglia, Carol Cheng Mayer, Janki Lalani Gandhi, Tamalin Srisook, Karen Israel, Laura Kim, Catherine Park, Alison Singh Gee, Paul Hemstreet, Greg Economos, Frank Lomento, Leslie Fram, Justin Ching, Rich Ross, Adam Sanderson, Barbara Jones, Laura Takaragawa, Janet Hsu, Selina Meere, Katie Workman, Catherine McCord, Melanie Kosaka, Mary Aggarwal, Nora Wong, Rita Drucker, Ellie Shapiro, Rolland Ryan, Marianne Szymanski, Steve Patscheck, Amy Castillo, Lori Tabb, Sue Ann Hong, Jason Wong, Shubhi Rao, Katy Spillars, Michael Now, Jayzen Patria, Joe Keenan, Kathi Sharpe-Ross, Mark Workman, Holly Workman, Adam Drucker, Tanya Altman, Leila Lee, Rachel Small, Rulivia Wong, Anna Roca, Sabrina Ironside, Alan Schwarz, Michael Dagnery, Susan Safier, Katie Clavette, Mandy Lile, Andy Chi, Marissa Panlilio, Devery Holmes, Wendy Diamond, Raghavan Iyer, Josh Madson, Kate Jonas, Emily Siegel, Sharon Graves, Kris Steig, Tina Moore, Carlota Espinosa, Kelly Lynch, John Banks, DJ Cathy Michele, Scott Joyce, Laurie Chesler, Terrie Silverman, Mark Reis, Bob Bell, Richard Ellinghausen, Andrea Rojo, Isabella Ovalle, Adam King, Helene Mullin, Doug Haase, Dayna Coronado, Michael Kent, Sophie Ali, Rosemary Tarquinio, Barbara Balik, Alan Locher, Laura McHolm, Joy Chudacoff, Gina Raphael and Kalika Yap.

Special shout out to my Game Night Goddesses: Stella McShera, Laura Gerson, Hilary Gadsby, Jen Mayo, Julia Rose, Christy Moody, Amy Robertson, Jyoti Sarda, Amy Stanton, Kristin Nicholas, Mary Sadeghy, Maria Sechrest, Sandra Hsu, Liz Svatek, Carrie Murray, Laura Keller, Schenae Rourke and Sheila Darcy.

Lastly, I'd like to thank the editorial, production, sales and marketing team at Tuttle Publishing and Periplus who encouraged me to write this book and brought my dream into reality.

Published by Tuttle Publishing, an imprint of Periplus Editions (HK) Ltd.

www.tuttlepublishing.com

Additional Photo Credits
13 Elaine Lee Photography
200, 202 Jon Falcone
2/3, 204–205 Amy Herold
25–28, 81, 113, 134, 144, 163, 176, 182–185, 186 top Masano Kawana
Front cover (spices), front/back endpapers top left, bottom left and right middle, 9, 11, 14 top, 187 bottom, 188–189, 196–197, 201 Matthew Jonas
190–191 Yakir Levy
1, 180 Hugo Rojas

ISBN: 978-0-8048-5225-8

DISTRIBUTED BY
North America, Latin America & Europe
Tuttle Publishing
364 Innovation Drive
North Clarendon, VT 05759-9436 U.S.A.
Tel: (802) 773-8930
Fax: (802) 773-6993
info@tuttlepublishing.com
www.tuttlepublishing.com

Japan
Tuttle Publishing
Yaekari Building 3rd Floor
5-4-12 Osaki
Shinagawa-ku
Tokyo 141-0032
Tel: (81) 3 5437-0171
Fax: (81) 3 5437-0755
sales@tuttle.co.jp
www.tuttle.co.jp

Asia Pacific
Berkeley Books Pte. Ltd.
3 Kallang Sector #04-01
Singapore 349278
Tel: (65) 6741 2178
Fax: (65) 6741 2179
inquiries@periplus.com.sg
www.tuttlepublishing.com

25 24 23 22 21
10 9 8 7 6 5 4 3 2 1

Printed in Malaysia   2102VP

TUTTLE PUBLISHING® is a registered trademark of Tuttle Publishing, a division of Periplus Editions (HK) Ltd.

Books to Span the East and West

Our core mission at Tuttle Publishing is to create books which bring people together one page at a time. Tuttle was founded in 1832 in the small New England town of Rutland, Vermont (USA). Our fundamental values remain as strong today as they were then—to publish best-in-class books informing the English-speaking world about the countries and peoples of Asia. The world is a smaller place today and Asia's economic, cultural and political influence has expanded, yet the need for meaningful dialogue and information about this diverse region has never been greater. Since 1948, Tuttle has been a leader in publishing books on the cultures, arts, cuisines, languages and literatures of Asia. Our authors and photographers have won many awards and Tuttle has published thousands of titles on subjects ranging from martial arts to paper crafts. We welcome you to explore the wealth of information available on Asia at **www.tuttlepublishing.com**.